T0311213

ISRAEL'S BLACK PANTHERS

ISRAEL'S BLACK PANTHERS

The Radicals Who Punctured a Nation's
Founding Myth

ASAF ELIA-SHALEV

UNIVERSITY OF CALIFORNIA PRESS

University of California Press
Oakland, California

Library of Congress Cataloging-in-Publication Data

Names: Elia-Shalev, Asaf, 1987– author.
Title: Israel's Black Panthers : the radicals who punctured a nation's founding myth /
   Asaf Elia-Shalev.
Description: Oakland, California: University of California Press, [2024] |
   Includes bibliographical references and index.
Identifiers: LCCN 2023032761 (print) | LCCN 2023032762 (ebook) |
   ISBN 9780520294318 (hardback) | ISBN 9780520967496 (ebook)
Subjects: LCSH: Panterim ha-sheḥorim (Israel) | Mizrahim—Israel—Social
   conditions—20th century. | Jews, Moroccan—Social conditions—20th century. |
   Mizrahim—Political activity—Israel—History—20th century. | Jews, Moroccan—
   Political activity—Israel—History—20th century. | Protest movements—Israel—
   History—20th century.
Classification: LCC DS113.8.S4 E385 2024 (print) | LCC DS113.8.S4 (ebook) |
   DDC 322.4/0956940904—dc23/eng/20230826
LC record available at https://lccn.loc.gov/2023032761
LC ebook record available at https://lccn.loc.gov/2023032762

33 32 31 30 29 28 27 26 25 24
10 9 8 7 6 5 4 3 2 1

Contents

Preface

ON A TUESDAY morning in 1972, residents of Jerusalem's upscale Rehavia neighborhood expected to start their day as they would any other, by stepping outside to collect the fresh milk that was delivered before they awoke. But on this particular morning, where there should have been bottles, they instead found a note. It referred to the missing milk as a donation. "We thank you for giving away your milk to hungry children, instead of to the dogs and cats in your homes," the note read. "We hope this operation inspires you to contribute to the war on poverty."

A short while later, across town in Asbestonim, an impoverished neighborhood named after the asbestos sheets used to hastily erect the local dwellings, residents woke up to a pleasant surprise. On their doorsteps, they encountered what was an almost obscene luxury for them—freshly delivered milk. Another note was attached. "This is a reminder to all citizens and to the government, and especially to you, that we care," the note read. "The children here don't have the milk they need. Meanwhile, in the rich neighborhoods, the cats and dogs have milk every day and lots of it."

Known as Operation Milk, this stunt represents the most enduring true story from the time of the Black Panthers in Israel. The novelty of the act and the flouting of the law neatly encapsulate the spirit of these Israeli Robin Hoods. And their message about inequality, implying that some families were thirsty for milk, undercut one of Israel's cherished myths. If the country was founded as a socialist haven for the Jewish people, why would one group need to take from another?

I heard this story in my twenties while sitting down to interview Reuven Abergel in one of countless moments that left me delighted, surprised, or confounded. The Moroccan-born radical with a walrus mustache and a guttural accent is one of the original Panthers. His roots in a country of the Middle East mean he is a Mizrahi Jew, part of an ethnic group making up about half of Israel's Jewish population. As I write these lines, Reuven is 80 years old. I met him about ten years ago, but the origin of this book goes farther back.

Raised in Israel and California, I came upon the story of the Israeli Panthers as a college student at the University of California, Berkeley. I was writing a paper about the Black Panther Party of the 1960s and '70s and learned that the African American militants had inspired a group of Israelis to take up the Panther name for their own cause. I was fascinated that a movement of Mizrahi Jews had struggled against poverty and discrimination in a country dominated by European, Ashkenazi Jews. It was a narrative so different from—and obscured by—classic stories like Leon Uris's *Exodus* or the legend of the Six-Day War. The idea that such a movement existed in Israel whet my curiosity, but, at the time, there was little about the Panthers online, even in Hebrew. Galvanized to search further, I decided to act on a lead: an odd blog post crediting the founding of the group to Angela Davis, the African American revolutionary, who was said to have visited Jerusalem in

1971. A friend was going to attend a talk by Davis, and I had her ask Davis about this story. She was amused at the question, and to our embarrassment, we soon realized why. Davis, famously, was incarcerated at the time on trumped-up charges of murder.

As I went on in my professional life, the story of the Panthers stayed with me. I returned to it over the years, including on visits to Israel. In part, the passion was personal. I used to consider myself an activist, and my background is Mizrahi, with grandparents who immigrated to Israel from Iraq. But my interest in the Panthers was about more than that. I was captivated by how a group of kids with criminal records and a provocative name helped redirect the course of the national conversation and forced Israel to face issues it had been denying. What I was slowly learning about the Panthers seemed deeply consequential, and in their forgotten story, I saw the roots of the country that Israel has become.

Over several years, Reuven gave me many hours of his time. We walked the cobblestone pathways near his childhood home and toured the courtyards of Jerusalem's city hall, where he pointed out the pockmarks from the bullets that used to buzz overhead when he was young. We lingered on Jaffa Street, the bustling commercial artery of the city, running errands and chatting with his acquaintances. These are the places where much of this book takes place, and exploring them together, my feet always tired before those of my elderly but indefatigable companion. I also visited Reuven for long conversations at his government-subsidized one-bedroom apartment in East Jerusalem. It was an ironic place for him to end up given that he is a hardcore leftist who regards the area as occupied Palestinian land.

During our interviews, he cut me off, redirected my questions, and raised his voice, reflecting an impatience with how little I knew and a lifetime of feeling unheard. He was also incredibly caring and warm, often answering questions over his shoulder as he brewed me coffee or chopped vegetables to throw into a pot for our lunch. He believed that not knowing English kept him trapped and prevented his story from being more widely known. Being interviewed by me, an American, felt like "smuggling a letter out of prison," he once said. Through stories like the one about Operation Milk, he wanted me to understand the injustice that gave rise to the Panthers. At his most heated, he used words like "holocaust" and "apartheid" to describe the racist treatment Mizrahi Jews had experienced in Israel.

I decided to build on Reuven's recollections, aiming to get as complete a picture of the Panthers as possible. I combed through more than a dozen archives in Israel and the United States. One of the key sources of information would take two years to obtain—a cache of classified police intelligence files on the Panthers. Meanwhile, I collected thousands of news articles—nearly every single story that mentions the Panthers from at least 20 periodicals. I also tracked down dozens of individuals, many of whom had never been interviewed before. Reaching them was a triumph, but subsequent interviews produced mixed results. Many Panthers survived childhood poverty and malnourishment and went on to experience trauma from drug addiction, violence, and incarceration; their recollections were often meandering, inconsistent, and abstract. Five of the people I interviewed have died since I started working on this project. I feel especially indebted to them.

No one has told the full story of the Israeli Black Panthers before, at least not at this length, and certainly not in English. But the project of this book is not only to plug a shameful hole in the public record. It is to provide readers with a unique vantage point on Israeli history. The narrative avoids the typical tropes and ideological cliches regarding Zionist triumphalism. And, to the extent the story represents an indictment of Israel, it does not reproduce the most common critique, which tends to come from a Palestinian perspective. With its focus on Jews of Arab backgrounds, this narrative breaks the binary of Arab and Jew, offering a fresh intervention into a topic that has been debated ad nauseam. Learning the story of the Panthers is key to understanding the rise of right-wing politics in Israel over the past several decades as well as the ongoing polarization and instability of Israeli public life.

Perhaps it's important to pause and spell out the meaning of "black" in the context of the time and place in which this book takes place. In the first few decades following the country's founding in 1948, there was almost no one in Israel who would appear racially black to American eyes. The Jews of Ethiopia had not yet arrived nor had the non-Jewish refugees and migrants from Africa. Mizrahi Jews are typically a few shades darker than most Jews of European origin. In the Israeli context, however, they were commonly referred to as black, by themselves and others. For derogatory purposes, Ashkenazi Jews sometimes turned to Yiddish and called their darker-skinned countrymen *shvartse khaye,* meaning "black animal," in the language of European Jewry. By picking the name they did, the young Mizrahi radicals were saying, "Yes, we are, in fact, black animals—we're the Black Panthers."

It wasn't just ordinary Israelis who spoke in racist terms about their fellow Jews. So did Israel's towering founding figure, David Ben-Gurion. In 1950, while serving as prime minister and presiding over a military command meeting, he complained about the Jewish immigrants arriving from Muslim lands. "We must educate the young man who has come here from these countries to sit properly on a chair in his home, to take a shower, not steal, not capture an Arab teenager and rape her and murder her," he said. "The ingathering of the exiles has brought us a rabble."

The exodus of more than 700,000 Jews from places like Yemen, Iraq, Kurdistan, Morocco, Tunisia, Egypt, and Iran in the 1950s and their arrival in Israel turned out for many to be a story of alienation, not redemption. These immigrants entered an Israeli narrative that assigned them no role. The young country had forged its identity upon the horrors of Europe and the rejection of the old diasporic Jew, who was seen as meek and stale. There was no accounting for the rich, diverse, and long history of Jews in the Middle East; Europe, for all the harm it had done, was still embraced as the model. Even the term originally used to refer to these non-European immigrants was something of a misnomer. They were dubbed "Sephardim," a historical identity for people with ancestry in the Iberian Peninsula before local rulers signed edicts expelling Jews at the end of the fifteenth century. While many of the Jews expelled from Spain and Portugal migrated to various countries in the Middle East, Jewish communities in the region existed before the expulsion and continued to maintain their distinct customs long after the influx of Sephardic Jews. Over time, the term "Mizrahi" took over in Israeli public discourse, and while it used to be translated into English as "Eastern" or "Oriental," that is no longer the practice today. Even though most of this story takes place when the terms "Sephardi" and "Mizrahi" were used differently than they are today, the book uses "Mizrahi" outside of direct quotes.

In their anxiety over the quality of immigrants from the Middle East, Israel's leaders constructed a binary separation between Arab and Jewish identities. Mizrahi Jews who had once inhabited both identities fluidly were now compelled to shed the former. Perhaps no one expressed this concern as directly as senior Israeli statesman Abba Eban. In his 1957 book *Voice of Israel,* Eban argued against cultural integration with the wider Middle East and warned of "the danger lest the predominance of immigrants of Oriental origin force Israel to equalize its cultural level with that the neighboring world. So far from regarding our immigrants from Oriental countries as a bridge toward our integration with the Arabic-speaking world, our objective should be to infuse them with an Occidental spirit, rather than allow them to draw us into an unnatural Orientalism."

Galvanized by such concerns, Israel attempted to legislate and otherwise enact the segregation of Mizrahim from the Ashkenazi population. Mizrahi immigrants were housed in dusty transit camps in remote areas for years even while Ashkenazi immigrants were moved into proper housing. When the state did provide housing to Mizrahim, that usually meant assigning them to homes abandoned by Palestinians who had fled or shacks in the far reaches of the country, away from economic opportunity. In the area of education, the curriculum offered where Mizrahim lived was distinct, designed to strip away their Arabness and track them into vocational training rather than academic degrees. Israel's racist policies created an underclass of Mizrahi citizens, an inequality which persists to this day, even as Mizrahi representation in media and commerce has improved. No prime minister, for example, has been Mizrahi, and relatively few have occupied senior ministerial positions. Academia, the media, and the justice system are all dominated by Ashkenazim, while prisons house far too many Mizrahim.

For a generation of Mizrahim of a certain socioeconomic class, the Panthers represented a rare public airing of one of the gravest pains of their lives: the feeling of devotion to a country that seemed to reject them. If the American Black Panthers challenged the notion that the United States is a country where all are created equal, their Israeli peers showed that the self-labeled Jewish state failed to heed the words of its declaration of independence promising "freedom, justice, and peace as envisaged by the prophets of Israel." The Panthers taught the Mizrahi public to take pride in their identities and assert a rightful place within their country. The consequences of this painful history—and the tradition of activism it inspired—continue to unfold today.

1

GOLDA'S DILEMMA

ON THE EVENING of February 28, 1971, Israel's aging prime minister, Golda Meir, summoned a group of advisers and senior officials to her office for an urgent meeting. Those who filed in included the mayor of Jerusalem, the national police chief, the minister of police, and the minister of justice. Together, they would have to resolve a dilemma: what to do about a new group of troublemakers who were calling themselves the Black Panthers.

The problem started two months earlier with a handful of youths from one of the country's impoverished neighborhoods. They had no resources or benefactors, and though they claimed to represent Israel's poor, dark-skinned Jewish masses, there was no way to know whether the masses would rally to their cry. Now, the so-called Panthers were planning to stage their first demonstration, a test of their appeal. Seeing this possibility as a threat, the police commanders were proposing a response—but even they could tell their plan was heavy-handed. They knew they needed to seek the approval of Israel's civilian leadership. From the precinct level, the matter went up through the chain of command all the way to the minister of police. He couldn't come to a decision, either, so he phoned the prime minister. Meanwhile, the press had contributed to the escalation by inflating the seriousness of these activists. Given the explosive reputation of the group's American namesake, it was an easy story to sensationalize. What started as a police matter was quickly transforming into a threat to Israel's domestic stability, if only because political leaders perceived it as such.

Meir and her deputies began debating. The first question they faced was whether to allow the protest to take place at all. Under Israeli law, public demonstrations required permits, and the Panthers had dutifully applied for one. From a legal standpoint, the officials could move to reject an application by presenting the case that such a protest would likely result in violence or disorderly conduct. As they began debating, an aide stepped into the room to interrupt. He came to deliver an update on the very issue they were discussing. Hundreds of incendiary flyers signed by the Panthers had just come off the press, and police had arrested two activists for illegally wheat-pasting the flyers on the exterior walls of Jerusalem's city hall.

The news about the flyers and arrests added to an already hefty surveillance dossier police had compiled on the group. Citing this collection of intel, Israel's national police commissioner, Pinhas Kopel, recommended that the Panthers' permit application be denied. Otherwise, he argued, violence and chaos would likely unfold. Kopel enjoyed a reputation as an experienced and capable lawman, and Meir could have accepted his recommendation and moved on. But the reason she had summoned some of her closest advisers was that she recognized the matter was too delicate to determine on narrow or technical grounds. One of her advisers had more reason than the others to be wary of running roughshod over the Panthers and their civil liberties.

Meir's minister of police, Shlomo Hillel, was an immigrant from Iraq. He was one of only two cabinet officials not of European origin who served as ethnic tokens in the Ashkenazi-dominated government of a country where more than half of the Jewish population was of Middle Eastern, or Mizrahi, descent. At least nominally, then, Hillel and the Panthers shared an identity.

Fourteen years earlier, when he was a junior member of parliament, Hillel became involved in an incident that would foreshadow the current crisis. An informal group of poor Mizrahi newcomers to Israel staged a protest against housing discrimination. They sensed they were being unfairly passed over when apartments became available. The police responded aggressively, dispersing the restive immigrants with force. Outraged by the reports of the crackdown, Hillel compelled a committee of lawmakers to investigate the incident. He knew some of the protestors and considered them fellow patriots who deserved better from the government. "The public must have confidence that the police is run not by hot-headed officers but by people possessing wisdom and a sense of public responsibility," he said at the time in a speech to parliament. To heed the advice of his younger self, he would need somehow to guide the situation toward a conciliatory outcome.

The rest of Israel's seasoned statesmen—and the bureaucracies they controlled—should have been prepared to handle unrest and contain Mizrahi disaffection. They had practiced when protests broke out at the immigrant camps in the 1950s amid an influx of hundreds of thousands of Jews. This decade of turbulence culminated in 1959 with an eruption that became known as the Wadi Salib Uprising. The rumored police killing of an unarmed Mizrahi resident in the city of Haifa triggered mass outrage and led to a period of dramatic confrontations between police officers and protestors. The memory of those clashes was worrying officials now as they debated what to do with the Panthers. "[The Black Panthers] could ignite ethnic tensions, possibly producing a rerun of Wadi Salib," the prime minister and her advisers realized, according to a police memo summarizing the discussion.

What the housing protesters, the Wadi Salib rioters, and, now, the Panthers shared was an existence outside of respectable society. These rebellions originated in distressed communities that lagged behind in a country that was rapidly Westernizing and industrializing. Their grievances were repeatedly dismissed because the protesters were on the margins. The Israeli government considered the people calling themselves Panthers to be "social rejects," as a police memo put it, reflecting long-standing attitudes toward Israeli's Mizrahi poor.

In other ways, however, the government was facing a new type of adversary. The Black Panthers were not communists with fealty to political parties or ideologies like those of some past protest leaders. Nor were they angry immigrant fathers and mothers who perhaps could be counted on to settle quickly in exchange for relative stability and marginally better conditions. The new menace emerged from what were being called "street corner gangs." Any urban dweller in Israel would have recognized them. Not mere delinquents, but rather bands of teenage boys and young men with flagrant disregard for social norms. The alienation that manifested itself in their separate style of dress, speech, and manners had never before translated into a political identity—until a street gang from the Jerusalem neighborhood of Musrara suddenly proclaimed its ambition to become Black Panthers.

To make matters worse, the Panthers were not acting entirely alone. The politicians were told that dangerous leftist provocateurs, from a group known as Matzpen, were attempting to hijack the nascent Panther movement. Matzpen was a Marxist organization with a few dozen members, and in keeping with the fashion of the far left, the tiny group had recently split into three factions. Their fringe views included hardline anti-capitalism and, more alarmingly for Israeli officials, a rejection of Zionism. After 1967, Matzpen was almost alone among Israelis in daring to speak out against the country's rule over conquered Arab territories. Yet, unlike the Panthers, Matzpen was not made up of society's rejects. Its activists all came from "good families," as one Israeli newspaper put it at the time, using a code that usually meant people of Ashkenazi descent with strong family ties to Zionist centers of power. Because they came from the establishment and disavowed it, their existence constituted a national shame. It didn't matter that they had no actual political clout.

One of the Panthers or someone close to them was feeding the police information concerning Matzpen's meddling. The intel was specific: Matzpen was holding "indoctrination" sessions for the Panthers about the necessity for violence, telling them that militancy was the hallmark of the American Black Panthers whom they hoped to emulate. There was even, reportedly, a plan in the works to have the Panthers wield nail-studded clubs against police. With such detailed intel, Kopel could feel confident in his case against allowing a demonstration to happen.

On the other hand, as the politicians realized, a rejection of the permit could backfire. The Israeli government had usually refrained from prohibiting demonstrations, at least those staged by its Jewish citizens. They recognized that protests served as a pressure valve for the disaffected and the aggrieved. The wider public, anyway, often responded to demonstrations with apathy. Denying the permit now would set a precedent and generate much-wanted publicity for both the Panthers and Matzpen. The officials also agreed that "it is very likely the protest would take place despite the prohibition out of a desire to clash with police."

Withholding a permit was not the only tool at their disposal. The discussion turned to what "positive measures" the police and city hall could take to placate the Panthers. Perhaps the military could be persuaded to accept some of them as recruits. If not military service, then authorities could help with job placements. Jerusalem mayor Teddy Kollek took it upon himself to work his connections with the media. His job would be to emphasize Matzpen's involvement and tell reporters that the Panthers were just "social rejects" who are undeserving of attention.

There were less than three days to go until the planned protest, and the permit application was pending. The officials were determined not to let the matter drag on. Within an hour, which is how long the meeting at Meir's office lasted, they would make their decision. If the officials were to approve the permit, they risked emboldening elements of society they considered to be illegitimate. Such a move would also alienate the police force, especially in light of intel assessments forecasting violence against officers. Denying the permit carried its own drawbacks, chiefly that doing so would resolve the matter only from a bureaucratic standpoint. The Panthers could defy authorities and hold a demonstration anyway—and that could end up being the worst of all scenarios. A decision to deny the permit would therefore also require some form of enforcement, which carried its own risks. Whatever choice they would make, the goal of the government was the same: to contain the threat of social turmoil.

2

1948

They Promised Us Jerusalem

ROBERT REUVEN ABERGEL was five years old when his parents decided it was time to move out of the Jewish quarter of Rabat, Morocco, and leave behind a country that countless generations of the family had called home. The year was 1948 and, in the faraway Holy Land, war had broken out. When the fighting was over, the entity known as the British Mandate for Palestine became a partitioned territory: on one side, the State of Israel, and on the other, the West Bank, ruled by the Hashemite Kingdom of Transjordan. The Abergel family knew little about the war or about the Zionist militias that fought to establish Jewish sovereignty over the land. Nor were they much informed about the wider ideological movement that was desperately lobbying international governments to recognize the creation of a Jewish state. But David and Esther Abergel had read their scripture and recited their prayers and they longed for an imagined

Jerusalem where Jewish brotherhood prevailed and material abundance was divinely ordained.

For the time being, the Abergels were in the minority among the hundreds of thousands of Jews in Morocco. The overwhelming majority preferred to stay put; there was a price to be paid for being the first to leave. The Abergel family with seven children, and still adding more, became wards of the Jewish Agency, the international organization arranging to bring Jews to the Land of Israel. The journey across the Mediterranean from Morocco to Israel would take the family two years. First, they traveled across the desert sands of North Africa for hundreds of miles to reach French-ruled Algiers. From there, a ship carried them to the shores of France where they moved into a decommissioned World War II camp. The family persevered even as their savings were siphoned away and their lives settled into the drudgery of collecting rations, negotiating for petty privileges, and obeying directives handed down by camp bureaucrats. Every day they waited to be cleared for passage to Israel. The excuses for the delay varied but usually centered on the medical condition of the children. In the crowded and unsanitary conditions of the camp, the migrants struggled to maintain their health. The elderly were rejected outright under a policy of screening immigrants for the fittest among them. The new state wanted only bodies capable of settling frontiers and fighting wars.

Meanwhile, in Tel Aviv, debates were raging within the nascent government and on the pages of newspapers about whether absorbing Moroccan Jews was worth the trouble. *Haaretz* journalist Aryeh Gleblum, for example, published a series of reports attempting to characterize people like the Abergels. "Among the Africans living in the camps, you will find filth, card games played for money, drinking for the sake of getting intoxicated, and prostitution," Gleblum wrote in the newspaper. "Anyone possessing any degree of responsibility must not be embarrassed or afraid to confront the problem head-on. Have we considered what would happen to this country if this were its population?" Only a handful of years after World War II, a newspaper in Israel was using the type of language that preceded the atrocities of the Holocaust—against fellow Jews.

If his parents understood little about the abuse they were suffering at the hands of people speaking in the name of Judaism, Abergel was only a child and knew nothing about it. Those early years of his life were a blur of fenced enclosures, sleeping in tents, and playing on the muddy ground outside with the children of other Moroccan families, all stubbornly hopeful about starting their lives over in Israel. When Abergel was seven years old, his family was finally cleared for immigration.

The ship that would transport the family to Israel docked in the French port of Marseilles in May 1950. It was called the *Negba*, a name that hinted at the eventual fate of many of its migrant passengers. In the Zionist imagination, the Negev Desert, which gives the vessel its name, was an empty desolation begging for intervention by the muscular Jewish state. David Ben-Gurion, the country's founding father and its first prime minister, famously envisioned that the desert would blossom if it were settled by Jews—the indigenous Bedouin population was seen as background noise or perhaps an impediment. Unsurprisingly, not many Israelis found the prospect of making their home in desolate reaches of the desert attractive. The group of people left to carry out the back-breaking labor of planting trees and building towns and roads in the dry sands were the masses of Jews from North Africa.

The *Negba* had been purchased a few years earlier from the Netherlands, and equipped with a ceremonial Torah book gifted by Amsterdam's wealthy Jewish community, to form part of Israel's small merchant marine. Sea access was critical because it was the country's only connection to the rest of the world. All the inland borders faced enemy countries: Jordan, Syria, Lebanon, and Egypt. Immigrants, tourists, and goods were delivered by the *Negba* to Israel weekly as it shuttled between Marseilles and Haifa. On the return journey, the ship carried government emissaries, commercial cargo, and, increasingly, Moroccan Jews who were horrified at conditions in Israel and had decided to go back. By 1951, 6,714 Jewish immigrants from North Africa and the Middle East had left Israel, with many returning to their native countries.

Embedding reporters among the passengers of the *Negba* offered a surefire way for the Tel Aviv press to generate attention-grabbing stories, such as when a band of communists took over the ship, removed the Israeli flag, and hoisted a red one in its stead. On another occasion, four veterans of the Spanish Civil War, on the Republican side, snuck aboard the *Negba* in Marseilles, hoping to arrive in Haifa and join the Israeli ranks fighting the Arab armies. And in 1949, a journalist decided to investigate the phenomenon of the Moroccan Jews leaving Israel and signed up for the *Negba*'s voyage to France. He reported that he attempted to talk the emigrants into changing their minds. Failing to do so, he concluded that they belonged to "an ethnic group of complainers and whiners. They gripe against Israel and do not distinguish between a nonsensical objection and a rational complaint."

On May 10, 1950, the *Negba*, with the Abergels on board, departed Marseilles on a five-day journey. The family spent the time confined to the lower decks; tourists and notables were up top. On the fifth day, the white steamship finally arrived within sight of the wooded hills of Haifa Bay. As the passengers spotted land, they broke out in song. For Abergel, it was a relief to know that his seasickness would soon be over. His mother gathered him and her other children and announced, *It's time to get dressed.* She opened a suitcase and pulled out their finest outfits, the ones usually reserved for Shabbat. She washed the children as best she could and had them change. *We must look our best when we greet Eretz Yisrael,* she said.

When the bridge was lowered onto the pier, prominent members of the Israeli Bar Association were assembled at the port. They had come to receive the bodies of Russian Zionist lawyer Oscar Gruzenberg and his wife for burial. For the Abergels and the other migrants, Israel reserved a different type of welcome ceremony. As they prepared to dis-embark, strange men boarded the vessel. Some wore plain clothes while others wore workmen's overalls and carried metal tanks on their backs. The officials ordered the immigrants to separate into three groups: men, women, and children. Without warning, the uniformed men began spraying bodies, faces, and hair with a white powder. The passengers screamed and panicked, and their Shabbat clothes were ruined.

During the two and a half years since they had left Morocco, the Abergels spent long months in makeshift camps, periods interrupted only by transportation to another camp, another port. But perhaps the wait—and the final humiliation of being sprayed with DDT as if infected with a contagious disease—was the price of admission to their reconstituted Jewish state. At least, now, they were home.

From the port, they were delivered by truck to a dusty outpost known as Pardes Hanna. The place seemed eerily familiar to Abergel. He recognized the fenced-off tent city, the desolation beyond the perimeter, and the brown-skinned Jewish kids playing in the dirt while their parents loitered around aimlessly. They slept ten or more to a tent on cots that they would fold up each morning to make room inside. In the sweltering heat of the summer days, they took refuge in the shade of the tent, while the mothers prepared food on Primus stoves. Esther cried through the first night in the camp. She was terrified because of the howling of jackals outside. This moment almost broke her and she demanded that her husband, David, find a real home for them or else she would return to Morocco.

Esther's defiance—of her husband, of camp clerks—and demand for proper housing was emblematic of a growing agitation among the camp dwellers. They noticed that as soon as European Jews arrived, the clerks whisked them away without regard to the established waiting list. By favoring the Ashkenazim at this junction, the Israeli state began to forge their counterpart: an underclass consisting of Jews from Asia and Africa, today referred to as "Mizrahim." Coming from countries as culturally and linguistically diverse as Morocco, Iran, and Turkey, they had little in common with each other when they arrived. But in Israel, suddenly, the breadth of their backgrounds was compressed into a single one, defined by their common experience of being treated as lesser than their fellow citizens with lighter complexions.

In Abergel's recollection, his parents and members of their generation were so demoralized that they generally accepted their conditions of destitution, passively putting their faith in God's salvation. The historical record indicates something a little different. Police records and newspaper clips from the time reveal that while some Moroccans clamored to leave—an act that itself can be considered political—many stayed and organized for collective action. The landscape of Abergel's early childhood in Israel was punctuated by uprisings, strikes, and protests.

Just months before the Abergels arrived at their camp, thousands of camp residents had come together to form the General Committee of Immigrants of Pardes Hanna. In a manifesto published in Hebrew, Arabic, and French, the committee railed against the harsh conditions in the camp and decried the humiliations residents were forced to endure. Authorities were accused of neglecting to provide medical care or schooling for the camp's children. And when people died, their corpses would rot for days before the arrival of transport, typically a garbage truck infested with rodents. The manifesto described the relationship between camp workers and immigrants as that of "master to slave." Years before the radical theorist Frantz Fanon published his ideas, these forgotten activists were speaking a language that sounds like postcolonial theory.

Tensions continued to build, reaching a peak when residents learned that Avraham Harush, a 49-year-old immigrant from Egypt, died during a visit to the camp's office. Newspaper accounts and a police report offer conflicting versions of what happened. But what has been established is that Harush came to the office demanding a housing assignment. He was desperate for his family to leave the temporary dwelling situation at the camp. There was yelling, an altercation, and two police officers intervened. Some immigrants saw the officers throw Harush to the ground and kick him until blood spattered out of his mouth, according to an account in a communist newspaper. The official investigation into the matter, however, declared the cause of death a brain hemorrhage and said the body had shown no signs of a beating. The stories converge again when relaying what happened in the hours following Harush's death. An angry crowd of hundreds gathered outside the office. The staff and police retreated, barricading themselves inside. Migrants stormed the structure, pelting it with rocks and attempting to light it on fire. After a few hours, police mustered forces from five nearby stations and managed to suppress the rebellion.

It is unknown how Abergel's parents reacted to the controversial death at Pardes Hanna, nor whether they joined the agitators. But within a month of the siege on the camp office, the family staged an escape. Leaving was not explicitly illegal—some lawmakers did propose making it so—but it was difficult and discouraged.

For one thing, transportation and navigation posed a hurdle because private vehicles were scarce and public buses did not serve the transit camps. Moreover, camp officials pleaded with and pressured immigrants not to leave. They threatened to make leavers ineligible for employment and public benefits. In some cases, families that left anyway, by foot or by hitchhiking, were rounded up by police and returned to the camp. Luckily for the Abergels, they had help from relatives on the outside. A few young men from the Abergel clan had arrived in Palestine in 1947 to enlist in Zionist militias during the war effort. Known as Machal, or overseas volunteers, they came to fight for the establishment of Israel and then stayed. The camp clerks agreed to let the Abergels leave with their Machal relatives but only late at night under the cover of darkness lest others catch on. They smuggled out a few foldable cots, a Primus stove, and a kerosene lamp, and hopped onto the back of the getaway truck. Now, they were finally headed where they had meant to go all along: Jerusalem, the city of biblical Zion.

Many Machal fighters lived in a military barracks in Jerusalem near the front line, which after the fighting ended became the de facto border between Israel and Jordan. The fighters had seen the surrounding neighborhoods empty out of their Palestinian inhabitants. Refugees for whom the founding of Israel was not a miracle but a *nakba,* or catastrophe. The war displaced nearly a million Palestinians. After the fighting subsided in 1949, rather than let them return, Israel seized Palestinian homes for the use of Jewish immigrants.

In Jerusalem, many of the wealthier Palestinian districts were now bombed out and they came under Israeli control. The city itself was split through the middle with a militarized no-man's-land separating the Israeli half from the Jordanian one. A string of Palestinian neighborhoods straddled the border zone on the Israeli side. In these areas, the stone houses were pockmarked with bullet holes and prone to collapse. They were also in the direct line of fire of Jordanian troops.

It was in the remains of a house in the border zone that Israeli commander Moshe Dayan and his Jordanian counterpart Abdullah al-Tall sat down to negotiate a mutual ceasefire in November 1948. They laid out a map over an uneven surface, and each commander drew a jagged line representing the front line claimed by his respective forces. Dayan used a green grease pencil to mark the boundary of Israeli-held territory and al-Tall used a red one to draw the line of Jordanian control. The space in between was the no-man's-land. They negotiated in good faith, but the result was what one deputy mayor would call "a cartographer's nightmare and a geographer's catastrophe." When magnified to

Immigrants pouring into the Jerusalem neighborhood of Musrara in the aftermath of the 1948 war encountered the rubble of bombed-out buildings and a militarized border with Jordan. Meitar Collection, The Pritzker Family National Photography Collection, The National Library of Israel.

the scale of reality, the grease pencil marks translated into strips of land 200 feet wide running through the city for which there was no accounting in the agreement.

In the preceding decades, the debate about Jerusalem had been about how to ensure universal access to places of worship. The cleaving of the city into two insoluble parts was a tragedy that compounded the war's toll in human suffering.

In 1949, the *Palestine Post,* as the *Jerusalem Post* was known until 1950, compared the aftermath of the war in the holy city to Berlin after World War II. "There's a new iron curtain going up in Jerusalem," the newspaper lamented.

A few months after the ceasefire agreement, in the spring of 1949, Dayan lifted some of the military restrictions over the abandoned residential areas. What followed was a scramble for real estate. Desperate for housing, small family groups from West Jerusalem poured across the former military lines into the abandoned lands. "It was an atmosphere reminiscent of a South African or California gold rush and the laws of the game are practically the same: you must stake your claim by pinning a piece of paper with your name to the door of the selected house and it won't do any harm (and may not do much good either) if you add a few imposing titles and official stamps," the *Palestine Post* reported.

The most central of these debris-choked border neighborhoods was called Musrara. It was made up of large stone houses with four-sided, sloping red-tiled roofs. The high, arched windows of these villas looked out to gardens that were lush with roses and fruit trees—pomegranates, almonds, mulberries, and medlars. Well-off Palestinian Christians had established Musrara at the end of the nineteenth century as one of the first built-up areas outside the confines of the Old City walls. All the Palestinian residents fleeing the shelling of their neighborhood in the 1948 war remained stuck on the Jordanian side of the city, forever separated from their homes.

The most famous Palestinian refugee from Musrara is probably Sirhan Sirhan, who was a little boy when his family left. Years later, he would gun down Robert Kennedy in Los Angeles over his support for Israel. As part of Sirhan's defense, his father gave a lengthy interview describing the family's idyllic life before it was disrupted by the trauma of explosions and dismembered bodies. "In 1948, [Sirhan] saw many things . . . woundings and sufferings," the father explained. "Sirhan was injured in the war . . . in his head and heart." After the Sirhans fled from Musrara to the Old City, they settled into a home formerly occupied by Jews.

Even as the homes abandoned by the Sirhans and others filled up, Jewish immigrants continued to arrive. The Abergels were among those who came a little late to the Musrara housing rush. The only homes available were the ones closest to the Jordanian border, situated beyond Dayan's grease pencil-drawn ceasefire line. The house they managed to claim had an underground reservoir to store rainwater and an old-fashioned pump to draw it back up. Miraculously, the house was still receiving electricity from Jordanian power lines. The Abergels now numbered ten and they packed into the tiny space of two rooms and a kitchen. A feeling of relief washed over Esther. After more than two years in transit, she had finally found a home. More than a roof and four walls, she wanted and obtained a community of neighbors like her old one in Rabat. With virtually every family in the vicinity having also come from Morocco, it made for a hamlet of familiar sounds and scents.

For David, the pious patriarch of the family, settling in Musrara brought him within mere hundreds of yards of Jerusalem's most sacred site, the place that had beckoned every time he prayed. Whenever he stood on high ground and gazed eastward, David's eyes would now catch sight of the walls of the Old City and above them the Dome of the Rock, the imposing Islamic shrine that dominates the city's skyline and marks the location of the Temple Mount.

As close as he was, the holy sites remained off-limits, rendered inaccessible by a carpet of barbed wire and the watchful guards of Jordan's Arab Legion, who occupied concrete pillboxes and sandbag forts atop the walls and towers of the Old City. Israeli snipers took position opposite the Jordanians on the rooftops of monasteries, churches, and hospitals. Abergel, who was born during World War II in Morocco as Allied forces prepared their invasion of North Africa, now faced a childhood on the front lines of another conflict.

In the 1950s, hundreds of thousands of Jews followed in the footsteps of the Abergels and left their native countries for Israel. It was a mass exodus that eventually siphoned away nearly all North African and Middle Eastern Jewry, bringing a conclusive end to two thousand years of Jewish life in a massive region that spans from the west, where Africa meets Spain, to the southeastern tip of the Arabian Peninsula. In countries governed by Islamic law, Jews had been relegated to a secondary, if protected, status. Long periods of coexistence, to borrow a term from contemporary parlance, were interrupted by periods of violence or repressive policies. Circumstances varied widely from country to country. In Morocco, French colonialism offered Jews opportunities for advancement and integration. By 1948, on the eve of Israeli independence, hundreds of thousands of Jews lived in cities and throughout the towns and villages of the countryside, occupying every rung of Moroccan society. This Jewish community produced advisers to the Moroccan king, singers of widespread appeal such as Zohra el Fassia, and prominent anti-colonial critics like Abraham Serfaty.

Until the mid-1950s, most Moroccan Jews remained in Morocco even as the struggle over Palestine increasingly permeated public discourse throughout the Middle East. Expressions of solidarity with Israel were forbidden and many Jews faced accusations of disloyalty. The rise of Zionism and Arab nationalism eventually rendered the shared existence of Jews alongside Arab Muslims untenable or, at the very least, mutually undesirable across much of the region.

It was a swift transformation. Until the end of World War II, Zionism's Ashkenazi leaders had all but ignored the existence of Middle Eastern Jewry. They envisioned the founding of a utopian society in Palestine modeled after their own native environs. This European project would draw its population from the millions of Yiddish-speaking Jews living in western and eastern Europe, who had suffered for centuries under repressive regimes surrounded by antagonistic Christian neighbors.

Theodor Herzl, the father of modern political Zionism, outlined at the end of the nineteenth century the contours and goals of the movement. "I am a German Jew from Hungary and I can never be anything but a German," Herzl wrote in what became a seminal text of Zionism. "At present, I am not recognized as a German. That will come soon, once we are over there!" His proposed idea, subsequently adopted by the movement at large, was that colonizing—a word used commonly and unabashedly at the time—Palestine would upgrade the status of Jews. They would be invited to join the "worthy" races of the world; they would become German. And, as early Zionist leader Ze'ev Jabotinsky, the Russian-born intellectual forefather of Benjamin Netanyahu's right-wing Likud Party, believed, Jewish settlement in the Holy Land was meant "to expand the frontiers of Europe to the Euphrates River."

But Herzl's and Jabotinsky's plans did not exactly pan out.

In the early twentieth century, Russia and eastern Europe were home to millions of Jews, whom the Zionist movement hoped to lure to Palestine. And millions did uproot and leave their countries behind. But for the vast majority of them, the destination was not the nascent Jewish settlement in Palestine. They amassed on American shores instead, directing their political energy into U.S. labor movements, not Zionism. In the decades that followed, with Europe still home to major Jewish communities, the Nazis came to power in Germany. After the Holocaust, Europe had six million fewer Jews, further depleting Zionism of its pool of potential pioneers. Finally, after World War II, the last major reservoir of European Jewry was located in the Soviet Union. But the Soviets lowered the Iron Curtain and locked the Jews in. Israel's pre-state Jewish community numbered only about 600,000. It was a small number in absolute terms but even more precarious relative to the 1.3 million non-Jews who lived in Palestine.

Under the pressure of this demographic imbalance, it began to dawn on Zionist leaders that the Middle East, the region where they wanted to build a Jewish state, was inhabited by an additional million people who called themselves Jews. The new country would need the extra bodies to man its factories, fields, and infantry forces. Perhaps more urgently, Israel would need a mass of people to help bolster its case for establishing an ethnic state to the exclusion of the indigenous population of Palestinians. Nearly a million Arabs fled or were expelled from the country in the 1948 war. Within a few years, Israel repopulated the land with about a million Jewish immigrants from the surrounding Arab countries. These new Jews were uncomfortably similar to the Palestinians who had been pushed out. From their complexion and facial features to their Arabic tongues and Oriental manners and predilections, the Mizrahi population posed a threat to Herzl's vision of a European state in the Middle East.

In response to that threat, Israeli leaders enacted policies that marginalized the masses of incoming Mizrahi Jews. For example, as part of its effort to secure a hold on conquered land, Israel designed a policy to populate its remote border region with dozens of new settlements. Almost invariably, immigration authorities sent Mizrahi Jews to build and live in these sites, while assigning Ashkenazi immigrants housing in and around Tel Aviv, where employment options and services were concentrated. In the area of education, the government built a multi-tracked system, based on the explicit idea that Mizrahi children are cognitively deficient. Mizrahi children received inferior schooling that led them into vocational schools rather than academic and professional disciplines. Meanwhile, the country's education ministry congratulated itself on rescuing Mizrahi youths from the backwardness that had supposedly accrued in their communities over hundreds of years of Oriental influence.

The discrimination of this period is immortalized in the chorus of a popular 1960s tune by musician Jo Amar, who sings about visiting a government employment office. The clerk asks him where he's from. When he answers, "Morocco," he's shooed away, but when he returns and responds, "Poland," he's welcomed in.

Most of the newspapers of the era acted as official mouthpieces of political parties and guarded with zeal the limits of acceptable dissent. One exception, a weekly paper named *This World*, pilloried the chumminess of press and government, running exposés that embarrassed politicians and undermined the carefully crafted image of Israel as an egalitarian society. For a cover story that ran on September 17, 1953, for example, the paper's Iraqi-born editor Shalom Cohen investigated conditions in the transit camps where immigrants even less fortunate than the Abergels languished for years. Cohen coined a phrase that would enter Israeli parlance when he wrote that "the blacks are getting screwed." In doing so, he was one of the first in Israel to color the nascent Mizrahi community "black." Despite Cohen's efforts, the mainstream press adopted a different approach to covering intra-Jewish tension, preferring to report on "the feelings of inferiority" which they found bafflingly common among Mizrahi immigrants.

The Abergels' ghetto of Moroccan immigrants in Musrara, located at the edge of the country's territory but within walking distance of the capital's wealthier districts, such as Rehavia and the German Colony, attracted more than its share of such coverage. A journalist touring the neighborhood's tight alleyways around the time of the Abergels' arrival encountered a group of men gathered on a stoop. He asked them about their job prospects and their families, and they volunteered details of their poverty. At one point in the conversation, one of the men mentioned that his daughter could not get herself admitted to a hospital despite a condition that left her deaf and paralyzed. "It's because I am Sephardic," the man said, using the more prevalent term at that time for Mizrahim. That line triggered a response from the rest of the men, and they began excitedly talking over each other until reaching a consensus: in Israel, everything requires a *protektsya*. The word, which comes from Russia, means "protection," but it refers to the nepotism governing access to opportunities. In Israel's Ashkenazi-run institutions, Mizrahim didn't have the right social influence or elite connections.

The linguistic mishmash of those days is also evident in the word "Musrara." The neighborhood was named after the Arabic word for the jagged pebbles found in its vicinity. But to the ears of immigrants speaking the Moroccan dialect of Arabic, "Musrara" sounded just like their word for "lovely."

In the 1950s, because of the width of Dayan's grease pencil, no one knew exactly where the neighborhood ended and no-man's-land began. Israel and Jordan quarreled over the position of the line at countless meetings of the Mixed Armistice Commission that was set up by the United Nations.

From the center of Israeli Jerusalem, the streets leading to Musrara slope downhill through the neighborhood until reaching the edge of the demilitarized zone in the lowlands. There, Israel built concrete barricades known as "dragon's teeth" to block the way for Jordanian tanks and mechanized infantry units. Before the city's division, the main thoroughfare running through Musrara led to the Damascus Gate of the Old City, where pilgrims performed their rites and ordinary residents did their grocery shopping. Now, the road was empty save for an Israeli soldier, who stood 40 yards across from a Jordanian legionnaire, each charged with turning away all who approached, aside from the few who were authorized to cross.

Children raced makeshift carts down the deserted road. They claimed the barricades, rubble, and uninhabitable houses as a playground. As they played, they yelled to each other in Moroccan dialect, the only tongue they had in common. Hebrew phrases slowly infiltrated their speech, likely by the influence of the soldiers stationed nearby; contact with other kinds of Israelis was minimal at first.

One of Abergel's favorite activities as a child was helping a kite maker who worked in one of the neighborhood buildings nearest the border. One hot summer day in 1951, Abergel remembers that he was flying kites from a rooftop when the sound of three gunshots echoed from the direction of the Old City. The Arab soldiers atop the walls cocked their rifles. Scurrying along the ramparts, they yelled unintelligible words in panicked voices. The news soon spread across both sides of the border. An assassin had killed King Abdullah of Jordan while he was attending Friday prayers at the Old City's Al Aqsa Mosque.

The stately stone houses of Musrara emptied when their Palestinian owners fled during the 1948 war. Soon, Mizrahi immigrants arrived in large numbers, and overcrowding defined life in the neighborhood. Central Zionist Archives, Jerusalem.

On more ordinary days, Abergel often became curious about the children living on the other side of the border. He studied them and they studied him back. Separated dozens of feet at the narrowest points, the children exchanged smiles and, sometimes, rocks. "We became friends through our eyes," Abergel later said of these moments.

With entire families sharing one or two rooms, the only space for children to play was outside. In one particularly bad case of crowdedness, 120 people lived in a two-story building that had one common bathroom. Despite these conditions, parents continued having children, obeying their rabbis and government officials who emphasized the biblical commandment to be fruitful and multiply. Esther Abergel would give birth to 14 babies, of whom ten survived into adulthood. But she was far from the neighborhood record-holder. That honor belonged to a woman named Amalia Ben-Harush, who had managed 20 births, the last of which earned her a check for one thousand liras and a letter from Israel's prime minister, David Ben-Gurion, valorizing her accomplishment as "unique in her generation and perhaps in all generations." The press also participated in the commendation of Amalia and her husband, Meir, portraying them as the ideal Moroccan immigrants for contributing to the country's birthrate.

Immigrants, roads, and children—all things flowed downhill toward the no-man's-land. So did the sewage. An open drainage ditch a few feet wide carried refuse from Ashkenazi West Jerusalem through Musrara along an alleyway called Mishmarot. The Abergel home was located there, on the good side of the street. People living in the buildings on the other side had to traverse the canal by leap or plank every time they headed out the door or came back home. In the 1948 war, Jordan, not feeling obliged to accept its enemy's flow of sewage, had permanently blocked the ditch. Clogged like a sick artery, the sewage line soon flooded, forming a pool at the lowest part of the no-man's-land. Musrara residents referred to the fetid body of water as "the swamp." In the summer, swarms of rodents and mosquitoes from the swamp invaded the neighborhood, overwhelming attempts at sanitation.

On rare occasions, outsiders ventured into Musrara to behold the ethnic ghetto and its hungry masses. These visits—by audacious reporters or campaigning politicians—produced some of the few existing accounts from the neighborhood's early years under Israeli rule. One of the most telling accounts involved a visit by Israel's founding father, David Ben-Gurion. The coincidence of his name—that the modern prime minister of the Jewish state was called David just like the greatest of the Hebrew kings in the Bible—contributed to the reverence for him among the immigrant population. As part of his visit, he met recent arrivals from Iran, the Yair family.

In their two-room apartment, he asked one of the Yair boys, "What do you want to be when you grow up?"

"A prophet," the boy responded. Being raised in a traditional Jewish household, the prophets of the Bible populated his imagination. Their proximity to God and miraculous feats made them role models.

Ben-Gurion stroked his cheek and said, "We'll see what happens."

His reluctance to endorse the child's dream underscores his secularism and points to his vision of a nation instilled with pioneer spirit, not pious passivity. The exchange also underlines the vast distance between the observant Jewry of the Middle East and the secular Zionist leadership of the country. Their spiritual yearnings notwithstanding, Israel had devised decidedly material plans for such immigrants.

For Ashkenazi journalists, visiting Musrara could be a somewhat traumatic experience. As one reporter for the *Jerusalem Post* wrote, the neighborhood was home to "hundreds of families living in conditions reminiscent of the Middle Ages: small children, half-dressed and covered with dirt, play in the middle of the streets or in trash-littered plots; on the pavements, and often in the streets, women stoically wash the laundry or cook over charcoal burners, throwing slops into putrid streams of sewage." Adding to the scene were the sounds blaring from the radios: "They are turned on full blast, usually to the wailing chants of the Orient. The music hangs thickly over the entire quarter, penetrating every nook and cranny."

The government had situated its Ministry of Education in Musrara, which was ironic given that many of the local kids went virtually unschooled. For years, the only school in the neighborhood was a religious institution run by teachers from the Orthodox movement of Agudat Yisrael, and as such it was unsupervised by the ministry. The education it offered consisted mostly of Torah lessons by teachers who spoke Yiddish among themselves and who sometimes beat the students for allowing Arabic to slip off their tongues.

Some students managed to scrape together enough of an education to advance to the secondary school level, but tuition for high school cost more than most families of the border zone slums could afford. The *Jerusalem Post* dispatched a reporter to investigate the phenomenon of slum youths hoping to escape their circumstances. "They actually starve themselves to pay for secondary school tuition," the paper reported. "They rob themselves of sleep, poring over books whose meaning they cannot grasp." From the perspective of education officials, such efforts only served to subvert government policy. No amount of striving could alter the students' designation as future farmworkers, plumbers, and mechanics.

The government considered the hope for social mobility, increasingly common among some of the youths, as a doomed form of "educational escapism" to borrow a phrase from the *Jerusalem Post*. Almost invariably, the students failed to surmount the hurdles they faced and their graduation rates remained low. The explanation of one Jerusalem school principal was that these children "have no thirst for true learning . . . either they have never developed the capacity for critical thinking or they are afraid to display it." Instead of university, they were diverted to vocational programs.

Many years later, Abergel described his own experience of leaving the educational system. He was speaking to a reporter for a story investigating what went wrong with Abergel's life: an attempt to identify the moment that society irrevocably failed him and set him on a path of trouble and adversity.

The story Abergel shared centered on the first sentence in the Bible: *In the beginning, God created the heavens and the earth.*

It was the second grade, and his teacher was trying to deliver a lesson about the book of Genesis. Abergel raised his hand to ask a question. *If God created "the earth,"* Abergel asked—in Hebrew, "the earth" is a synonym for the "land" of Israel—*then who created "the abroad"?* The unholy pun only works in Hebrew, but it was inappropriate enough to get him kicked out of class. He never returned.

Abergel and many of his fellow would-be Panthers dropped out in early elementary school. By the mid-1950s, the Israeli authorities took increasing notice of immigrant youths, who became known as delinquents or street corner kids. The papers began reporting on teenage girls turning to prostitution, overcrowding in juvenile detention centers, and a court system ill-equipped to handle young offenders. Less than a decade after arriving, Israel's North African immigrants began exhibiting the criminal tendencies falsely ascribed to them in the racist press reports of Israel's first years. In other words, those reports were turning out to be a self-fulfilling prophecy.

The government set up various commissions to study the problem of delinquency. In 1956, one body of experts recommended that the government raise the age of criminal culpability from 9 to 12. The change came too late for many Musrara youths who by then had been led by police to face scornful judges over stealing fruit at the souk or illegally salvaging metal fittings from the no-man's-land for sale to merchants. Several of Abergel's brothers got caught up in the juvenile justice system and were sent away to reform schools. The papers eventually published exposés about the abuses at these institutions, committed by staff who compensated for their lack of training with extra aggression.

At the age of 14, Abergel got caught up in the system too. Abergel recalls vandalizing a motorbike by painting his name and the word "Musrara" on the seat—a dumb, self-incriminating move—while in other accounts, he was said to have stolen the motorbike. Whatever the case, the police found him: he was facing a possible sentence of incarceration at one of the reform schools. Fortunately for Abergel, his probation officer convinced the court of the boy's potential, and the judge agreed not to send Abergel to a juvenile facility. Instead, he sentenced Abergel to spend the remainder of his school years at a program of rural immersion on a kibbutz.

The program took place at the Mishmar Hanegev kibbutz in Israel's remote and semi-arid south. There, Abergel split his weekdays between work that started at early dawn—milking cows, picking fruit in the orchard, cleaning out the chicken coops—and class, which occupied some two hours each afternoon. Abergel took a special liking to Hebrew, Bible studies, and chemistry. On Saturdays, instead of letting the boys in the program rest, the kibbutz gave custody over them to two kibbutz men who became known to the boys as "The Sheriffs." They dubbed them that because The Sheriffs carried rifles, barked orders, and exuded a kind of swagger that they had only seen on screen. Nearly every weekend, The Sheriffs loaded the boys onto the back of a truck and headed to the desert. After the dust from the wheels settled and the boys were assembled, The Sheriffs would mark off an area for the day's dig. They would instruct the boys to scrape away layer after layer of earth and to stop whenever they reached something unfamiliar.

Abergel was clueless about the purpose of the work, but in hindsight, it became clear that the kibbutz was harvesting ancient artifacts. The most daring such acts of archeological excavation took place at Masada. Years before the inaugural expedition of 1963 that introduced the site to the world, The Sheriffs and the boys hoisted themselves up the rock plateau with ropes to conduct an unofficial excavation, Abergel recalled. In those years, every inch of soil in the Holy Land seemed to contain secrets, and each month ushered the discovery of magnificent mosaics, forgotten settlements, and archeological lodes full of coins, daggers, and other bronze relics. Dayan, the fabled Israeli commander who wore an eye patch and delivered stunning military victories in 1948 and then drew the borders that would create the no-man's-land, was the most famous of the country's tomb raiders.

At age 16, after about two years on the kibbutz, Abergel embarked with his group of fellow teenage parolees on a four-day hike from the lowland desert up to Jerusalem. Armed with Sten guns, they climbed mountainous terrain, marching past villages and forests until reaching the Valley of the Cross, where an ancient monastery stood. They set up camp in a historic stone structure that seemed like a fairy-tale castle to Abergel. He knew he was within walking distance of his family and he begged to take time off to visit since he hadn't seen them in two years.

Perhaps he hadn't realized how much he missed home, but a sense of desperation built up within him. His chaperones didn't seem to care; they refused to let him visit. Finally, Abergel took a piece of rope and tried to hang himself. He was stopped in time, and to calm him down, they promised to grant him leave after the group returned to the kibbutz. Instead, back at Mishmar Hanegev, officials handed Abergel a letter assigning him to another kibbutz. They sent him off with a pack of clothes and a bus ticket. At first, he complied, reaching the road leading to the new kibbutz. But then he paused and decided he was done with that life. Hitchhiking to Jerusalem, Abergel soon returned to the neighborhood of his childhood. No officials came looking for the missing teenager. "No one ever came to look for me," he later said. "It was as if I was never there."

3

1959
The Rebellion of Wadi Salib

THE HOT SUMMER day of July 8, 1959 was rough for Akiva El-Karif, but by evening he managed to find some respite at Café Rosolio near his home. A resident of one of Haifa's poor immigrant districts, El-Karif settled down at a table and listened to the record of Arabic tunes the staff had agreed to play for him. As he sat there, a police officer from a nearby precinct, Asher Goldberg, walked in. He approached El-Karif, ordered him outside, and said, "Get in the patrol car."

The station had dispatched Goldberg and another officer, Karol Segal, to pick up El-Karif, who was known around town as a drunk. Earlier that afternoon, reports had trickled in painting a picture of a man in dire need of help. El-Karif had been spotted throwing himself at cars in traffic. "I have more money than Ben-Gurion," he'd been yelling, referring to the prime minister, "and I don't want to live." Later that day, he also smashed some bottles at a bar after a bartender refused to sell him alcohol. It is unclear what had triggered these outbursts. Little is known about his background, except that he was a Jewish immigrant from North Africa who worked as a laborer in the city's wholesale market.

El-Karif disobeyed the patrolman's order to get into the police car. Instead, he stepped back inside Café Rosolio, grabbed some bottles, and started hurling them at the police car, hitting the windshield, according to reports submitted to the minister of police in the following days and weeks. El-Karif also threatened to kill himself and the two officers. Eventually, Goldberg and Segal opened fire. One of the bullets struck El-Karif in the midriff, burrowing through his gallbladder and into his spinal column. The officers would later say they had been aiming for El-Karif's legs. He was evacuated to the hospital in critical condition.

Moshe Gabay, a fellow resident of the tight-knit neighborhood known as Wadi Salib, was at a nearby café that evening, he later testified. He was chatting with friends about their difficulty in finding proper employment when he suddenly noticed a commotion outside. People were yelling, "They killed him!" Gabay joined the crowd in front of Café Rosolio where word was spreading that El-Karif had been shot five times by police. The police were gone by then. Confronted by angry onlookers, they had retreated into their patrol car and driven away, barely evading a barrage of rocks.

Hundreds of residents assembled that night at a local synagogue. From there, they marched out and staged a spontaneous protest, chanting slogans about "police murder" and about the overall treatment of their community. Haifa's police chief arrived and listened to their grievances, managing to quell the outrage, at least momentarily. That night, however, David Ben-Haroush, a local 35-year-old with political aspirations, decided to galvanize the community to action. With the help of the members of his small group, the Union of North African Immigrants, he organized a gathering of residents. He told them he wanted to stage a demonstration the next day—emphasizing that it must be nonviolent. "He made us swear that even if the police beat us, we won't respond," Gabay later said. By morning, Wadi Salib was plastered with the news: "To have an existence in this country, we must get organized," flyers declared.

Virtually all of Wadi Salib went on strike that day. At 8 a.m., after staying up all night, Ben-Haroush led hundreds of demonstrators on a march toward the Haifa police headquarters in Hadar, an upscale Ashkenazi neighborhood nestled above Wadi Salib. They waved black flags and at least one Israeli flag. As they marched, one of the demonstrators ducked into a nearby butcher's shop, where he soaked one of the flags in chicken blood. The march's route could be traced in droplets. Finally, the protesters reached their destination, assembling in front of the police station. An officer snapped a photo of the moment, documenting a banner that read, "Where is the justice? The police have killed an innocent man."

The police tried to calm the crowd by informing them that El-Karif was alive. They invited Ben-Haroush to visit the hospital to see for himself. But the neighborhood would not be pacified. The day turned into an open revolt against the government and, more specifically, the ruling party, known as Mapai. Police cars were targeted with stones. A bank manager's car was set on fire. Clubhouses belonging to Mapai and its all-powerful labor federation, the Histadrut, were vandalized. Display windows of upscale storefronts were shattered. Destruction of property and impromptu demonstrations continued late into the night. The police responded with force, further aggravating the community. By the end of the day, 34 people had been arrested and at least 13 people injured.

Mindful of the public spotlight, the top brass of the police arranged to have officers of Mizrahi backgrounds sent to the front lines of the conflagration. This strategy served to downplay claims of ethnic suppression and drive a wedge between officers and their communities. One of the Mizrahi officers dispatched to Wadi Salib was Avraham Tourgeman, a young Moroccan-born policeman, who would climb the

The eruption in Haifa's Wadi Salib neighborhood in 1959 started with an impromptu protest march to demand justice after police shot a local resident. The Israeli flag flown by protesters became a potent symbol of the desire of Mizrahi Jews to be fully included in the national story. Photo by Oskar Tauber, © Josef Tauber.

ranks and go on to manage the police response to the Panthers. Later, he would be reassigned to the Tel Aviv district, where again he found himself at the center of police efforts against Mizrahi agitation.

The next morning, July 10, Israel's national police chief sent out a telegram labeled "urgent" and "top secret" to senior commanders across the country.

"A number of disturbances have taken place over the past 24 hours in Haifa," wrote Inspector General Yosef Nahmias. "It is possible that these incidents are the result of intentional incitement. False rumors about the incidents in Haifa could cause the riots to spread. Until further notice, you must act with heightened but inconspicuous alertness, especially in population centers."

If it were not for the alternative press, the news of Wadi Salib might not have spread outside of the city. Television broadcasting had yet to arrive in Israel. The government, perhaps wisely, was suspicious of most media and their potential to inflate incidents. Until the late 1960s, it banned all television broadcasting in Israel. For now, radio and the print media arrived several days late to the Wadi Salib story and covered it as a criminal matter, rather than a political or social one. There were two exceptions: the communist newspaper *Voice of the People* and the independent *This World*. Word of the uprising spread most effectively not through the alternative press, however, but through informal immigrant networks. Almost as soon as confrontations kicked off in Haifa, police reports started coming in about similar incidents at immigrant population centers like Migdal HaEmek, Be'er Sheva, Acre, and Tel Hanan.

Over the next few weeks, the police established intelligence-gathering operations within these Mizrahi communities. The few documents to emerge from these spy networks reveal the existence of at least two surveillance operations. One was code-named "Kochav" and the other "Eshel." Both explicitly targeted Jewish citizens based on their ethnic identity. Whether domestic spying on Israel's Jewish citizens had any antecedents remains unknown because the archives of Israel's police are sealed. Similarly unclear is when—and whether—these operations were ever terminated. What is known is that in Wadi Salib and at dozens of other locales, the police developed a network of informants and undercover officers. Regional headquarters assigned intelligence officers to process incoming information and coordinate operations. Officers tracked the comings and goings of various individuals, studied "internal social structures, cults, movements, and families," and sought out "inciters, criminals, and likely rioters."

The police seemed to believe that there was something inherently restive about the North African communities and particularly the Moroccan one. One memo from the time described "loyalty oaths administered by religious figures." These loyalty oaths, detectives wrote, were born out of a traditional practice among Moroccan Jewry in which individuals "pledged allegiance to their ethnic community." In an intensely patriotic country, any semblance of a divided loyalty could be construed as a threat. "You are being asked to provide facts that are as accurate as possible on loyalty oaths for North African Jews carried out by religious leaders that have occurred recently," a police memo said.

In early August, the police were close to completing a survey of target locations when commanders realized that their undercover officers were a little too conspicuous. Superintendent Aharon Chelouche, a senior intelligence officer, warned that immigrant communities were tensing up and closing ranks. He issued new guidelines on how to conduct surveillance: "Make sure that encounters with informants are clandestine, that their incentive for cooperating with us is clear, that meetings are set at regular times, [and] that the informants are well briefed about their targets."

One of the places profiled as part of Operation Kochav was the Musrara quarter of Jerusalem, home to a group of children who would one day become the Black Panthers. Police detectives drafted a document listing supposedly suspicious individuals and groups in the neighborhood. Among them were several community-run burial homes and a group known as the Independent Organization of North African Immigrants in Israel. The meeting places of the suspected rebels and lawbreakers were noted and included a café, an apartment belonging to an opposition party activist, and a community club. In hindsight, two names in the Musrara memos stand out: Eliyahu Marciano and Eliyahu Biton. They were the fathers of future Panther leaders Saadia Marciano and Charlie Biton.

Both Eliyahus left Morocco as adults and resettled their rapidly growing families in the part of Musrara that was closest to the border with Jordan. They were immediate neighbors of the Abergels. The characterization of the two men as likely agitators had merit—and not only because of their affiliation with a small neighborhood organization for ethnic advancement. In the 1950s and '60s, both men were implicated in passport and visa forgery schemes. In two cases that reached the press, the men were accused of providing counterfeit papers to individuals trying to leave Israel and travel to France; police discovered a passport forgery laboratory set up in Biton's apartment. They also found several dozen partially filled out French-Moroccan passports, consular seals, chemical agents for removing ink from paper, and foreign currency. Considering the prevailing stigma and bureaucratic challenges faced by Mizrahi immigrants who wanted to leave, passport forgery was not merely illicit but also a political act. Israel wanted to be the country Jews flowed into, not out of.

Biton also gave expression to his politics by joining the Herut party, the main Zionist faction outside of Israel's governing coalition, and a predecessor to today's Likud party. This move is probably what earned Biton his description in the memo as a "political provocateur." Mapai, the party representing Zionism's labor movement, ruled Israel with an almost Soviet-like iron fist and expected nothing short of obedience from poor immigrants who depended on state welfare for survival. In the early years after Israel's founding in 1948, Mizrahi voters supported Mapai at the ballot box. They were sometimes forced to do so by party bosses. Over time, many in the Mizrahi community began supporting the right-wing Herut. They weren't necessarily voting according to an ideology. To a certain extent, support for Herut came from Mizrahim who merely wanted to register their dissatisfaction with Mapai.

Evidence for Biton's dissidence also survives in a long-forgotten government survey of the population in Musrara. The data collected from hundreds of households in the survey included such items as family size, country of origin, and occupational status. Virtually everyone voluntarily participated. Only one household was noted as resisting: the Bitons. The note entered for their entry said, "This family refused to answer any questions and the neighbors also refused to provide information on them." This kind of recalcitrance was rare among Mizrahi immigrants both because of their dependence on the state and due to a genuine and prevalent desire to belong to a collective Jewish society.

It was a short while before the Wadi Salib revolt that Abergel, now 16 years old, terminated his own kibbutz sentence and returned to Musrara. When the protests started, Abergel heard about them through men in the community with whom he worshipped at synagogue every Shabbat. One Saturday after service, the adults gathered Abergel and several other teenagers. They handed them buckets of wheat paste and stacks of political flyers bearing expressions of solidarity with Wadi Salib and told them to cover every bare wall they encountered. The wheat-pasting was followed by a plan to stage a protest. But before it could materialize, the police caught wind of it, and 200 officers descended on the neighborhood in a show of force. After having been away for about three years, Abergel felt proud to belong to the atmosphere of collective action in his community: "I didn't realize exactly what it was we were fighting against, but I felt the spirit of a common struggle," he would say decades later.

When the civil unrest started to subside, the Israeli government wanted to know what had caused it. A commission of inquiry was established, informally referred to as the Etzioni commission because it was chaired by a judge named Moshe Etzioni. The stated goal was to determine the root causes of the uprising—and to answer the question of whether ethnic discrimination existed in Israel.

Over the course of a month, 17 public sessions were held and several closed ones as well. Forty-six people gave testimony and documentation was amassed. The commission had no power of subpoena so all testimony came from those who volunteered to speak. They included residents of Wadi Salib, teachers, police and probation officers, the mayor of Haifa, and the chief of police. All of them were men except for one, a woman who was called up to speak only after complaining about having been excluded.

Gabay, the Wadi Salib resident who provided valuable eyewitness testimony of the immediate ruckus following the shooting of El-Karif, also gave an account of his own life. He told of blatant prejudice that affected every aspect of his development as a person. "At school, they didn't call me by my proper name," he said. "They would call me 'Morocco' and it weighed on me. I was a child."

After serving in the military, he returned to Wadi Salib and got married. "If I knew life would be this way, I would have never gotten married. I left the military and from that moment on, the trouble started. I signed up at the employment office. For the first three months, I had no job. My mother has been in Israel for five years. She lives in a transit camp and has no way of making a living. I have a wholehearted desire to help but I have no way of doing so. A few times, she came over to my house and cried: 'I have nothing to cook Shabbat dinner with.' I told her, 'Don't come here anymore. I don't want to hear about your suffering anymore. I suffer enough myself.' I feel like I could lose my mind. Enough with all this misery. If I could find a ship, I would get on it and leave the country."

Gabay talked about his experience at the employment office, echoing the themes in Jo Amar's popular song. He was there so often it felt as if "he lived inside that office." Whenever he did get work, he always seemed to be assigned menial labor. "Right now, I am working for the city of Haifa in sanitation. If a guy like me has to work in trash collection, that's fine. I'll do it . . . but if I had a *protektsya* I would already be sitting at an office somewhere long ago. Unfortunately, no one even asks me how I am doing."

He continued: "I believe all the Sephardis are being deprived, not just the Moroccans—Baghdad, Persia, Iraq. At the factories and plants in Haifa, they let us work only for three weeks before Passover or Rosh Hashanah so that we'll have a way to pass the holiday. The rest of the time, it's either no work or make-work jobs.

"I don't have it in my blood. I don't have the courage, and I don't know how to steal. If I'd want to steal, I would go become a thief instead of seeing my wife and child in agony. When I come home, my wife tells me, 'You don't want to work.' And I fight with her and some-times my blood boils and I want to murder her.

"Here in Israel, I should also be entitled to more after having served in the military. I know how to write and I know two languages. I curse the day that I was born Moroccan. They sent me to the post office to apply to be a mailman. They said to submit my resume in writing. I wrote it and they asked me where I learned how to write. I said in Israel. He asked me, 'Where are you from?' I said from Morocco. He said, 'What a wonder, a Moroccan who writes like that.' I said, 'What's the matter, are all Moroc-cans ignorant?' He asked me to write in French and I did. I got the job."

Gabay said he then began shadowing a veteran mailman as a trainee. "But the man tried to dissuade me, saying, 'It is not a job for you. You'll be moving around all the time. You'll get tired, going up and down the stairs. You're a young man, maybe go to vocational school.' So, I said, 'Why didn't you go to vocational school?' He began to tell me about what happened to him—wars in Germany. And I felt sorry for him because he said his children were killed over there. It really pained me. I remember when we were kids . . . We used to pray and cry and do a little [ritual] for our brothers in the European diaspora . . . we'd walk barefoot in the street and pray to God to save them. We worried about them. Now they look at us sideways, because, for them, 'Moroccan' is like saying you are an international criminal."

The testimonies of Gabay and others provide a rare and profound window into the experience of racism during the first decade following Israel's founding in 1948. Almost equally revealing are statements made by low-level government officials who interacted with Mizrahi immigrants.

On the evening of July 28, for example, a day after Gabay testified, a probation officer for juvenile offenders in Haifa addressed the panel. His name was Levy Cohen, and he was born in Germany and raised in Switzerland. He had been a social worker since before the founding of Israel and the mass immigration of Mizrahi Jews that followed. The commission wanted his perspective on why the country had divided along ethnic lines. Why were North African immigrants feeling so alienated and disgruntled? Cohen began talking about the distrust he encountered among immigrants, tracing the perception they had of being discriminated against. The judges asked him repeatedly if such perceptions were merited.

"I cannot say so with absolute certainty but I do believe that government institutions do not discriminate against immigrants from North Africa," Cohen said. "But one thing I am convinced of—among the Israeli population, there are prejudices against immigrants from North Africa, and it is possible that these prejudices engender these feelings of deprivation and discrimination." After some further questioning, Cohen allowed that there was some responsibility on the part of the state: "I cannot say that there is deliberate discrimination on the part of those public institutions, but because of the prejudices, indirectly, there is discrimination."

With the encouragement of the commissioners, who seemed to hang on to his every word, Cohen allowed his answers to meander. His testimony at times evolved into a theoretical discussion about what prevents Moroccan immigrants from building collective capacity and adapting to their circumstances in Israel. While allowing that poverty is one part of the explanation, he said, "the primary factor, in my opinion, is in the area of mental hygiene among immigrants from North Africa in Wadi Salib."

He used a term, mental hygiene, that may sound peculiar to contemporary ears, and one that was already falling out of fashion in 1959. Originating in the United States at the beginning of the twentieth century, the mental hygiene movement sought to increase awareness of mental health as an issue of public and scientific importance. Ostensibly based on empirical methods, the mental hygiene movement often promoted a definition of well-being that corresponded with whiteness. Some leading proponents of the movement also promoted eugenics. In the Israeli context, mental hygiene was equated with being Western, with the shedding of so-called Oriental characteristics.

One of the proclaimed goals of Zionism was to forge in Israel the New Jew, as distinct from the diasporic Jew. The New Jew would be a free citizen, muscular, and connected to the soil of his homeland. The old Jew, having internalized the oppression he suffered, was seen as meek, weak, and unfit for hard work. In Israel, therefore, mental hygiene was associated with the shedding of diasporic attitudes and manners, and the adoption of an assertive, confident, and fresh Israeli identity. The Zionist leaders who came from Europe sought a break with the Orthodox Jewry of eastern Europe, characterized by life in shtetls and ghettos, the Yiddish language, and traditional garb.

Talking about North African Jews and mental hygiene led Cohen to an anecdote from his childhood. "In my professional experience I do not know discrimination—Negro, Christian, Arab, Jewish—to me everyone is a person," Cohen said. "But if I have to admit it . . . when I was a little boy in Germany one time, I walked down the street with my father, and suddenly we saw a man with a beard and a *kapoteh* [a type of frock coat worn by Orthodox Jews]—and I confess that to this day, if I encounter a diasporic type, an *ostjude* or *yehudon,* it is in my blood."

What he divulged in this story was a deep-seated aversion to diaspora Jewry, or at least to the stereotype of diaspora that Zionism had cultivated. *Ostjude,* meaning Jew from the East, and *yehudon,* which is roughly like saying "little Jew boy," were common derogatory terms, and Cohen was aware he shouldn't use them. Following that anecdote, he described his disappointment upon his first encounter with newly arriving Mizrahi immigrants. This sequence of his testimony suggests that on an emotional level, Cohen could not help but see immigrants from North Africa as another version of that detested diasporic Jew he encountered on the street in Germany as a child all those years ago.

His testimony also provided more empirical explanations for the difficulty immigrants experienced in Israel. "A large portion of the North African youths arrived in Israel as part of the Youth Aliyah," he said, referring to a program that brought Jewish teens to Israel without their parents. "At kibbutzim and institutions, they tried to educate the youths and show them a different lifestyle," he said. When the children and parents reunited, there was "a clash between the parents and the child who had already come to know different values than those of the parents. This led to conflicts. . . . The child no longer sees in the father a positive father figure. We managed to break the values but we did not succeed in creating new ones."

If fathers had lost authority in the family, mothers felt helpless in their new environs. "Adult women, mothers to ten children—and still she misses her parents. They were used to *hamulot,*" he said, referring to the extended family structures common across the Middle East. "The mother would live with a married sister and with mom and dad, and when she needed to go someplace she had no problem finding someone to watch over the children. Certainly, in our society, we cannot return to a regime of clans and patriarchal rule by parents."

Throughout his testimony, he used the United States as a foil. "The problems of the Puerto Rican population in New York could arise here as well," Cohen warned. Children and teenagers were beginning to organize into gangs "like in the United States."

Even if it were just for the testimonies collected, the Etzioni commission would have deserved credit for creating a rare moment in Israeli history. At no other time before or since had the country held such a forum for an extensive public conversation on racism and discrimination toward Mizrahi Jews. But the commission also made other contributions to the historical record. On orders from the commission, the police sent three plainclothes officers to tour the Mizrahi neighborhoods of Haifa and interview people. These visits were called "reconnaissance missions" and involved "state-sponsored, ethnographic research into Haifa's Mizrahi population," according a historian of the era.

The other significant accomplishment was the collection of hundreds of letters that immigrants from Morocco sent to relatives and friends who had stayed behind. These were letters that had been intercepted by a shadowy government office called the Censorship Bureau, whose surveillance was justified by national security considerations. Letters that immigrants sent back home were deemed harmful and confiscated if they contained negative assessments of life in Israel. Now, however, the government commission found these confiscated letters helpful, a repository of unadulterated public perceptions among immigrants.

On July 31, at the end of the first week of the Etzioni commission's deliberations, leaders of the ruling Mapai party arrived on the outskirts of Wadi Salib. The party scheduled a campaign event at a local movie theater as clashes between police and the community continued. It was a challenge and a test. Would the neighborhood submit?

Police intel suggested that it would not. Ben-Haroush and his Union of North African Immigrants were organizing to disrupt the event. On the day of, the police mustered crowd-control forces. But in case police officers weren't enough, Mapai also summoned its militia. Established in pre-state times, Plugot Hapoel were squads of thugs used by the Mapai-dominated labor federation to disperse unsanctioned strikes and protests.

It was a Friday evening. Officers stood guard in the area and used walkie-talkies to coordinate. An order came in through the wireless sets and more police arrived, equipped with steel helmets, shields, and batons. Fifteen minutes into the event, a crowd of several dozen Mizrahi men gathered outside the theater. They shouted and hurled a few stones, which triggered a police order to disperse. When the crowd ignored the command, six officers wielding batons advanced on the group. They were met with more stones. The men broke away toward the side of the building where loudspeakers had been set up to relay the speeches from inside the venue. About 200 people gathered to shout together and drown out the voices from the speakers.

Next, a rock smashed through a theater window and demonstrators threw projectiles toward the officers. The police commander shouted an order and a group of officers marched on the agitators in battle formation. The ensuing street fight lasted less than an hour. Most of the locals managed to get away, blending into the nooks and shadows of Wadi Salib. Some were arrested, having been chased down alleyways and over rooftops. The neighborhood soon settled into an uneasy silence. The silence broke suddenly as bricks, cinderblocks, and pieces of burning wood began raining down on the police. The union had turned the neighborhood into a fortress, erecting barricades and amassing makeshift munitions on strategic rooftops. One of the projectiles hit a water main, which broke and flooded the streets. By midnight, after a couple of hours of clashes, the police had seized the rooftops and installed searchlights on them. Many officers were injured and all were drenched in sweat from the exertion on this hot summer night. By 1:15 a.m., the police had completed large-scale arrests and news reporters left the scene.

They left too soon. Two hours later, the police noticed suspicious movements from the window of one of the neighborhood homes. A squad of officers was dispatched. They tried to enter but the door was locked. They knocked and hollered but no one answered. As they broke in, someone from an inner room fired a shot in the direction of police. The bullet hit a picture hanging on the wall. Before retreating, the police spotted two women and several children inside. Then, a voice that was familiar to the officers bellowed from the apartment: "I'll kill myself and kill you if you come near." It was Ben-Haroush. He had avoided arrest and was holed up inside. Police reassembled and prepared to deploy tear gas. But within a short while, he and his fellow organizers surrendered. Ben-Haroush told the officers he never meant to hurt anyone.

On Sunday morning, Ben-Haroush and his accomplices appeared in court. He was pale and unshaven and his hair was disheveled. He wore blue slacks and the shredded remains of his white t-shirt. Overnight, Ben-Haroush had torn his shirt and tried to use the fabric to hang himself. A guard who had been walking by managed to stop him just in time.

In parallel with the protests, the Etzioni commission's hearings, and subsequent legal proceedings, the government cabinet held internal discussions on the state of ethnic relations in Israel. Minutes of these conversations were unsealed only recently. Nearly all members of the cabinet were Ashkenazi, and the two who weren't came from Sephardic families with long-established roots in the country. They ruled over a population that was more than 50 percent Mizrahi. The ministers remained steadfastly deaf to the substantive grievances raised by the protesters. Reactions were universally dismissive and defensive, with ministers alternately accusing the activists of being self-seeking criminals and drunks, puppets of right-wing politicians, or ingrates.

Minister of Police Bechor-Shalom Sheetrit, for example, whose family had come from Morocco a century earlier, briefed the cabinet on what he believed was the true character of the people behind the mayhem. He called them "political hacks, persons of degraded morality, who are known for their ties to criminality and prostitution, and random bystanders." Prime Minister Ben-Gurion was on vacation and missed a related cabinet meeting, but he provided his assessment of the matter in a letter to Judge Etzioni. "An Ashkenazi gangster, thief, pimp, or murderer would not gain the sympathy of the Ashkenazi community (if there is such a thing), nor would he expect it," Ben-Gurion wrote. "But in such a primitive community as the Moroccans—such a thing is possible."

At a meeting that took place a day after the arrest of Ben-Haroush, Golda Meir prepared to give her own assessment. She was serving as foreign minister, but, previously, she spent most of her career in government working on immigrant issues. She had been charged with organizing housing, employment, and basic welfare for the masses arriving to Israel. Her biographers describe her as a restless champion and her efforts as heartfelt. Now, faced with a manifestation of Mizrahi anger and alienation, Meir dismissed the case of Wadi Salib as "a riot that must be crushed all the way to its foundation." In her assessment, Ben-Haroush had been given everything an immigrant could ask for and yet was unsatisfied. "What happened here was not based on a societal issue," she told the ministers. "Kill me and I won't admit that it's a societal issue."

On August 10, the trial of Ben-Haroush and his fellow conspirators opened with a declaration of the judge's own bias. "Any man who comes to me and announces he is Moroccan will get twice the sentence," she announced. "You are dividing the people." In response, Ben-Haroush demanded that the judge be disqualified. This sort of well-publicized wrangling characterized the initial phase of the trial. The judge tried to downplay the trial's political significance and the defense moved to frame the whole affair as an act of persecution. When the proceedings concluded in late September, Ben-Haroush was found guilty and sentenced to two years in prison on charges of obstructing police and illegally possessing and discharging a firearm. The sentence was reduced on appeal to ten months.

The more important verdict came in early during the Ben-Haroush trial when the Etzioni commission presented its official report. In 22 pages submitted on August 17, the commission laid out its conclusion that there was no deliberate discrimination against Mizrahim in Israel. Meir did not conceal her satisfaction with being officially vindicated. Speaking to the cabinet a few days later, she said, "there is an important thing in the report that I haven't seen headlines about in the papers. . . . there is a decisive ruling that there is not a policy of discrimination and that government offices assist extensively in housing, education, and other areas. These are good words for the government." The Etzioni commission endorsed her view that Wadi Salib was not an uprising by an ethnic community but an outburst of anger by ungrateful outcasts.

Moments later, in this self-congratulatory atmosphere, the ministers moved the discussion to the issue of Mizrahi representation in government. Apparently unaware of the irony, Minister of Trade Pinchas Sapir told the group he would automatically rule out the appointment of a North African jurist to the Supreme Court. Fully confident of their virtue, Israeli leaders continued blindly to advance policies and practices that were starkly racist and discriminatory. In its defense, Mapai had yet to see any punishment at the ballot box for its condescending and authoritarian style. Indeed, at the parliamentary election that November, the public gave Mapai its biggest electoral victory yet. Ben-Haroush, while in prison, ran for office as the head of Union of North African Immigrants but failed to cross the electoral threshold and didn't secure a single seat in parliament.

Musrara was in many ways like Wadi Salib: a community of impoverished North African immigrants living in a densely built-up area whose homes had belonged to Palestinians until 1948. Through the 1950s,

Jerusalem's civic leaders and journalists observed the increase in delinquency in the city and ruled Musrara the source. At the same time, the neighborhood's youths were seen as a prime target for alleged Christian missionary activity. There were dozens of hastily established synagogues in Musrara, but the area was dominated, architecturally at least, by churches and Catholic institutions dating back to the nineteenth century.

The most famous of these was the French Notre Dame compound, which included a hospital, a chapel, a monastery, and extensive living quarters for pilgrims. In the absence of a framework for services for youths or other welfare services, these Christian institutions stepped in to fill the void. Musrara's children received free meals and healthcare from the institutions, and though no attempts to proselytize were ever revealed, the mere potential of such a threat sufficed to mobilize municipal budgets and Jewish philanthropists.

The confluence of public concern over delinquency and proselytization generated an opportunity in Musrara for a crop of idealistic, youth-focused social workers to step in. Employed through the city's social aid office, they installed themselves as permanent fixtures among the street youths in Musrara and other slums. Unlike Cohen, the German-born probation officer in Haifa who testified in front of the Etzioni commission, social workers in Jerusalem were almost exclusively Mizrahi, and some even spoke Moroccan Arabic.

The man who led these trailblazing social workers was Avner Amiel. By the late 1950s, Amiel earned a reputation as Musrara's "foster father and father confessor." Under an array of job titles—including coordinator of the Jerusalem's Municipal Youth Clubs for the Social Welfare Department—he worked to divert "slum youngsters" from a life of delinquency.

A reporter shadowing Amiel in 1958 described Amiel's first encounter with a 14-year-old boy "whose semi-wild, semi-impudent look shone through several layers of dirt."

The boy opened his mouth to curse, and "as he did so, his personality split into two: his mouth and the rest of his body."

He kept his head trained on Amiel but twisted the rest of his body in the direction of escape. "The boy delved deep into the youth leader's genealogy. He started with the youth leader himself. He traced his canine traits back to his father, and his father's father."

As Amiel glanced at the boy, he let his face form into a grin.

"The boy imputed him guilty of a series of vile sex offenses."

In response, Amiel simply laughed. When the boy finally ran out of breath, Amiel said, "If you've finished, let's go to the movies."

That was the end of the tantrum. Amiel had passed the same test countless times before.

Amiel descended from a line of distinguished Moroccan rabbis. His parents had immigrated to Israel as religious pilgrims in the 1920s and settled in a Jewish neighborhood outside the Old City. They groomed their son for a lifestyle of religious observance, sending him to a noted yeshiva school. But when he was a teenager, Amiel chose a different path. It was the days of the British Mandate when Palestine was ruled by decree from London. Amiel joined the Jewish Underground, helping with the armed resistance to the British. In 1946, when Amiel was 16, British intelligence discovered his role with the Haganah militia, secretly stashing weapons. They arrested him and tossed him into a detention camp where he encountered a book by Mahatma Gandhi. It propelled Amiel toward a life of community organizing.

Early in his career, Amiel began searching for the reason behind the deep alienation and demoralization he sensed among Mizrahi street youths. Poverty and age alone could not explain the gushing angst. He concluded that it had to do with a particular difficulty faced by immigrants from North Africa trying to acclimatize to Israeli society. The men, expected to be breadwinners, "are crushed by poverty," he said in an interview at the time. "They see wonderful job opportunities here, jobs they cannot have because they have neither the training nor the connections." It was especially frustrating because they had successfully adapted to the French system in Morocco, but in Israel, "they are thrown back."

Meanwhile, members of the younger generation are "anxious and eager to learn," he said. "But they are met by barriers on every side." As a result of this frustration and anger, boys increasingly formed into gangs that roamed the streets. "This will be an inevitable development if the process of demoralization in the quarter is not halted and reversed," Amiel warned.

In doing his job, he tried to navigate a path between two types of community leaders who he thought did more harm than good. "The first is the aggressive kind who wins a following by harnessing their bitterness—the type organizes demonstrations which degenerate into riots," he said in the wake of Wadi Salib, offering a thinly veiled criticism of Ben-Haroush. The second is the "Westernized" immigrant expressing fealty to the ruling party and doing its bidding ahead of election day. Amiel's goal was to get first-generation children as well as their immigrant parents to organize into a sustainable movement and demand change from the government.

Amiel could not have known how close to the mark he was when he made a particular prediction in 1959—validated 12 years later with the emergence of the Panthers. He believed that the Mizrahi community would awaken one day and develop new young leaders. At that point, the Mizrahim "won't have to be force-fed Western ideas, they will accept them readily," he said. "And once they do, they will throw off the thrall of the past with a vengeance, releasing a burst of energy which will astonish everyone."

4

1967

The Fall of the Wall

ABOUT 250 FEET from the walls of the Old City, in a shack whose doorstep marked the internationally recognized edge of Israeli territory, Reuven Abergel was sleeping in. It was the morning of June 5, 1967, and, outside, a war was happening. Still, Abergel remained asleep. He finally woke up when the door to his home burst open. Armed men in military fatigues rushed inside. They yelled at him in what sounded like Arabic. He looked at them through his still crusty eyes and noticed mustaches on their faces and dark complexions. Seeing these features only heightened the confusion and surprise of being abruptly awakened. *Was this an invasion by Jordanian legionnaire soldiers?* Abergel wondered. He too, like these soldiers, had a mustache and brown skin. And he spoke Arabic—so he blurted out in the language of the enemy, *Who are you? Is this an invasion?* No, it wasn't. The two sides had mistaken each other for Arabs.

In defense of the soldiers who couldn't tell whose territory they were in, Abergel was quite an odd thing to encounter. *Was he out of his mind?* they asked him. How could he be asleep when war was about to break out? And how the hell had he not been conscripted into military service by now?

The fighting had begun at 7:45 a.m. hundreds of miles away. Israel scrambled a squadron of jet fighters to the Sinai Peninsula; explosives fell on Egyptian air bases and obliterated most of the enemy's aircraft before they could take off. Abergel was in deep slumber when this happened, but, by then, civil defense sirens had alerted the rest of the Israeli population to the military escalation. In the preceding weeks, the military had fully mobilized its reserves. Civilians, especially those close to the border, had been busy for days stacking sandbags on window sills and filling bomb shelters with provisions. In Jerusalem, the *New York Times* reported, preparations had been made with a "certain deliberate calm" and "little or no panic."

Everyone in the city of 200,000 people helped: "both ultra-Orthodox and militantly liberal Jews, members of a larger number of Christian denominations than can be found in Rome, thousands of immigrants ranging from faculty members at the Hebrew University to illiterates from North Africa, and the squabbling representatives of seven political parties. This mixed bag has been molded together by the threat of war." The supposedly illiterate North Africans were most accustomed to the tension, of course, having sustained sporadic barrages of Jordanian gunfire for almost two decades; they referred to themselves, sometimes hopelessly and sometimes angrily, as the nation's "cannon fodder."

For the first few hours of fighting, Israeli leaders were intent on persuading Jordan to stay out of the war and spare Israel the need to defend an additional battlefront. What gave them hope was that Jordan's King Hussein had done Israel the courtesy of tipping them off that war was becoming unavoidable, based on what he was hearing from other Arab leaders. But by midday, Jordan's own decision to enter the war became clear and most abundantly so in Musrara. First came bursts of machine gun fire. Then, the neighborhood absorbed a barrage of shells from mortar and howitzer guns. The Jordanians trained their barrels on the entrances to buildings where people sheltered and on exposed open stretches of street.

Abergel was a 24-year-old able-bodied man. The soldiers' expectation that he should be in uniform and attached to some battalion was reasonable. Or at least that he would be contributing to the war effort in some capacity. But this was Musrara, and its men, by and large, did not get drafted. That's because the military had a policy against enlisting people with juvenile records. It would have been difficult to find a single young man in the neighborhood who hadn't been arrested, whether for theft, pickpocketing, or simply because the police had to pin a crime on someone. But even in Musrara, Abergel represented a special case. He did not share in the Israeli feeling of togetherness, the solidarity in the face of border skirmishes and war. He belonged to the most neglected age group of young, poor immigrants, those who had arrived before the authorities even noticed it had a delinquency problem on its hands. Abergel was so outside society that the war caught him by surprise.

Amid the Jordanian bombardment, Abergel slipped away from the border zone rather than join the war effort. He sought out and found his wife in a government bunker farther away from the border in the West Jerusalem and spent the war safely holed up with her.

Thirteen-year-old Koko Deri wasn't able to escape the area as easily. He was at his home on Musrara's eastern edge, mere steps away from no-man's-land, and had somehow gotten separated from his parents and the rest of his family. All that stood between him and the dozens of Jordanian positions was a landscape of fences and barbed wire entangled with overgrown vegetation and decaying stone buildings. He wanted to make a run for a bomb shelter, but each time he took a peek outside, he became a magnet for fire: the bratatat of machine guns became a constant soundscape, punctuated by the even louder booms of mortar shells.

For whatever reason, there was suddenly a lull, and Deri dashed uphill toward the center of Jerusalem, utility poles collapsing around him and water bursting out of broken pipes. He eventually found his parents. They huddled together on the dirt floor of a basement. But he stayed there for only a short while. Curiosity got the best of him, and Deri joined other teenage boys who had decided to venture outside. They encountered a convoy of Israeli tanks and armored vehicles heading east toward Jordan. "Get out of here!" the troops inside the vehicles yelled to no avail. Israel was launching its offensive and had begun invading Jordan.

The Old City walls that stood impervious for 500 years were vulnerable to the destructive power of modern munitions. But as long as the warring sides respected the holy city as singular and irreplaceable, the walls would remain a strategic defense and all fighting would circumvent them. Musrara, long exposed to warfare, was suddenly sheltered by its proximity to the Old City, and Jordan trained its artillery on more important targets farther away.

Israel's ground attack on East Jerusalem came from two directions: one to the south of the Old City and one to the north. Deri followed on foot as the armored battalions to the north blasted into the no-man's-land through Mandelbaum Gate. At the head of the convoy, the combat engineers were detonating explosives known as Bangalore torpedoes to clear barbed wire and other obstacles blocking the way into East Jerusalem.

With a few curious and intrepid civilians in tow, Israeli troops advanced on the closest Palestinian neighborhood to the border. The homes they reached were empty. Deri and the thrill-seekers entered—and so began the looting. His entire life, Deri had had nothing. No material possessions besides a set of clothes, some soap, and whatever he managed to scavenge or steal. With gusto, he grabbed a white sheet off a bed and tied the ends together to make a sack. He tossed inside every manner of food, drink, and clothes. Some people made off with faucets. He saw one man carrying a television set and another a typewriter. Deri thought of it as a game. For the next few days, his objective was to infiltrate East Jerusalem, pilfer from abandoned homes, and escape without setting off landmines or catching blows from Israeli border police officers charged with keeping civilians like him away.

The war lasted six days. By the third day, Israeli forces had already captured the Old City. Soon, all the land stretching to the Jordan River was under Israeli control. In the north, Israel took control of the Golan Heights from Syria, and in the south, it took the Sinai and Gaza from Egypt. Israel had waged one of the most effective military campaigns in history, multiplying its territory several times over.

Anywhere in the world, when Jews pray, they face the general direction of Jerusalem. It's a ritual that signals the longing for return, nurtured over 2,000 years of exile. In Musrara, worshippers do not need to consult a compass to orient themselves toward the proper direction of prayer. They can simply turn their bodies to the omnipresent walls of the Old City, within which stands the sacred Wailing Wall. For 19 years of Jordanian rule, entry into the Old City was restricted, and that banishment only strengthened the pull of the ancient and the sacred. With the war over and the barricades coming down, the masses would soon be arriving. But the first civilians to cross over in a wave that has never ended were the residents of Musrara.

"Ahalan" and "tfadal," Palestinian shopkeepers called to Deri as he wandered through the ancient winding alleys soon after the fighting ended. "Hello." "Welcome." He accepted an invitation to sit down from a man who looked as old as his grandfather and ran a small café. Deri, only a teenager, felt a little embarrassed as the man's wife and children hustled to put coffee and food on the table in front of him, treating him as if he were their superior. As the Palestinian man spoke to him in Arabic, Deri found that he understood what was being said. The dialect was a bit strange, but patience and mutual curiosity smoothed over the linguistic differences between their Arabic and that of his Moroccan upbringing.

The old man shared his experience during the Israeli military's invasion of the Old City. In the buildup to the war, Jordanian radio stations and newspapers had waxed arrogantly about Arab armies crushing Israel in battle and repelling the Jewish colonizers from Palestine. The outcome of the first few days of the war, when the exact opposite happened, turned that confidence into fear. The café owner recalled that as the soldiers poured into the Old City, he gathered his family to shelter at home, dreading what would come. *We waited for them to come and kill us,* he told Deri.

Of all the interactions Deri had with Palestinians in the immediate aftermath of the war, his conversation with a man who was relieved not to be butchered remained etched the most clearly in his memory. It gave him an explanation for the deference the Old City residents showed him and other Israelis upon their arrival. In the following months, Deri kept coming back, but not to loot or merely to be served. He began feeling at home among his Arab neighbors, united by language, customs, and the scents wafting from family kitchens.

Deri's experience was not unique. Ayala Marciano, who lived down the block from Deri and had brothers his age, also vividly recalled crossing into the other Jerusalem. Her mother, Aliza, loaded a backpack with candy and fruit. She took an Israeli flag and fastened it to a stick and attached it to her bag. Grabbing Ayala, Aliza marched down to the Old City. Soldiers were still stationed everywhere, and she blessed them, stuffing sweets into their hands. "May God protect you," she repeated again and again. Palestinians were in their homes, behind green metal doors in the favored style of the area. If they peeked their heads out, Aliza charged over to meet them. "I come in peace," was how she introduced herself. Her overwhelming and effusive greetings almost inevitably earned Aliza an invitation to come in and have some tea. It was impossible not to let your guard down when she spoke of Morocco and her beloved Muslim neighbors. In a short time, Ayala made friends and spent much of the rest of her childhood among Palestinian children of the Old City.

Today, when fellow Musrara-raised Reuven Abergel thinks about the experience of crossing into Palestinian East Jerusalem for the first time, he sees a milestone in his political consciousness. The encounter with the Arabs across the border was a revelation: "Something awakened in my DNA," he said. He felt more at home among the enemy than he did in West Jerusalem.

No one documented these encounters between residents of Musrara and East Jerusalem at the time they happened. Israel was busy lionizing its paratroopers and generals—the narrative of heroes liberating the Wailing Wall and reunifying Zion. It is only in the past few years that this alternative history is being excavated in interviews with aging people whose memories of events have faded. Nostalgia, political bias, and other factors have likewise degraded the factual reliability of these stories. At the same time, it is also clear that many residents of Musrara shared in the general Israeli suspicion toward Palestinians and other Arabs, and many voted for hawkish, right-wing parties, representing the start of a pattern of Mizrahi voting that prevails to this day. But whatever the larger politics, something remarkable did occur between these two communities: a rare, genuine instance of what today is called coexistence. Until the war, residents of the neighborhoods lining the border, areas almost exclusively populated by Mizrahi Jews, saw daily warning signs: Danger. Stop. Border. Living so close to that territorial edge engendered curiosity and mystique. The act of crossing over in postwar Jerusalem helped dissipate some of the tension built up in previous years.

As Mizrahi Jews from Morocco, many in Musrara had lived among Muslims for years. Count their ancestors and the time frame extends back many centuries. Then, the community uprooted itself and moved to Israel. Many in Musrara grew to miss the camaraderie they felt with their bygone Muslim neighbors. For a honeymoon period after the war of 1967, the Palestinians became proxies for these lost Arab neighbors and friends. Palestinians may have viewed the amiability of Moroccan Jews with different eyes, but they, too, ventured across the former border. One day, for example, a family of Palestinians strolled into Musrara and pointed at the Abergel family home. *"Hada beiti,"* one of them said. "That is my house. We used to live here." Abergel's mother, Esther, invited them in and offered them a meal. They shared the story of 1948 when they evacuated their home, and Esther told them of the exodus from Morocco. The families kept in touch for years, Abergel recalled.

While the division of Jerusalem into two by the no-man's-land may have represented the most tangible partition in the city, the formal border was not the only one that came down in the wake of the war. With its victory over the Arab armies that encircled it, Israel instantly shed its identity as a besieged backwater and became a society triumphant, delusional with self-importance, geographically expansive, and eagerly receptive to foreign imports. In an instant, the entire world rushed in, impressing itself upon Musrara's youths in a way that was all but irresistible to its teeming reservoir of restless teenage boys and young men.

The grown-ups and elders in the community were more firmly anchored to the traditions of the old country and shackled by their poverty to their established routines. The girls remained for the time beholden to the expectations of their parents and to gender roles prescribed in their community. It was the thousands of Mizrahi boys

In the late 1960s and early 1970s, formative bonds developed between the boys who would become Panthers and American Jewish girls studying in Israel or visiting on extended stays. Courtesy of Vicky Judy Free-Cannatello.

crowding Jerusalem—variably referred to as outcasts, marginalized youths, street kids, ruffians, gang youths, and slum youths—who could reap something from the sudden influx. They took their pick of music, fashion, political radicalism, drugs, and other, less tangible novelties introduced by visitors from the United States, Europe, and South America. They explored their sexuality with female and male foreigners whose notions on the matter were far more open than what was customary in Musrara.

Jerusalem writer Susan Bellos belongs to the small class of expatriates from the English-speaking world who immigrated to Israel, settled in Jerusalem prior to the 1967 war and stayed long after. She became an astute observer of the city's transformation. She had arrived as a young woman from the United Kingdom and encountered a community of "offbeat, unusual characters who came to Jerusalem because it was an extraordinary place." What made it special to them was the same thing that repelled tourists, that kept away the throngs of Israelis living in the coastal population center of Tel Aviv. Like an open wound, the border through Jerusalem was marked by barbed wire, armed sentries, and battle-ready cannons. The brutality of it both repelled people and commanded their attention. To Bellos, Jerusalem was alluring and extraordinary because "it was cut off—it was actually the end of the world."

Lacking the privileges of Western expatriates, the residents of Musrara experienced life in the border zone as a given. For 19 years, they were entrapped within it. They raised their children in an ethnic enclave, speaking Moroccan Arabic at home and broken Hebrew outside. It was practically like growing up in the *mellah,* or Jewish quarter, in Casablanca and Marrakesh.

The youths' interactions with the broader Israeli society consisted to a large extent of run-ins with the law and arbitrary beatings by police officers. Once detained, police interrogations routinely included physical abuse, ranging from punches to the torso to blows to the genitals.

Bellos worked at that time as a reporter for the *Jerusalem Post,* where editors' attitudes about gender dictated that she could only cover areas like education, welfare, and health—rather than the supposedly masculine beats of national security and politics. She made the most of her position in the newsroom. Rather than sticking to surface-level coverage of institutional announcements, Bellos mined Jerusalem's underbelly for stories and produced a substantial body of reporting on poverty, unjust policy, and the daily struggle of life in the slums. In the course of this work, the youths of Musrara and other poor districts often shared with Bellos accounts of their painful and sometimes humiliating encounters with police. Many were stories she never managed to get into print: "Any reference to police violence or alleged brutality inside the lockups was simply removed from my copy," she later recalled. Out of Zionist sentiment, editors feared that such stories gave Israel a bad name abroad.

Many decades later, a retired police commander named Avraham Tourgeman, who served in the Jerusalem precinct in those years, agreed to be interviewed. At 85 years old, Tourgeman had trouble moving around his apartment, but his mind was lucid. He spoke in slow and deliberate sentences. Tourgeman had immigrated to Israel from Morocco, like many Musrara residents, but he had managed to secure placement in the police force's officer corps. After serving in Israel's northern region and helping put down the Wadi Salib protests as a junior officer, he transferred to Jerusalem. By the late 1960s, he had climbed to the rank of chief inspector, perhaps the only Moroccan among the top brass. By all accounts, including his own, Tourgeman instilled fear in the youths of the city's poor districts. At the time, the fact that he shared an ethnic background with the population under his wardship engendered in him no apparent sympathy for them. Now, however, long after it would make a difference, Tourgeman had softened to their complaints of neglect, discrimination, and repression. "They would get beaten up," he said. "Physically speaking. By cops. Because they were from Musrara."

As soon as the fighting ended, Jerusalem adopted an urban development plan that resembled the action of a centrifuge: from the central axis of the Old City, the plan accelerated the movement of people— only Jewish people, that is—toward the farthest reaches of Jerusalem's expanding municipal boundaries. The most important expansion happened less than two months after the war, in a deliberately quiet vote by the Israeli cabinet. The item being voted on was described dryly as a "declaration regarding the expansion of the jurisdictional area of the Jerusalem municipality." This seemingly harmless language, meant to deceive international observers, was not really about municipal land, but about the formal annexation of 27.4 square miles of conquered territory. Only 2.3 square miles of those included the Old City and the built-up area around it. The rest was mostly agricultural and undeveloped land belonging to 28 outlying Palestinian villages. These were the lands Israel was determined to fill with Jews as part of the Israeli doctrine known as "creating facts on the ground."

The new Jerusalem, a reunited city in the grips of a construction mania, spun out around the central axis of the Old City. Musrara abutted its walls on the northwest and therefore formed part of the city's new core. West of Musrara, past a small commercial area, were the wealthy Ashkenazi neighborhoods. To the east were the Palestinian Arabs. Before the war, foot and vehicle traffic through Musrara was nil. On the rare occasion a car passed by, children would clap their hands in excitement. Now, everyone seemed to be passing through. Ashkenazi students commuting by foot to their campus on Mount Scopus traversed Musrara to get there. So did visitors going to the Wailing Wall and other Jewish holy sites previously sealed off by the border. Meanwhile, there were also the masses of Israelis entranced by the foreignness of Arab Jerusalem. The Orient, elusive and imagined, suddenly presented itself in the Old City to be seen, heard, smelled, and tasted. It had an intoxicating effect on them.

Crossing the 1967 line in Jerusalem opened up the possibility for mixing between Israelis and Palestinians. But it also, ironically, allowed Israelis to mix among themselves. Meir Wigoder was a teenager from an affluent, Ashkenazi background when he began visiting the Old City. Recalling that time, he said that most Israelis making the journey eastward reminded him of soldiers on the march—even though they were just civilians on a leisurely visit. "The Israeli way of walking had to do with conquering," he said. "They took very assertive steps."

There were two groups of Israelis whose gait stood apart to him. One group was what Israelis used to call "bohemians": artists, writers, and undifferentiated free spirits, who typically came from well-off families but who had rejected the norms of mainstream society. The others were the Mizrahi street youths from neighborhoods like Musrara, youths who would go on to become Panthers. For Wigoder, these groups had "a completely different type of walk," which brought to his mind the French word *flânerie*. He'd spot them strolling down the street as if time were of no concern. "You'd see them walking slowly, ogling what's happening and who is doing what," Wigoder recalled. "It was a curious type of walk." In 1967, Wigoder was yet too close to the moment to fully grasp the impact of the city's reconfiguration on his own identity. But he was already far along a path that would have him join the tribe of idle walkers.

Wigoder first encountered the war in the sky: an enemy aircraft sweeping above and Israeli jets trailing closely behind. From his boarding school near Netanya, a city on the country's Mediterranean coast, he saw the Arab plane take a hit and dive uncontrollably. The war was soon over and so was his school year. Meir returned to his home in Jerusalem and found it in the process of profound transformation. The city's boundaries now encompassed 65,000 new Arab residents who had lived on the other side of the former border. From north to south, bulldozers were in the process of tearing down the ugly concrete and steel barricades. The curfew on East Jerusalem was being lifted, and Israel's urban reunification program was proceeding rapidly.

The Zionist dream of Jewish sovereignty over the land, and over Jerusalem in particular, is what had brought his parents to the country in 1949. That ideology's hold was strong enough that they left the relative comfort of New York City for the opportunity to make a life in an impoverished, postwar Israel. In the years before 1967, his mother would often take Meir and his brother Shimshon on drives to a hilltop in the Abu Tor neighborhood, one of the only vantage points from which it was possible to behold a sliver of the stone walls, magnificent domes, and ancient cemeteries of the Old City. She would extend her arms and cry out, "Oh, I could just hug that view!" Her romantic notion was somewhat lost on Meir because he couldn't brook the notion of hugging a view—inevitably you would be left empty-handed.

After the war, when he came home for his summer break, Meir and his family went to see the Old City together. They passed under one of the seven ancient gates and walked the tight cobblestone alleyways. Muslim worshippers filed past them on the way to prayer. Incense burned in dimly lit Coptic churches, releasing an unfamiliar scent into the air. Everywhere, vendors sold things: splendidly colorful spices displayed in overflowing piles, carcasses of butchered animals hanging off hooks, but also electronics, household items, textiles, and all manner of consumer goods. It was an overwhelming sensory experience for a sensitive boy. But not so overwhelming as to stop him from coming again and again.

On a subsequent visit, Wigoder found himself locking eyes with an old Arab man. A street vendor, he was climbing up the uneven steps toward Meir, all his merchandise in tow. In one hand, the man held rosary beads and with the other, he presented his various goods. He stopped advancing when he reached one step below Meir, making it so that the boy stood taller than the old man. The vendor presented postcards for sale. Meir noticed something strange. Newly minted, these festive postcards marked the Israeli triumph in the war. Here was a man who belonged to the losing side hawking the victor's Six-Day War mementos. For the first time he could remember, Meir experienced a deep feeling of shame. Or rather, he felt ashamed that the vendor did not seem to feel shame. It was a lesson about the power he had come to possess through conquest.

The Old City is also where Meir was first introduced to drugs. In 1960s Israel, and for many years afterward, the word "drugs" represented an undifferentiated specter. Narcotics, in any quantity or type, and whether inhaled, injected or ingested, were all just "drugs" and were all heavily criminalized and stigmatized. That conservative attitude was easy enough to maintain before the war, when there were few drugs on the market. That changed with the incorporation of the West Bank and East Jerusalem, where the use of hashish, and to a lesser extent, opium, had been normalized.

About 13 years old at the time, Meir sat down at a café, one of the countless Arab venues where patrons smoked hookah. Expecting to be served flavored tobacco in the water pipe, he held its tentacle and took leisurely puffs. When he left, he thanked the proprietor and told him he would be sure to come back again. He didn't yet realize the reason he felt so good was that hashish had been mixed in with the tobacco. On his next visit, Meir figured out the special ingredient and bought some to take home with him.

The most common unit of measurement for hashish was known as a finger: seven grams of cannabis resin tightly packed in an elongated bag. When he went back to his boarding school, Meir cut up one finger of hashish and started giving it away to his friends. Somehow, the principal found out and called in his parents. But he didn't end up in a criminal justice program for youths, as would almost certainly have happened for Musrara's street boys. Instead, the incident was covered up and forgotten.

As a Palestinian who grew up mere feet away from the militarized border separating East and West Jerusalem, Philip Farah spent nearly his entire childhood within close range of Israeli cannons. But when war did eventually break out in June of 1967, 15-year-old Philip was a safe distance away. The war had turned the Jordan River, a waterway known as the site of Jesus's baptism, into a fault line of geopolitical significance and left the Farah family stranded on the Jordanian side.

They had planned to be away from home for a short trip when the war broke out. Now, they were forced to remain in the crowded quarters of their relatives in the Jordanian capital of Amman, not knowing when and if they would be allowed to go home to Jerusalem.

As the cash they brought with them dwindled, the family decided to dispatch one member to sneak across the border and retrieve money stashed away in their home. The mission fell to Farah's mother. Crossing the Jordan River undetected would be a challenge, but it was 75 miles long and authorities could not hope to stop all traffic. Mary found a local farmer who moonlighted as a smuggler. At the appointed time, she climbed into his tractor, and they started descending into the water. Mary and the smuggler could only hope that Israeli border sentries were nowhere nearby. The sound of flowing water provided cover for the hum of the engine but also made it difficult to listen for patrols. They managed to traverse the river without being spotted and emerged from the water in the West Bank.

Fortunately for Mary, she slipped into her home in East Jerusalem right before the first postwar census of Palestinians. It was June 26, and Israel had placed the area under an all-day curfew. By 9 a.m., hundreds of civilian volunteers accompanied by armed soldiers set out on their assigned routes. They went door to door registering the population of about 66,000 that had come under Israeli rule in the war. The census takers filled out basic questionnaires with the details required for the issuance of identity cards. Now she had, at least, an Israeli paper acknowledging her claim to her house, while others, who remained stranded outside Israeli-controlled territory, were absent for the census and risked losing their homes.

Nineteen years earlier she had not been so lucky. It was 1948 and the Farahs were living in Musrara. Their home was built by skilled masons who gave it an arabesque facade with arched doorways and windows. The home had proved a refuge before: in Ottoman times, Mary's father once hid in a secret compartment in the house to avoid military conscription. But in the war that broke out over Palestine in 1948, that house did not provide a haven. The Farahs fled the fighting, and their home ended up on the side of the city controlled by Israeli forces. Almost as soon as a ceasefire was reached, Israel let the masses of Jewish immigrants move in, and they occupied the Farahs' abode and houses like it.

Philip Farah was born a couple of years later. His father worked as an inventory manager for a United Nations aid agency, and his mother was a teacher in the refugee camps that had cropped up after the war. With the help of partial scholarships, Farah and his three siblings enjoyed a quality education. They studied at the best Christian schools in Jerusalem, where they learned to speak perfect English and participated in renditions of Shakespeare plays. The family did not own real estate or a car but had enough money to hire domestic help. A girl who had survived the massacre of Deir Yassin and had a bullet permanently lodged in her ankle came to work for the Farahs as a maid.

Like the boys and girls on the Israeli side, Farah discovered in the no-man's-land a source of adventure, surprise, and refuge from the world. One time, a Jordanian soldier on a nearby rooftop had accidentally let a grenade slip from his grasp and it landed beyond the barbed wire of the border. He asked if one of the kids would crawl underneath and fetch it. Farah volunteered. On another occasion, Farah and his friends set off exploring decrepit old structures beyond the border and happened upon one particularly ornate building. There they found pipes with flammable liquid. Farah was convinced he had struck oil. The no-man's-land was also where he snuck away to spend time with a girl in a case of puppy love.

He grew up in a house that was surrounded on three sides by the no-man's-land. On the fourth side, the house faced the UN outpost near the only border crossing between Israel and Jordan. From the unique vantage point of his house, Farah could see haredi Orthodox Jews going about their lives in the Mea She'arim neighborhood, which sat adjacent to Musrara. He also had a chance to watch Israelis every other Wednesday, when the border crossing was opened for convoys heading east to resupply the Israeli exclave on Mount Scopus. It fascinated him to catch sight of those he was told were "the evil people who had taken over our land."

With the 1967 war and his exile in Jordan, Farah's curiosity about the Jews only grew stronger. One of the first books he chose to read after the war was *Exodus*, a work of historical fiction by novelist Leon Uris. It told the story of Israel's founding from a Zionist perspective and became a massive worldwide hit. Quickly adapted into a Hollywood film, Uris's vision of Israel as a real-life miracle came to shape public perception of the country across the West.

As a teenager in Amman, Farah was exposed to plenty of writing that contradicted the *Exodus* story and focused on the plight of the Palestinians. But for Farah, the best source of information on the injustice perpetrated by the Israeli regime in the West Bank was not the local Arab papers. He managed to get his hands on newsletters published by a Jewish dissident from within Israel. These dispatches by Israel Shahak, a Holocaust survivor and chemist, kept Farah informed about issues like land confiscations by Israeli authorities. He was also interested in issues internal to Israeli society. Two books he read around that time informed him about the fissure dividing Ashkenazi and Mizrahi Israelis: *The Aryanization of the Jewish State,* a 1967 polemic written by journalist Michael Selzer, and *Reluctant Pioneers: Village Development in Israel* by anthropologist Alex Weingrod, a 1966 study of immigrants from Morocco. These works, along with a reading of Frantz Fanon's *Wretched of the Earth,* convinced Farah that Palestinians could find natural partners in the Mizrahi masses.

He nurtured such ideas in Amman, where the family stayed for seven months until being allowed to return to Jerusalem under a family reunification program. His political education continued a year later when he was sent to study at the American University in Beirut. But it was not only intellectual input that shaped Farah. It was the experience of the war itself. Israel's resounding victory over the Arab armies in 1967 was as traumatic as it was formative for Farah and other young, well-educated Palestinians. It was the moment in which "all the gods collapsed," as he put it. The defeat made evident the hollowness and corruption inherent to their parents' generation and cemented Farah's embrace of the radical left. He considered himself an internationalist, a peer to the student revolutionaries of the 1960s in France, Pakistan, and the United States.

Jerusalem, where he would come to visit on summer breaks from college in Beirut and where, after graduation, he would choose to live, was the perfect place for Farah to live out his ideals. In his mind, the revolutionary stakes, the players, and the nature of the conflict could not be clearer. The vast majority of Jerusalem's population was Palestinian and Mizrahi. He believed they would join together to fight the racism and colonial project of the Israeli state.

5

ORIGIN STORIES

AMONG THE COUNTLESS reverberations of the 1967 war and its aftermath was the impact on a particular set of young men in Jerusalem. The first person to record that reverberation was veteran journalist Itzhak Shorr. He worked for the newspaper *Al Hamishmar,* which was affiliated with the Mapam party, the left-wing ally and sometimes adversary of Israel's ruling political faction. It was early January 1971, and Shorr was scouring Jerusalem for his next story when he received a tip. The tip came from one of the newspaper's patrons, a Mapam party insider named Miriam Meyuhas. A city council member, she wanted to improve social welfare services but was faced with a mayor who wavered on whether he had the budget for it. To make the issue salient in the press and crank up the pressure on the mayor, Meyuhas suggested to Shorr that he look into the city's proliferation of gangs of youths and locate a certain group she had been hearing about.

Shorr obliged her and on January 13 wrote a story that publicized Meyuhas's policy proposals. But this wasn't the typical piece of party propaganda masquerading as a news item. The headline of the story was a quote gathered by Shorr and attributed to boys from one of the city's street gangs: "We want to organize against the Ashkenazi government and establishment. We will become the Black Panthers of the State of Israel."

Judging by the tiny space allotted to the story and its location on the paper's back page, the editors of *Al Hamishmar* didn't seem to think much of the news. National security, foreign affairs, and parliamentary politics—these were the beats that mattered. But as it turned out, this story was not the usual stuff about poverty, youth alienation, or Mizrahi-Ashkenazi relations. The announcement of a homegrown version of the Black Panthers was immediately sensational. Shorr took to calling the item the "scoop of his lifetime."

It was a scoop that yanked the street gang from the clutches of obscurity while at the same time providing almost no details about who they were—neither their identities nor which part of the city they were from. Shorr gave his readers lots of sentiment and very few facts. The youngsters were angry, he reported, that the Israeli establishment seemed more concerned about the pending execution of "white Jews in Russia" when the recent hangings of "Black Jews in Iraq" had been all but ignored. Matzpen, a far-left organization that readers were primed to detest, was reportedly in touch with the Panther group: long, hippie hair and hashish consumption had brought them together.

After Shorr published the story, it was left to others to determine how the group became politicized and why they had chosen a name inspired by the movement of African American militants in the United States. For the Israeli Panthers and their supporters, it would become a question of who deserved the credit for the idea and its implementation. For their detractors, it would be a question of whom was to blame. After the initial newspaper headlines, in subsequent years and decades, various origin stories emerged. Some explanations are fuzzy or incomplete, and others too pat. But they all contain at least part of the larger truth.

The informal and, initially, unrivaled leader of the street gang that started the Panthers was Saadia Marciano, whose prominent jawline, dark eyes, and long black hair would make him a favorite subject of the photojournalists in those days. It would be tempting to locate the first sign of his rebelliousness very early, for his officially listed birth date was May 1, 1950—a neat and symbolic coincidence for a would-be revolutionary to have been born on May Day, the international holiday of labor and the left. His true birth date, however, and whether he was born in Morocco or Israel, are a matter of confusion, each account of his life offering a variation that is inconsistent with the others.

What is known for certain is that Marciano grew up in the part of Musrara that was located within the border zone splitting Jerusalem into an Israeli half and a Jordanian half. His parents and 12 siblings lived in a two-room home whose walls could hardly keep the wetness out in the winter or provide respite from the heat in the summer. He made it through a few years of school but quickly dropped out. Marciano and many other boys on his street found escape from dreariness by venturing into the no-man's-land separating the territories of Israel and Jordan.

To pay for things like movie tickets and candy, they scavenged the no-man's-land for whatever they could sell. A local university lab was in constant need of cats, for example, and some boys made a business of supplying them. More typically, the plunder came in the form of glass sheets, copper fixings, and plumbing fixtures that could be sold to a number of buyers in West Jerusalem. Sometimes, the valuables were trafficked in the opposite direction. Marciano and his friends would steal little things like cigarettes from stores in the city and stash them at their camp, confident no one would dare pursue them past the signs that declared, "Danger: border ahead." But when Marciano was about 12 years old, the police did exactly that. He got charged with theft and was sentenced to a few years at a reform school.

Virtually all the boys of Marciano's age and background passed their teenage years the same way. They drifted in and out of detention, spending significant chunks of time away from home in various penal institutions. When they came back to Jerusalem as adults, there was no place for them. Employers rarely offered them work. Even the military wouldn't take them. An exception was made for Marciano, perhaps because it was early 1967 and the country was gearing up for war. But a few months after he enlisted, Marciano was discharged under unclear circumstances. He was not yet 20 years old and every societal institution had given up on him. He felt that he was barred by outside forces from having any kind of meaningful future. His life, he believed, would continue to consist of run-ins with the law and crushing poverty. Struggling against these limits seemed futile.

Marciano's only reprieve from complete despair was that he was not alone. There were thousands of young men in his situation in Jerusalem, and they were organized informally into groups of 10 to 15 and known as street gangs. The exact size and composition of each group fluctuated with the churning of the criminal justice system. Within his set, Marciano established his leadership through the power of his charisma. His friends trusted his ideas and guidance. He did not need to carry out dangerous feats or perform spectacles of brute strength as might have been the case in other gangs.

Starting in the late 1960s, a year to two before he started identifying as a Panther, one of Marciano's regular haunts outside Musrara was a municipal clubhouse for youths called the Basement. It was located in Jerusalem's tiny downtown area, in a building with vaulted ceilings and whitewashed walls. With tables for playing pool and ping pong, a

Saadia Marciano in Jerusalem, 1971. © Meir Wigoder.

television set, a music room, and a zero-judgment vibe, the Basement lured the capital's teenagers. Technically, Marciano and his friends were too old for the club, but city workers didn't stop them from coming. What mattered was they were off the streets. One of the few formal programs offered at the Basement was literacy classes. The Musrara set attended those regularly. With the help of the Basement's counselors, the boys worked to parse newspaper stories. But these lessons were not just about reading; they offered exposure to information about the wider world.

On one occasion, for example, Marciano and his friends read a story about an immigrant who had recently arrived from the Soviet Union. It's impossible to know which exact news article this was, but the topic of Soviet Jews was capturing the attention of the press because the Kremlin was refusing to let the bulk of them leave. In December 1970, the tension was at its height with a high-profile court case involving nine Zionist activists who tried to escape the Soviet Union by plane but were caught. The Musrara boys, instead of feeling solidarity with the activists and enmity toward the Soviet Union, focused on something entirely different. When they read the news story about the immigrant, they responded with indignation. Israel, they realized, was lavishing public benefits such as tax breaks and housing allowances on the new arrivals from the Soviet Union. How was this treatment fair, Marciano asked his friends, when Mizrahi communities continued to languish in poverty? A city inspector present for the reading lesson was so appalled by the conversation that he intervened with a lecture on the national imperative of attracting Jewish immigration.

It was during these sessions that Marciano first learned of the Black Panther Party. What Marciano probably didn't realize is that his life ran along remarkably similar lines to the original Panthers' founder, Huey Newton. They were both products of historic migrations. In the mid-twentieth century, the Marciano family uprooted themselves from Morocco, joining the massive movement of Jews from various Middle Eastern countries to Israel. Around the same time, Newton's family arrived in Oakland as part of America's Great Migration, the movement of millions of Black Americans from the country's rural south to its urban north and west. Both grew up poor but benefitted from having tight-knit families that scraped by. Their early teenage years were marked by entanglements with police and, by the time they reached adulthood, each had begun to awaken to the role racial discrimination played in their lives. Newton was illiterate until after high school. Learning how to read turned out to radicalize him. Four years after Newton launched his movement 7,400 miles away, Marciano, too, started learning how to read. The Israeli press did not devote many column inches to Newton's background, and Marciano would have likely been unaware of these similarities. One message he would not have missed, however, was the notion that the American Black Panthers were bad for Israel and bad for the Jews.

"American Jewry faces a terrible peril," reads one article typical of the views published in the late 1970s. "Anyone who reads the declarations by leaders of the Black Panthers, who have found refuge in Algeria, knows what they are preparing for the Jews. In the United States, there are around six million Jews, among them hundreds of thousands of military veterans. Should these Jews unite in time and prepare for the terrible and awful judgment day, they may accomplish much." A smattering of other news headlines from the time would have produced the same impression:

Panthers Plan Anti-Israeli Propaganda Campaign
The Terrorists—Idols of the New Left in the United States: White
    Radicals and Black Panthers Join Forces to Support Terrorism and
    Condemn Israel as a Racist Country
The Challenge: How to Tame Panthers?
The Black Panthers: Violent Revolutionism

Marciano read these stories or ones like them and soon began to remark in conversations with the street gang workers who ran the Basement that "we're going to be like the American Black Panthers." These were the words of a young man who was learning to understand and channel his anger. Upon reading of faraway extremists condemned for the threat they posed to his people, he identified with the extremists. Marciano had an entourage of like-minded friends but no organization. And at this point, he imagined behaving like the Panthers, not necessarily adopting their name. Their essence, he believed, was to use the threat of violence to advance the interests of poor people—and that was an idea he found attractive. Just days before Marciano and his crew were outed by a newspaperman, their plans were still so preliminary that they were considering adopting another name entirely. This other name came via Uruguay where, on January 8, 1971, a group of leftist guerrillas called the Tupamaros kidnapped the local British ambassador Geoffrey Jackson. Inspired by the act, someone in Marciano's group coined "Tupamarconos," a portmanteau of the Uruguayan group's name and "Moroccans." It was clever but the boys recognized the name's limitations. They were wise enough to realize that the name Tupamarconos would exclude Jews who came from Middle Eastern countries other than Morocco, such as Iraq or Syria. The coinage was quickly abandoned.

According to another version of how things started, the Musrara gang first learned of the American Black Panthers from a chance encounter with a darling prince of the Jerusalem bohemia. One day in 1970, some number of months before the gang's debut in the newspapers, Avi Bardugo ran out of kef. At first, he sought out his regular hashish dealer. But the dealer turned out to be away spending time in Sinai, the desert peninsula that Israel had conquered a few years earlier and which now served as a low-cost vacation destination. So Bardugo went on a stroll down to Musrara, where he was guaranteed to find many other dealers of kef.

Bardugo didn't have to advertise his intentions. Based on his appearance alone, anyone in the neighborhood could have guessed his objective. His style was gratingly countercultural, especially in Israel: long unkempt hair, sideburns extending so far down they nearly connected to his horseshoe mustache, and round wire-rimmed glasses framing his eyes. However foreign the hippie aesthetic, it was starting to catch on among Musrara's youths, a group of whom was now loitering in the street. Bardugo approached them and struck up a conversation.

He tended to speak quickly and confidently but in a way that was charming rather than arrogant. He would smile generously and share in hearty laughter with anyone he met. These qualities had made him popular among his fellow law school students and across Jerusalem's nightlife scene. And since people always seemed to congregate around him, he figured that his sociability could help him earn a living. Soon after he arrived in Jerusalem, in the early 1960s, Bardugo became one of the city's most prolific nightlife proprietors, opening a string of trendy cafés and clubs for 20-something-year-olds. The most famous one was an establishment called Bacchus, named after the ancient god of revelry. Bardugo decorated it eclectically, painting tiger stripes across the venue's curvaceous ceiling. Another space in the club was a mirrored alcove lit by gargoyle-shaped lamps. It was a style he once described as "Middle Eastern psychedelic." Above the dance floor, Bardugo had hung a blow-up doll of Marilyn Monroe and positioned her so that she was flashing her coquettish smile at a giant photograph of a hippie character—himself.

Bardugo's ubiquity was such that he regularly got mentioned in newspaper columns on nocturnal Jerusalem and many people thought they knew him, even though his background remained a mystery. If he didn't exactly conceal his identity, he also didn't tend to volunteer too many details. His name is the best example of this pretense. When they called him "Bardugo," everyone assumed it was a moniker he made up. Bardugo, after all, was a distinctly Moroccan name, but with his manner of speech, light complexion, and European features, he allowed people to believe he was Ashkenazi. Adding to the confusion, some people recalled that he had introduced himself as Avri HaCarmeli, a name that would have registered as sabra, or Israeli-born.

In Musrara, Bardugo's simple mission of buying hashish turned into something more. After chatting in the street for a few moments, Marciano and his friends invited Bardugo to continue loafing with them somewhere else: their secret lair. To get there, they walked down to the end of Mishmarot Street, past the crypt-like apartments most of them called home. The density of the neighborhood left few places for young people to hang out. Luckily, however, the youngest of the crew, Koko, had a spare room. It was a dark and shoddily built shed on the roof of a three-story building where the air was always thick with smoke emanating from cheap tobacco and Arab hashish. Bardugo suddenly felt free to shed some of the pretensions he had erected while mingling with Jerusalem's socialites and bohemians. In this crowd, Bardugo recognized his younger self.

Though his appearance may have suggested he was Ashkenazi, Bardugo was, in fact, Mizrahi. He was born in 1940 outside of Haifa to a Moroccan Jewish father and an Egyptian Jewish mother. His family was poor and religious. At school, he often got in trouble. Instead of enrolling in high school, he went to work as a delivery boy for a local factory. The labor union at the factory had set up a library, stocking it with leftist tracts. In his spare time, he read through the selection, inhaling many titles including the whole opus of Karl Marx. When he was 19, the faraway and theoretical revolutions from his book reading seemed to leap out of the page and consume his city. The Mizrahi neighborhood of Wadi Salib was in revolt and refusing to cower to police batons. Bardugo didn't participate directly but he did observe what was happening and read commentary about it in the independent press. He noticed an overlap between what the Marxists called the working class and Israel's Mizrahi underclass. He felt solidarity with the residents of Wadi Salib but he also saw a personal way out of the Mizrahi predicament. It was at this time that he constructed the identity of Avri HaCarmeli, or Avri the Carmelite. Carmel refers to the mountainside where Haifa's upper-middle-class Ashkenazi families lived, situated right above the Wadi Salib area.

This transition from Bardugo to HaCarmeli has been recorded in history thanks to two reader-submitted letters published in the newsweekly *This World*. The first came in 1962 when Bardugo signed his real name to an impassioned diatribe against the "whites." It ends with a threat in the name of all Mizrahi youths: "We will join the underground, and then the country will awaken as it did in the days of Wadi Salib!" In 1963, another letter appeared under Bardugo's Ashkenazi pseudonym. Again, he pledges himself to fight for liberation. This time, not for Mizrahi rights, but rather for Kurdish independence. His ability to activate his new identity helped propel Bardugo out of a working-class job and into a production gig with a theater company in Haifa. Soon he brought his book smarts and artificial identity to Jerusalem where he enrolled in Hebrew University's law school. In Jerusalem, among the bohemians and students, his camouflaged Mizrahi identity never fully receded. It still stung when he overheard his new peers mocking the Moroccan families they were gentrifying out of downtown neighborhoods.

Now, on Koko's roof, enough of Bardugo's upbringing remained that he saw in his younger peers not just juvenile delinquency but revolutionary potential. So began their political education. Bardugo listened to their grievances and as the smoke whirled about the room, he threaded into the conversation stories from the United States. In that country, there were young men not unlike themselves, he said, who decided they had had enough with police beatings and destitution. A turf gang of Puerto Ricans from Chicago, for example, had transformed itself into a political force known as the Young Lords. And don't you want to hear about a group of black American men your age calling themselves the Black Panthers? he asked. When the police brutalize their people, they fight back—by any means necessary. Do you understand what I am telling you? he asked.

They were starting to. Marciano and Koko, Charlie, Eli, Meir, Haim, and Eliezer. They had known each other and each other's families for as long as they could remember. They experienced the same fear of growing up in a war zone under the threat of sniper fire, the same damp walls, and ceilings that didn't keep the rain entirely out. Each of them was well versed in the daily routine of crowded living quarters: beds folded away to make room for eating breakfast, a hop over the stream of sewage running just outside the front door, days spent in the streets, late nights spent waiting for bed space to free up as family members were forced to sleep in shifts. All of their childhoods were cut short by the criminal justice system, which spit them out as teenagers who attracted crooked looks from employers and government clerks. On the faces of their parents, the Musrara boys saw permanent expressions of resignation and surrender, and the premature arrival of old age. Bardugo now lived a life far removed from these conditions. He could hardly be their peer, but at least he showed he understood them. The boys took to calling him "the intellectual."

After the ad hoc lecture on Koko's roof, the Musrara crew began to frequent Bardugo's newest nightlife venture. At the Yellow Tea House, named after the vivid color of its walls and furniture, they joined a mixed crowd that ranged from left-wing lawmakers like Uri Avnery to American college students eager for authentic experiences during their sojourn in Jerusalem. A traditional tea house by day and a bar by night, the venue was located on King George Street, one of the three roads marking the edges of Jerusalem's Downtown Triangle. The Basement, where Marciano and his friends expressed indignation at what they read in the paper, was in the same area. The boys became a permanent fixture at the Yellow Tea House. At first, they kept to themselves. They would sit in a corner and indulge in Bardugo's animated tales or they would try their luck at the pinball machines he had installed. From a vending machine, they bought cigarettes piecemeal and sometimes cracked them open to lace them with hashish. Music from a jukebox, one of Israel's first, introduced the Musrara boys to both canonical jazz tunes and the latest amplified guitar sounds from the United States.

The potently hippie atmosphere at the Yellow Tea House provided its visiting American customers the perfect opportunity to cash in on their cultural capital. They were, after all, living specimens from the land that had produced the Black Panthers, Young Lords, and rock 'n' roll; Bardugo was but a second-rate rendition by comparison. For a period in 1970, no one exemplified this American stereotype better than a tall young man with long curly hair known simply as Steve, who hailed from Borough Park in Brooklyn. With his sheepskin jacket protecting him from the crisp mountain air, he would wander around Jerusalem as if he were on a perpetual pub crawl. From Café Ta'amon to the haunts near Jaffa Gate in the Old City, the rambunctious Steve conversed in fluent revolutionary with everyone he met. At Bardugo's café, however, Steve and his ilk got what young visiting radicals crave most: direct and unfiltered dispatches from the oppressed and downtrodden.

Over cigarettes and aromatic tea, Marciano and his sidekick Charlie Biton gave testimony of their lives in Israel, a country, they said, that sentenced them from birth to confinement in crumbling slums and fickle employment as manual laborers. The establishment may talk a good game about Jewish brotherhood, but why, then, do Moroccans fill the prisons as Ashkenazim dominate the universities? The distance was short between grasping Israel's social stratification and recognizing its American echoes. Building on Bardugo's teachings, Steve and his friends fed the Musrara boys snippets of incendiary rhetoric and shared tales of daring exploits by Malcolm X, Angela Davis, Huey Newton, and others.

Another critical component in this exchange was the young Israeli activists who acted as interpreters between Hebrew and English—and as provocateurs. Identifying with the New Left, they had watched with envy as their peers in France managed to occupy factories and universities in 1968. They followed along as the anti–Vietnam war movement intensified, which dovetailed with another phenomenon: the rise of black radicalism. The Israelis' efforts at promoting conscientious objection in Israel produced nothing like the widespread draft-card burning in the United States. But perhaps they wouldn't miss out on the global moment after all. Listening and egging the Musrara gang on, the Ashkenazi radicals held out hope.

Right as Marciano began reading newspapers at the Basement and started holding court with radicals at Bardugo's Yellow Tea House, the first stranger who had ever gained his trust reappeared suddenly in Marciano's life. According to some accounts, it was this man, a social worker named David Meiri, whose boyish face and charm belied his formal job—rather than Bardugo or Steve or the press—who introduced the idea of the Panthers to Musrara. Meiri represented the best kind of idealist: unflinching, crafty, and boundlessly empathetic. Marciano—and Jerusalem—were lucky to have him back.

Meiri's family arrived in Jerusalem in the first half of the twentieth century after a multigenerational migration that started in Syria and took a detour through Kurdistan. Theirs was not a story of Jews escaping persecution nor of Zionists heeding the call of the homeland. The Meiris came to the Holy Land as part of a centuries-old tradition of Jewish pilgrimage, long before and independent of Israel's founding. Hundreds of other families with the same story occupied the poor and crowded neighborhood of Ottoman courtyards called Nachlaot. Meiri's father was a respected rabbi in the community, the kind who expected his sons to eventually assume his mantle. And so, when an irreligious socialist-Zionist youth movement lured Meiri into its orbit, his father disapproved. The break with tradition intensified when Meiri left the city to volunteer on a kibbutz. Rather than studying at an Old City yeshiva, Meiri ended up in training to become a combat soldier for the newly established State of Israel in 1948.

In 1959, after completing his service, Meiri was contemplating a civilian career. As an Israeli in good standing within the circles that ran the country, he could have his pick of career paths; he had successfully overcome the impediment of his conservative Mizrahi ghetto background. His first choice was a safe civil service job. It soon bored him and got him thinking about an alternative. He remembered his youth movement and his time on the kibbutz where he had enjoyed working with immigrant kids from a nearby transit camp. He applied for a job with the city of Jerusalem as a social worker focused on street youths. His first assignment, if he would accept it, was a group of pre-teens from Musrara. They were attending a municipal summer camp, and all the other counselors refused to take them.

The group from Musrara had earned its reputation for disobedience and disruption during an earlier summer. A combat veteran turned sculptor volunteered to act as an art teacher for the children's camp in return for living and studio space in an adjacent Georgian-era monastery. He was a hulking man and always barefoot. His name was Menashe Kadishman and he would go on to become world-famous for his paintings of sheep. Already now, he was fixated on artistic representations of animal forms, and in particular, the calf from the biblical story on Mount Sinai. A critic described his works at the time as "forcefully carved, and stylized to reflect [the] spare Romanesque environs" of Jerusalem.

One day, the entire camp was startled by screaming. It was Kadishman yelling, "I'll kill them! I'll kill them!" It turned out that the Musrara boys had smashed a calf-shaped sculpture he had made. Fortunately for the boys, they had a brilliant defense—the Second Commandment. The Bible, they said, condemned ancient Israelites when they constructed the false idol of the golden calf while waiting impatiently for Moses's return from Mount Sinai. Like the original sinners, Kadishman had clearly done wrong when he violated "thou shalt not make unto thee any graven image."

Now, a few years later, Meiri was on his own in a wooded area of Jerusalem, approaching the same group of unruly boys. From the array of kids, their leader moved toward Meiri and they faced each other like two gunslingers in the Wild West. The child had dark and piercing eyes and a stern expression on his face. He was holding something in his hand. He directed his gaze at Meiri and said, "Take one more step and this rock hits you." Meiri froze in place. For a quick moment, thoughts rushed through his mind. He remembered his own experience as a child learning to trust his counselors. He recalled the lessons he learned from the *Pedagogical Poem,* a canonical Soviet text on juvenile delinquency. The lesson was that this was a test. He took a step forward in defiance of the boy's threat. The next thing he felt was ringing in his ears. Dizziness. A thin warm stream of blood running down his face. Quietly, he pulled out a handkerchief, pressed it to the wound, and then walked off to the infirmary. The test was not over. He still had to decide how to respond to being hit in the head with a stone.

He returned, his head wrapped in a bandage. He maintained perfect composure and the boys stared at him. They waited for him to react. *All right,* he told them, *let's sit down. It's about time we get on with it.* He pulled out a trumpet and played it for them. After that, he pulled out a book to read to them. Titled *Heart,* it was a nineteenth-century novel by Edmondo De Amicis written as a fictional diary of an eleven-year-old boy from an upper-class family. The moralistic tales the boy records in each entry are about youths from backgrounds different from his own. He learns that young boys, no matter how poor, can contribute to the makeup of the nation. Meiri's story-telling stunned and enraptured his audience, especially the boy who threw the rock at him. But even more than what he did, it was what Meiri didn't do that shocked them. He didn't lecture them and he didn't call the police. The boy who lobbed the rock was Saadia Marciano and Meiri had passed his test.

In 1967, in the summer after the war, Meiri left Jerusalem, losing touch with the boys of Musrara. For the next three years, he worked directing youth programs for Jewish communities in St. Paul, Minnesota, and Chattanooga, Tennessee. The young people in America,

Meiri once told an interviewer, were the country's promise. "They want peace. And when they are happy, there's music and dancing—it's like that in Israel," he said. Meiri spent most of his time among American Jews as well as among white American Christians who were financially comfortable or wealthy. The press taught him about how the other half lived. He read about the African Americans who, in their teens and twenties, were organizing into militant groups. The most prominent one was the Black Panthers.

Meiri's time in the United States coincided with a transition from the era of the civil rights movement to the rise of black militancy, with groups like the Panthers rejecting nonviolence as impractical and dogmatic. The new wave of activists believed that justice must be achieved "by any means necessary." The year Meiri arrived, riots broke out in black neighborhoods across the country, including in Minneapolis where he was stationed. The following year, 1968, Martin Luther King, Jr., was assassinated in Tennessee, a state whose Jewish community Meiri would go on to serve next. If the civil rights movement had managed to gain support from liberal media, what followed in its wake would not. The press almost uniformly castigated black radicalism and cast the Black Panthers as antisemites, an accusation driven in part by their support for the Palestinian cause.

The Israel that welcomed Meiri back in the summer of 1970 resembled little the country he had left three years earlier. The culture was increasingly out of sync with the provincial and idyllic but war-prone place that Meiri had described to fawning American audiences. Just days after he concluded his foreign assignment, Israel and its longtime nemesis, Egypt, signed a ceasefire agreement, bringing an end to the War of Attrition and heralding a period of calm along Israel's borders. This dissipation of military tension made another, far deeper change crystalize: in the 23rd year of its existence, Israel was in many ways coming to mimic America. Collectivism was giving way to individualism. Consumerism had arrived. Ostentatious wealth became more commonplace even as the poor grew desperate. In a letter to an American friend, Meiri described what he found soon after returning to Israel. "I am working as a community worker in a very poor Jewish neighborhood," he wrote. "There are many poor people in Israel." And the poor people that Meiri noticed were ever more aware of their poverty because they could see the imported cars and luxury housing of the nouveau riche.

One of the powerful ways that America had invaded Meiri's little corner of Jerusalem was through television. As he resumed his duties with the city's youth services office, Meiri found that Marciano and his crew were spending less time on the streets in Musrara. Now, they were embedded in the downtown scene where they could plop themselves onto a couch at the Basement and thoroughly enjoy the advent of broadcast television in Israel. Television transmission arrived only in 1968; political leaders feared the medium would be a corrupting influence. The Musrara boys found the televised drama of American boxing irresistible, and no boxer impressed them more than Muhammad Ali. They caught him right as he returned to prizefighting from the political blacklisting that had kept him sidelined for several years. Ali's message of black pride and racial justice was not lost on his young Mizrahi fans in Jerusalem. Perhaps the politicians were right to worry about the medium.

Amid all the changes, Meiri settled right back into his job with the city's Division of Community and Group Work, joining a team of social workers known as street gang workers. He reinstalled himself in the lives of Musrara's poorest families. Despite his long absence, his sway over the youths had not faded. The street gangs of Musrara once again gathered around him as he delivered lessons on history and civics through compelling storytelling. He got them to identify with significant historical figures such as Alfred Dreyfus by infusing past events with drama. Because he grew up in the same kind of neighborhood they did, he knew their vernacular. He made poetry and literature accessible, supplementing the newspapers they were already reading on their own. Together, they studied works like those by Hayim Nahman Bialik, who wrote poetry in high Hebrew about the pogroms of Europe: "On the Slaughter" and "In the City of Slaughter." He noticed something was changing in the boys. Following the Bialik lesson, for example, they got riled up and, uncharacteristically, pushed back against his teaching. Enough with the pogroms, with the blood libels, with Kishinev, they told him—the true city of slaughter was right there in Jerusalem.

The impact of these lessons became fully apparent to Meiri when he received a phone call late one night. Meiri's supervisor at the time, Yosef Meyuhas, rung.

The police commander is demanding to know who's been teaching your boys about the French Revolution, Meyuhas said, per Meiri's recollection of the conversation.

That was me. What's this about?

Your boys are causing trouble. They were out in the street tonight. They were slashing tires of expensive cars and chanting loudly: "liberty, equality, fraternity!"

The French Revolution incident didn't make it to the press, but the boys' pent-up energy was too great to be drained away by a single night of righteous hooliganism. Marciano and Biton and the group that congealed around them wanted to do something bigger—something to shock their oppressors into attention.

Still fresh from his time in the United States, Meiri began talking to them about the Black Panthers. Or, otherwise—according to another version—Marciano and Biton brought up the Panthers themselves, expressing their fascination with the group. Either way, a conversation developed and a plan was hatched. With the help of Meiri's media ties, the Musrara boys would make their debut. They would threaten to do in Israel what the Panthers had been doing in the United States.

So, which origin story is correct? One says that the Panthers were born out of the bitterness, boldness, and creativity of Marciano and his group of friends in Musrara. Another says that the sly bohemian Bardugo planted the idea in their heads, while yet another story suggests that a social worker returning home from time spent in a turbulent, late 1960s America brought "Pantherism" to Jerusalem. There's truth to all these versions. While there is no question that a tiny group of young adult-aged, second-generation immigrants living in Jerusalem slums declared themselves the Black Panthers one wintery day in 1971, the answer to the question of how exactly they coalesced is lost to the thicket of Jerusalem's urban mythology. However it came about, the first moment that someone publicly referred to them as Panthers was transformative, and the group may have adopted that name simply because they liked how it sounded on them.

6

THE DEBUT OF THE PANTHERS

AFTER THE FIRST headline in *Al Hamishmar* broke the news—"We Will Be the Black Panthers of Israel"—the rest of the press followed. The radio reporters, the tabloid columnists, and the most respected journalists in the country sought to verify and elaborate on a potentially explosive story. Meiri and Amiel were more than ready to provide the scoop-hungry press with tantalizing details about the Panthers. They could even provide the reporters with access to the Panthers themselves. Before that would happen, however, Meiri, Amiel, and other street gang workers began training Marciano and his friends for the eventual moment they would have to face the press. They held debates to flesh out the group's grievances, teaching the boys to talk not just about police violence but also about root problems like education and housing.

That social workers on government payroll were helping seed a cell of Black Panthers would have been outrageous in any city—and Jerusalem was no exception. According to the approach prevailing in the profession in Israel at the time, social work existed chiefly to alleviate and contain discontent. Welfare recipients were expected to passively comply with requirements. This attitude grew out of long-standing religious notions around charity and had become policy because, at the city and national levels, secular officials regularly ceded control over welfare to Orthodox parties in exchange for their cooperation on other matters. So when the street gang workers acted to galvanize Marciano and his friends, they were intentionally undermining their superiors and subverting the standard model for dealing with people on welfare. Their readiness to support the Black Panthers' plot cemented their role as the city's in-house agitators.

Already, just by virtue of their ethnic backgrounds, Jerusalem's community workers proved conspicuous among their fellow municipal employees, who were typically Ashkenazi. Many in the 40-person unit traced their heritage to Asia and North Africa. There was Amiel, for example, the head of the unit, who was of Moroccan ancestry and who could speak Moroccan Arabic. Meiri was a Syrian Kurd, and another colleague, David Zioni, a Yemenite. Yosef Meyuhas, a street gang worker of old Sephardic stock, referred to himself as "the only Jew who was ever born in Silwan," the Palestinian neighborhood in East Jerusalem. When a reporter, however, later went around asking them if they identify with the American slogan, "Black Is Beautiful," they all demurred. Their political philosophy did not derive from the foundation laid by the civil rights movement in the United States. It was a different American tradition that informed their activism.

After World War II, cities in the United States saw a rise in juvenile delinquency and the proliferation of youth gangs. Public and philanthropic agencies were not equipped to handle the problem. Police clampdowns failed to blunt it. Innovative social workers stepped into the void and introduced the concept of street gang work. In cities like New York and Wilmington, young idealistic social workers embedded themselves in poor neighborhoods. They became trusted adult figures in the lives of vulnerable teenagers, a position from which they would help settle gang fights, obtain jobs for their clients, and intervene on their behalf with police and judges. The goal was to redirect the youths toward productive pursuits. By the 1960s, after some demonstrable successes, street gang work inspired proponents abroad. Aryeh Leissner, for example, helped introduce it in Israel, eventually publishing a book titled *Street Club Work in Tel Aviv and New York* in which he pointed to common facets of youth delinquency that appear irrespective of the local context. Early on, Jerusalem gained its own champions of the hands-on approach in the figures of Amiel and Meiri.

Seeking to further professionalize his practice, Amiel left for Cleveland in 1962, enrolling in a graduate program in social work at Case Western Reserve University. He returned to his job in Israel three years later, equipped with the latest knowledge in the field, and a renewed sense of urgency inspired by his exposure to black activism.

Amiel expanded the mandate of the city's Division of Community and Group Work. He was no longer satisfied with simply saving individuals. To work holistically, he felt he had to address the underlying and interconnected injustices that produced troubled adolescents, neglected elders, and spotty healthcare. He had to change policy. To do so, he built up community organizations that could educate and rally constituents; he fostered friendships with liberal elites like university faculty; he found allies who would leak to him relevant government data; and he activated the media by feeding select reporters with sensational nuggets of information.

It was classic community organizing. Some of Amiel's earliest successes seem like they came right out of Saul Alinsky's playbook, *Rules for Radicals*. In 1967, Amiel organized 600 elderly clients into a spirited rally that marched on city hall to demand the reinstatement of neighborhood health care services. They vowed that the next funeral procession for an elderly client whose death was preventable would be staged in front of the homes of the mayor and health minister. On another occasion, Amiel's unit used the press to publicize the stories of several youths who couldn't pay their criminal fines and if sent back to jail would likely end up as recidivists. As expected, the move engendered both sympathy and shame. Donations to cover the fines flowed in from the public, including a check sent by Mayor Kollek himself.

Within a few years, Amiel and his staff earned a reputation as grass-roots heroes among large segments of the city's population. This sentiment is encapsulated in a newspaper profile of an American, James Torczyner, who became one of Amiel's protégés. With his leather jacket and long sideburns, Torczyner was "an archetypal street gang worker," a "rebel of the rebels' department," who was perpetually embarrassing city leaders. "Street gang workers are in many ways romantic figures," the newspaper profile said. "They are fighting the just fight against the establishment on behalf of adolescents who have been much wronged by society. They are not well understood, partly because they look too much like their clients, and, like them, they suffer from the permanent feeling that they, or their work, is not properly understood."

If only the reaction to them stopped at being misunderstood. Many fellow municipal employees derided them using terms as varied as "communists," "right-wing fascists," "homosexuals," and "emotionally unstable anarchists." Rabbi Moshe Porush, a deputy mayor in charge of social welfare activity, gave his opinion of Amiel's unit in the bluntest of terms. "Street gang workers! It's a whole lot of nonsense, and they all ought to be sacked," he said. Some newspaper coverage stoked the establishment's resentment of street gang work by publicizing some of the more salacious and sensational rumors about it. In April 1969, for example, an article chronicled lengths to which some street gang workers would go in their effort to gain the trust of their clients. "One of the counselors was made to witness sexual intercourse between the boys, the torturing of cats, and the smoking of drugs," the article said. "They showed him stolen goods, a haul of switchblades, and in one case, guns." The information was secondhand and almost certainly exaggerated but such reports served to bolster the perception that Amiel's unit was a failed experiment and one that perhaps abetted criminal activity.

Neither Porush nor anyone else in Jerusalem's establishment appreciated being undercut by subordinates who seemed dangerously out of touch with official norms and had apparently gone rogue. Under normal circumstances, someone in Amiel's position would have been fired long before he managed to build such a controversial reputation. He perhaps wouldn't have risked his career to indulge youths who were openly vowing to follow in the footsteps of a foreign group with a reputation for violence and antisemitism. Maybe, he wouldn't have gone behind the back of his employer and invited journalists to meet them. But in this instance, Amiel's coalition building, including his ironclad backing from the public employees' union, immunized him from repercussions. At least, so he hoped.

A correspondent for *Yedioth Ahronoth,* one of Israel's highest-circulation newspapers, met the group at their lair in the Basement. To Gabi Brun, their puny frames attested to their history of childhood malnourishment. But they didn't look weak. Their style of dress and manners were carefully calculated to counteract any such impression. Their leather jackets, denim pants, and long, slicked-back hair served as visual cues for an ethic of street grit. Encounters with their type in the past would likely have earned Brun standoffish postures and stares. In their lexicon, Brun was a "nerd" because he was Ashkenazi. Even more revealing was their term for the rare Mizrahim who had achieved social or economic status: "vaccinated," as if being Mizrahi were a disease that made you poor. By agreeing to talk to Brun, they chose to be vulnerable in front of him. Starting with Marciano, whose position as the leader was evident, Brun went around the room taking down notes.

They decided to trust him with their personal stories, revealing details that were a source of shame in their lives. They couldn't know how he would represent their plight nor whether he would keep his promise to protect their identities.

When the story was published a few days later, it became clear that Amiel was right to try to whet the press's appetite with an exclusive. The first journalist permitted to behold the Musrara rabble-rousers took them incredibly seriously. His story praised the "rare candor" with which they spoke to him. The headline was a quote composed of words Marciano had said to him: "We Won't Be Silent—Violence Will Stun the Government." In the article itself, however, Marciano's message appears to be more of a prediction than a threat. In his warning that "things will have to ignite eventually," there is a heartfelt plea for relief from poverty and racism, relief from the burden that makes it too hard for some to advance in life. "Why bury a man?" Marciano asked.

Later the same day, *Maariv,* the evening newspaper, published its own version of the story. The article summoned to the page nearly every bogeyman of the Israeli establishment. Under your noses, the article suggested to readers, there has emerged a scary phenomenon. Bitter and hate-filled street youths, who don't like Ashkenazim, could erupt in violence at any moment. A cabal of extreme leftists and foreigners is stirring them up. These youths are now talking about flying abroad to learn from African American radicals. But not only that. They also want to meet Soviet radio and television people.

Both articles framed the problem of the Panthers as one of rampant juvenile delinquency. The press cast blame on the government and its negligence. There were warnings about street gangs, the papers said, long before the Musrara gang diagnosed its own delinquency. "Why must we have street gangs threatening violence and brandishing ideological slogans [for someone to take notice of this plight]?" one columnist asked. Our slums are starting to resemble the "black ghettos in the United States," wrote another. A solution was prescribed: empower the community workers, end their chronic underfunding, and enable them to stem the brewing urban catastrophe.

Musrara's gang was but one of 30 in the capital, the reports noted, and there were only a handful of community workers to deal with them. To help do their job, they would need the city to invest in things like job training and mental health services. These headlines supplied Amiel and his unit with a major coup. The rogue social workers were being touted as champions of the poor—as the only ones taking proactive measures to solve a community-wide problem. A cynic, however, might have assigned the community workers ulterior motives. As with any city, the budget for social services had always been strained and the livelihood of social workers depended on it. Perhaps, the community workers were simply seizing an opportunity to protect their own interests. Strategically, they took advantage of a moment in which the public was paying attention to domestic matters; it had been five months since the end of the War of Attrition and the country was turning inward. That was certainly how city hall treated the matter at first. When asked about the talk of Black Panthers, Kollek told the press, "Here, among us, no such thing could ever happen." He said that the whole thing was concocted by the social workers and soon prohibited them from giving any more interviews.

Marciano read about himself in the papers. He noted the panicked tone and apocalyptic pronouncements. All of the coverage warned that the Musrara youths wanted to become *like* the Black Panthers. Being talking about in that way—and being referred to as Black Panthers— made Marciano increasingly resolute. He grasped the impact of his threat and searched for ways to oblige the alarmists. At first, he had only thought of the American Black Panthers as a frame of reference, an object of reverence and imitation. Now, he dared think of himself as a Black Panther. Among his gang, he steered the conversations toward politics, curbing talk of individual grievances. But they were facing a challenge. Even with all the attention they had gotten, they were still just idle, chattering nobodies. None of them knew the first thing about organizing a militant movement. It's not that they had never seen a demonstration. Representatives from their neighborhood had only recently campaigned against consumer price increases, and throughout their lives, a profusion of associations and committees had been claiming to fight for Mizrahi betterment. But such efforts struck them as passive and laughable, a surrender to the establishment rather than a challenge.

Far more prominent, in terms of news coverage and turnout, were the displays of solidarity with Soviet Jewry. Activists had recently staged a hunger strike at the Wailing Wall in protest of a show trial of the Jews who tried to flee. To witness the spectacle only minutes away from the slums they called home induced as much aggravation as inspiration in Marciano and his friends. They couldn't possibly expect to garner that level of attention. Soviet solidarity activism flourished because it was encouraged by the government, the same government they felt was oppressing them.

Amiel and his unit provided limited help to the Panthers, continuing the individual rehabilitation programs and allowing the use of the unit's office space and telephone line. But as he sought to draw attention to the underlying issues, Amiel downplayed the seriousness of the Panthers. Yes, there was a street gang that called itself the Black Panthers, but "they only become that way because they gave too many interviews to the press," he told a reporter, belying his role in setting up their media debut. A few days later, Amiel again cast doubt on the gravity of the threat. "These boys, unlike black people in America, want to be inside society, they don't want out," he said. For Amiel, the headlines about Black Panthers were the result of a publicity stunt that he hoped would compel society to reabsorb its outcasts. He wasn't interested in an actual Israeli rendering of black power, suggesting that he perhaps appreciated the rhetorical power of the concept but was not attracted to the idea of truly overhauling the system in Israel.

There was another key ally who had goaded Marciano on and now might have offered ideas about political organizing. But after months of conversations at the Yellow Tea House, Bardugo suddenly left. And since he wasn't there, he couldn't tell Marciano about the movement he envisioned, composed of many cells and modeled, no doubt, after some foreign revolutionary group. For the moment, Bardugo's considerable energies belonged to another, far less radical organization—the Israeli military. An imperfect specimen of the New Left, Bardugo was no draft dodger. When the military summoned him for reserve duty, he complied, expecting to soon pick his efforts back up. But Marciano didn't wait to break the news, and Bardugo only realized what he had missed when he read the first story about the Panthers of Musrara in the newspaper.

Portrayed as the unwitting puppets of exploitative outside forces, Marciano and his friends found themselves rather alone. Their initial threat wouldn't amount to much if they didn't know how to follow through with it.

The moment when they would force the attention of Israel's prime minister still lay more than a month away. At this point, if Golda Meir summoned advisers to her office for a late-night meeting, it would be to discuss the pending expiration of Israel's ceasefire deal with Egypt, not the insolent hooligans from Musrara. She had her minister of police focused on an insurgency in occupied Gaza, not on the potentially restive slums of her own capital city. And yet, there were a few reasons to imagine that Meir might have taken an interest in the particular and peculiar problem of the Panthers. She had grown up in the United States and traveled there regularly, which meant she was familiar with America's racial tensions. As a self-avowed socialist, she regarded the manifestations of American inequality as the inevitable product of capitalism. According to her biographers, part of what drove Meir to Zionism was her belief in the possibility of a Jewish utopia, a place where brotherhood could prevail over social hierarchies of race, class, and ethnicity. Her record of public service centered on housing, labor, immigration, and welfare, meaning that her interest in these issues was almost unimpeachable, even if decades in politics had largely dispelled her idealism.

At the age of 71, she was elected prime minister, offering her the best and final chance to contribute to the vision of her youth—of creating an egalitarian country for Jews. How would someone with such a background react to the sudden apparition of the Black Panthers? It is unclear whether she yet knew of their existence, let alone considered them a political threat. There still existed no political force that could cast doubt on her domestic policy credentials or challenge her social justice commitments. Soon, however, a serendipitous burglary would deliver Marciano a few key allies to help him do just that.

7

MAKING SULHA

NO ONE IN TOWN would have looked at the two young men and thought they could become close friends. If Marciano represented an archetype of deprived youths, then the person who perhaps best encapsulated the polar opposite was a 19-year-old stranger named Shimshon Wigoder. Marciano was living in the same crowded, damp apartment he had grown up in; Wigoder, who came from a family of four and was raised in the well-heeled neighborhood of Beit Hakerem, had promptly moved out to live on his own when he was just old enough. Wigoder spoke fluent English and was Ashkenazi. His parents worked in radio and newspapers, and his dad was the author of the *Encyclopedia Judaica*. As a teenager, Wigoder spent a summer touring Europe. Marciano's only major experience outside Jerusalem was a sentence in a faraway reform school. Without an ounce of self-awareness, Israelis referred to youths like Wigoder as *bnei tovim,* or "children of good folk." Marciano's parents were, therefore, the other kind of folk.

The disparity might also be measured by the size of the collection of vinyl records that Wigoder kept: he had about 350 of them. The music ranged from the jazz classics he listened to growing up to the recordings of contemporary stars like Jimi Hendrix, the Rolling Stones, and Bob Dylan. One morning, toward the end of January 1971, Shimshon woke up to find his collection had vanished. He didn't know the term yet, but Wigoder was the target of *tashesh.* In the vernacular of Israel's underworld, *tashesh* was a type of burglary carried out at night while the victim is asleep; they don't notice they have been robbed until the morning. The most professional of *tashesh* practitioners guaranteed incapacitation by applying sleeping gas to their targets.

Instead of reporting the theft to the police, Wigoder turned to a friend he had made from Jerusalem's so-called underworld. The contact was Morris Kaubilio, who was known as one of the city's most skilled pickpockets and purse-snatchers. They had been acquaintances but they became close after Kaubilio got caught for stealing a car and taking it on a joyride. That incident led to charges against Kaubilio and a potential prison sentence. Wigoder persuaded his mother to intervene. A tall, freckled white woman with an American accent, Devorah Wigoder showed up at court on Kaubilio's behalf. She vouched for him as a character witness. *I know Morris. He's a good boy. Let him go,* she pled. The judge couldn't easily dismiss someone like Devorah and so he offered her a deal. Instead of prison, Kaubilio would spend three months under house arrest—if she'd agree to help rehabilitate him by housing her at her own house. She agreed. Kaubilio and the Wigoders came out of the experience with a deep bond.

When Wigoder turned to him for help, it gave Kaubilio a chance to return the favor. He promised he would find the culprit and get the records back. Street justice produced results swiftly. That same afternoon,

Kaubilio found the thief, who was a teenager, and hauled him in front of Wigoder. The boy's name was Zion. He apologized and tried to explain: Both his parents were sick, and he had seven hungry siblings at home. That's why he was robbing people in the first place.

But I would have never stolen from you if I knew you were cool, he said repeatedly. *I had no idea you were cool.*

I'll tell you what, Wigoder responded. *If the story is true, I'm not mad and I'll even let you keep 30 records. But if not, Morris will deal with you.*

They all caught a bus across town to where the boy lived. It took only a few moments to see that the situation was far worse than the boy had described. Wigoder reacted by launching into a lecture on how they needed to rise up and organize for social change. Zion listened to Wigoder's zeal and realized it sounded familiar. There was a group of people in one of the slums, Zion said, that was talking about doing just what Wigoder was suggesting.

To signal that all accounts were settled, a *sulha,* or reconciliation party, was called for that same night. Wigoder brought his friend Yigal Noah, an art student whom everyone called "The Goat," and his younger brother Meir, who was known by all as "Pink." Zion was accompanied by Marciano's group, whose primary concern was that the police not get involved. As Marciano saw it, he had a responsibility to protect the younger boys of Musrara. As soon as they all sat down and began to talk, Wigoder dispelled any lingering worries. He had gotten his records back and he was angling to hear about the political awakening in Musrara. Over coffee and smokes, Marciano and his friends unspooled stories of their daily frustrations and crushed dreams. They shared their half-baked plan to emulate the Black Panthers. There was talk of Molotov cocktails and burning tires—of somehow forcing the establishment to reckon with them. They couldn't personally identify with the indignation, or endorse the threat of violence, but the Ashkenazim in the room affirmed the basic notion of politicized anger.

The encounter lasted for several hours. By the end of it, something much deeper than political affinity sprouted up and began to fill the enormous void between two groups of people who had grown up so differently. Marciano and Shimshon Wigoder, in particular, were smitten with each other. They would all meet up in big groups most nights for the next few weeks, whether at the rooftop lair of Panther Koko Deri, at someone's shabby apartment, or at the Wigoder family home. Hashish and music served as powerful binding agents, facilitating conversations about politics. "People from the bourgeois families and people from poverty areas came to parties," the younger Wigoder brother would explain in a video clip filmed about a year later. "Drug parties, usually. They began trying to understand the problem together. That was the first communication."

Ordinarily, a burglary doesn't end with a victim who, having retrieved his property, summarily exempts the thief of blame, asks to meet his friends, becomes enamored with them, and involves himself in their plans for violent revolution. But that's exactly what Wigoder did, roping into the affair his younger brother, Pink, a gentle and soulful 16-year-old. And just as unusual for its own mores, a Musrara youth gang opened itself up to outsiders. Only rarely had mentor figures like Meiri and Bardugo managed to penetrate this group. Even though they spent the better part of a year downtown among students and radicals at the Yellow Tea House, admittance to the clique required the credential of having grown up in Musrara.

Why the Wigoder brothers found it natural to mix with the Panthers and what unique qualities Marciano and Biton saw in them is a story that starts with Shimshon and Pink's mother.

Long before their mother became Devorah Wigoder, a woman who throws her blue-blooded weight behind juvenile offenders, everyone knew her as Jane Emmet MacDwyer. She came from the proud Irish Catholic stock of Long Island. So firmly were they embedded in that tradition that the family had a living speaker of Gaelic, Jane's father. Her brother was training to be a Catholic priest and her sister was headed toward life as a nun. But not Jane. Before she turned 20, she broke with Irish Catholic customs and left the suburbs of her extended family to move to New York City. Soon after, Pearl Harbor was attacked and Jane decided to aid in the war effort. She volunteered with air traffic command, which dispatched her to a control station located in the heart of the Jim Crow South. Already then, she tended to stand up for people of lesser status. One day, for example, while waiting for a bus, she witnessed a white truck driver berate a black man, who happened to be dressed in a military uniform. Outraged, she defended the man—and got herself arrested.

After the war, she found work back in New York City. She became a secretary at the New School for Social Research, a job that exposed her to the cultural traditions of a different community: Jews. It was the time of the Nuremberg trials and Jane followed the proceedings closely. She discovered in herself a desire to understand what had happened in Europe. She embarked on a self-guided study of Jewish history from ancient times to the present. What she learned about that history and about the Holocaust unsettled her. It seemed to Jane that history had condemned Jews to perpetual persecution. Why had Jews been targeted and what effect did that persecution have on their psyche? she asked herself. She came to believe that trauma had invaded the Jewish soul, producing certain bizarre patterns of behavior. In the Jews of Manhattan she met, she perceived a chronic sense of resignation, misplaced doubt, and self-hate. Her prime example was when she and a few friends decided to found a student chapter of the United Jewish Appeal, one of the leading Zionist organizations of the day, and were met with indifference and even skepticism from most Jewish students on campus.

On November 29, 1947, after nearly two years of involvement with Jewish life, Jane happened to be attending a rendition of *The Merchant of Venice* by a Yiddish theater troupe. The most dramatic moment of the night came after the final curtain had been drawn across the stage. That was when the lead actor, Maurice Schwartz, stepped out in front to the applause of the audience. But instead of bowing for the usual curtain call, Schwartz raised his hand to request that the crowd quiet down. Jane couldn't understand a word he said—she spoke no Yiddish—but she saw that he was gripped by emotion and almost unable to convey his words. She thought she heard him say the words "Eretz Yisrael." He was crying by the end. As he spoke, a wave of exhilaration swept through the audience, expressed first in murmurs and then more loudly. Suddenly, it dawned on Jane. She remembered hearing earlier in the day a bulletin on the radio about the United Nations and Palestine. The UN General Assembly must have had its vote on the Partition Plan, a decision of major consequence for the Zionist movement.

Jane realized that a majority of the world's countries had just endorsed the idea of a Jewish state. For a moment, she felt like a stranger, like she didn't belong, and she prepared to leave. But she didn't do that, she stayed, and when Schwartz motioned for the audience to stand up, she did so, too. She joined the ovation and the spontaneous singing of the Zionist anthem. It was a song about 2,000 years of yearning for home—and now, finally, there appeared to be an answer for that yearning. At that moment, Jane's identification with the Jewish people became complete. She decided she would discover the secret to "their enduring permanence in human history" by becoming one herself, as she later put it in her memoir. The Jewish secret, she believed, "would bind the loosened strands" of her own life. Jane—who soon took the Hebrew name Devorah—distilled her transformation into a simple but powerful idea: by converting to Judaism, she hoped to personally replace one of the six million Jews who were lost in the Holocaust.

Having broken with her Irish roots, Devorah ended up falling in love with a Jew from Ireland. His name was Geoffrey Wigoder. They met through a mutual friend on the campus of the Jewish Theological Seminary in New York, started dating, and got married. Eventually, they moved to Israel, where they soon had two sons. The firstborn was Shimshon, whose looks were Irish but temperament was Israeli. As his mother put it, he was "an extrovert, quick-tempered, generous, and a natural-born leader." The other son, Meir, was three years younger. Devorah described him as "sensitive, mobile, and handsome." In his default facial expression, she sensed a sadness reverberating from the depths of Jewish historical memory.

Geoffrey made a living as the head of a radio broadcasting station and as a writer. Devorah supplemented that income as a Zionist emissary and an official host of important visitors from abroad. The foreigners often stayed at the Wigoder home, and the family would joke about the irony of their decidedly un-Israeli, English-speaking family showcasing for foreigners what Israelis were supposed to be like. It was a stimulating and theatrical setting for children to be raised in and the atmosphere was happy. But while Shimshon felt comfortable in this lifestyle, Meir was overwhelmed. He needed structure, desperately, and when he was 11, his parents sent him to a boarding school.

Devorah was a convert to Judaism living in Jerusalem. Occasionally, people doubted or derided her religious sincerity. The experience of being questioned and the anti-racism she nurtured in America shaped how she raised Shimshon and Meir. She taught them to never attack anyone on account of their origin. She instilled in them an understanding of right and wrong that was universal—rather than focused on the plight of Jews—and an ability to empathize with victims. The other value she hoped to pass down to her children was a love for Judaism and the land. In their backyard in the Beit Hakerem neighborhood, quality time for the Wigoders often meant having their knees and hands in the dirt, planting an edible garden. It was, however, more than a simple green patch. Devorah insisted that the only seeds they put into the soil were of plants identified in the Bible.

The following summer, in 1968, Devorah was booked on a speaking tour in South Africa, whose sizable Jewish community generally caucused with the white side of apartheid. She invited Meir to come along. In Cape Town, Meir was taken to a museum that featured an exhibit of live human beings, acting out activities from their indigenous African culture. He saw a black man and a black woman on a podium set apart from visitors by a line of rope. They were weaving threads of cloth in a demonstration of native craftsmanship. It was the rope around them— "do not touch"—that stirred a reaction within him, imprinting an image of exploitation in his mind forever. In his young teenage mind, he realized that only someone of a much lower status than his own could be placed on display. After the museum visit, Meir started noticing the signs on public benches: "Whites Only," "Coloreds Only." His sense of injustice was developing step by step through his emotional processing of these moments.

Meanwhile, Shimshon received his political education in a much more direct way. He was 16 during the summer of 1968 and had been sent by his parents on a tour of Europe. Shimshon's trip took take him through London and Paris, where he encountered a generation of radicals seasoned in the recent wave of student uprisings. One of the most exciting places for a young leftist in those days was Czechoslovakia. The so-called Prague Spring had brought the election of a new independent leader and a move away from Soviet-style communism. Shimshon arrived to witness a flourishing of media, art, and social mobilization, a sort of laboratory experiment for revolution. But before he could get too involved, the Soviet Union and its Warsaw Pact allies began mobilizing for an invasion to put a stop to the reform government. Shimshon made it onto one of the last civilian flights out of the country.

The vast majority of Israelis did not have the means to leave the country, as the Wigoders did quite often. Foreign travel was reserved for the wealthy and for those on official diplomatic duty. In different ways, both brothers were well-ripened by their travels and upbringing for their encounter with the Israeli Panthers.

A month later, when the Israeli prime minister was meeting with some of her cabinet members and advisers to decide how to handle the Panthers, the debate lingered on the relationship between the Panthers and the Wigoder brothers. The two were labeled as members of Matzpen during the deliberations and in various police memos. As the government saw it, the brothers belonged to the far-left group and they only got involved with the Panthers after reading about the affair in the papers and only because they sensed potential for further propaganda. "By meddling in the matter," the government believed, Matzpen hoped "to ride the ethnic issue and use it to clash with the establishment and expand their influence."

Contrary to these oft-repeated claims, however, the Wigoders did not, in fact, belong to Matzpen. The older brother left the group a year earlier, after becoming disillusioned with its tendency to split ideological hairs. Pink was too young, anarchistic, and volatile to join any kind of self-appointed vanguard. Still, the government's impression was not entirely incorrect. The Wigoders did introduce the Panthers to Israel's radical left, including to Matzpen.

The public debut of the Israeli Black Panthers as members of that left—and not just as a group of anonymous youths from the slums making threats in the newspaper—came on February 1, 1971, soon after the *sulha* and three weeks before Golda Meir would face her dilemma. Shimshon invited the Panthers to see one of the typical leftist protests being staged those days. It was a demonstration against Israel's military occupation of the Palestinian population. He brought his new friends to a courtyard outside the parliament building, known as the Knesset. About a hundred protesters gathered there, holding up signs with slogans like "Occupiers—Get Out of Gaza" and "Stop Israeli Terror in Gaza."

The protesters were not alone. Opposite them were counter-protesters from right-wing groups like Beitar and Herut. At first, the Panthers stood back and observed the scene. Many of them had come from families that voted for Herut and were not inclined to side with the peaceniks. What started as a routine and forgettable showdown, suddenly transformed into a fight. Two large young men appeared and began shoving the leftists and tearing up their signs. They were instantly identifiable as Americans because they were shouting in English. The more prominent one wore a black leather jacket with a shoulder patch featuring a Jewish star. Marciano looked on as two thugs ravaged through the crowd, and asked Shimshon, *Who are these guys?*

Shimshon had only ever heard of them. He knew that in America there was a group made up of militant Jews. The Jewish Defense League was what they called themselves. Vowing to fight antisemitism "by whatever means necessary," the JDL had borrowed the slogan, as well as the uniform and insignia, of black power. A few months earlier, an Israeli paper had run a two-page spread on the group under the headline "Panthers in Yarmulkes." Natural enemies of the left, the JDL earned a reputation as violent and reactionary thugs who got into street brawls with black groups in Brooklyn. But even as members of the Israeli left kept tabs on the JDL through the press, none had ever encountered their kind in Israel.

Shimshon responded to Marciano: *These guys? In America, they fight against the Black Panthers.*

Within a few minutes, the Musrara gang intervened in the scuffle, sending the JDL guys running. It was the first violent confrontation between the Israeli Panthers and the yarmulke-wearing Panthers. More would follow in the coming months and years.

It was around this time that the first of a series of confidential sources materialized to assist the police. A member of the Panthers or "someone close to the group," offered the police what seemed like reliable and detailed information from within. A senior detective described the unnamed source as "primitive" and "criminal" but also pliable: "It is possible to manage him well if he is given specific tasks. To extract details from him, extensive questioning is needed."

One afternoon, the source and his handler arrived at the regional police headquarters. The Special Assignments Bureau had summoned them following a report that the Panthers were planning to stage their own demonstration in two weeks. Matzpen, the source said, naming the Wigoder brothers, Shimshon and Meir, was driving them to violence. He had heard one of them give a lecture about the Panthers in the United States, a group that is made up of "Negros, Puerto Ricans, Chinese who use violence and even weapons," according to a summary of the police meeting. The source said the Musrara gang was being urged to use the same aggressive tactics in their own struggle. Matzpen allegedly offered specific instructions: "Fasten black flags to poles and drive nails through the poles for striking cops if the cops use force." And according to the source, the Panthers accepted the advice and secretly amassed helmets and improvised weapons at one of their homes. Shimshon allegedly got his mom to donate money, which was used to purchase clubs.

Detectives did not identify their source in their memos but they did provide a few telling details. One clue, in particular, aids the process of elimination. The informant had served in the military and had been court-martialed over an unspecified infraction. Most of the Panthers were exempted from mandatory conscription because of their criminal history, a fact that had helped exacerbate their alienation. In the short list of people who were privy to events, had served in the military for a period, and were court-martialed, is one particularly interesting name: Saadia Marciano. Oddest of all was the following detail. Based on the informant's contributions, police drew up a list of the Panthers' seven key members. These included Charlie Biton, David Levy, Meir Levy, Eli Avichzer, Baba Sa'adon, Koko Deri, and Haim Turgeman. Marciano was not named. Could the omission of the undeniable leader of the group indicate that it was he who was the confidential source? Possibly, but not in any conclusive way. The informant could have been someone else, and the omission of Marciano's name could be explained in any number of ways.

But if it were Marciano, then the speculation would have to turn to his motives. By all accounts, Marciano genuinely believed in what he was advocating. Indignant and impatient, he wanted to confront the establishment over what he perceived as a grave social injustice. Betraying his cause so early on by informing on his group wouldn't make any sense—unless he was acting tactically. It is not impossible that he feigned cooperation and provided false and exaggerated information. In fact, if he were purposely playing up Matzpen's involvement and fabricating tales about caches of nail-studded clubs, then he was doing an effective job of amplifying the threat of the Panthers.

8

GET OFF THE LAWN!

GOLDA MEIR HAD RESOLVED the dilemma of what to do about the Panthers. Carrying out her orders, the police first told the Panthers that their permit to protest was denied. It was the morning of March 1, two days before the demonstration was scheduled to take place. For almost 24 hours straight, and still now after they had been turned down, the Panthers were in motion. In teams of two, one to hold a brush and a bucket of glue, the other to carry a stack of handbills, the Panthers plastered Jerusalem with their message: "Enough!" This simple slogan was the title of the flyers posted on every open patch of wall in the city:

> Enough
> We are a group of downtrodden youth appealing to all
>   those who are fed up.
> Enough not having any work
> Enough sleeping ten to a room

Enough watching as apartments are built for new immigrants
Enough jail and beatings every Monday and Thursday
Enough unfulfilled promises from the government
Enough with the deprivation
Enough with the discrimination
How much longer will they treat us this way while we remain silent
Alone, we can do nothing—together, we will overcome
We will demonstrate for our right to be like all the other citizens in this
    country.

The content and phrasing of these flyers echoed the messaging of the group's American namesake. Whether this was intentional or not has been lost to time. But consider the party platform of the U.S. Panthers. It was called the Ten-Point Program. Like the Israeli declaration, the program was a list of demands, preceded by an emphatic title. "Enough!" created a similar effect to the original's "What We Want Now!" with each of the ten points repeating the phrase "We want." Aside from the stylistic similarities, the platform tackles many of the same issues: housing, education, treatment by police, incarceration, and economic justice.

The protest literature didn't stop with the "Enough!" flyer. The Panthers also drafted an open letter and had messengers deliver it to the newsrooms of every major publication in the country. It was a single yellow page with large black typeface. The letter was addressed to the minister of police, Shlomo Hillel, but also contained direct jabs at the prime minister. There was no way for the Panthers to have known that the prime minister and her police chief were involved in the decision to deny them the permit. It was audacious of them to assume so, and yet they were right.

The irreverent tone of the open letter seemed to have caught the attention of news editors. In the next day's editions, all the papers quoted from it. It scandalized some publications, which decided to redact the letter's most colorful language and strident characterizations.

For Hillel, the Panthers reserved a special animus. An Iraqi Jew by birth, they felt he should have been more sympathetic to them. Without using the term, they described him as an Uncle Tom figure—the exact label they picked out for him was "Black Collaborator." As they had done with the choice of their group's name, the Panthers were most effective at garnering attention when they forced comparisons between American racism and ethnic stratification in Israel. "What gives you the right," the letter demanded of Hillel, "to prevent members of your own ethnic group from demonstrating for rights that you have received only by becoming Ashkenazi?" After "twenty years of discrimination against us," the Panthers were no longer going to wait to be offered a place in society. They vowed to protest no matter what—a point that none of the papers redacted. "The rejection of our permit request only encourages us to break the law." For good measure, the Panthers asked to meet the prime minister. They asserted that "Golda is interested in us."

The government had anticipated that the Panthers would not acquiesce to the denial of the permit. Officials interviewed by the press in response to the letter commented on the criminal records of the group's members and on the apparent involvement of the universally loathed Matzpen. The spokespeople also lied by denying that Hillel and Meir were involved in the police's decision to deny the permit. But the media narrative was now out of the government's control. The open letter was delivered on a Monday night, less than two days before the scheduled demonstration. The government was running out of time. It had failed to contain what it saw as a threat. Attempts to offer the Panthers employment and other perks had not dissuaded them from carrying on. Police reached out to community leaders in Musrara and other Mizrahi areas but that too failed to stem the determination of the Panthers. On Tuesday morning, with Meir's blessing, the police decided to do something they had never done before.

Five leading Panthers were invited to the police headquarters in Jerusalem. When they arrived, police placed them under arrest. They were not arrested for a crime that had occurred but for one that might occur: conspiring to stage a demonstration without securing a permit. According to a police official, it was the first time that police in Jerusalem had resorted to preemptive arrests. To justify this infringement of civil liberties, government attorneys dug up an obscure clause in the penal code. They found the clause not in Israeli law per se, but in the legal code that Israel had inherited from the British Empire, the previous rulers of the land. In covering the detentions, the *Washington Post* got into a knot attempting to explain the legal case: "Calling a demonstration without a permit constitutes incitement to commit an illegal offense and their request for permission was turned down on grounds that the demonstration raised fears of disturbing the public peace."

In their jail cell that morning, the Panthers came face to face with their nemesis for the first time. Not Meir or Hillel, but a person whose everyday job was to suppress them. A clean-shaven cop in a commander's uniform, he introduced himself to Marciano and the four other detainees. He said his name was Tourgeman, which was short for Superintendent Avraham Tourgeman. His was not just any last name. It was a distinctly Moroccan one, and he was hoping that their shared heritage would help generate rapport when he offered the Panthers a deal. They were to sign a declaration distancing themselves from the radical leftists of Matzpen and withdrawing their request for a permit to stage a demonstration. As he explained the deal, he also displayed some sympathy for their grievances, pleading that they be patient. The bigotry they felt was real but society would change over time, he promised. He even brought to the precinct a rabbi from Musrara to help press the young men.

Outside of the police station, word of the arrest was starting to spread. Shlomo Segev, a lawyer who agreed to represent the Panthers pro bono, got his friend at the radio station to mention it on air. Fighting their side of the propaganda battle, the police publicized the names of the detainees in attempt to tar the Panthers as criminals in the eyes of their neighbors. It was against protocol to do so—usually, names were only released after an arraignment.

When the Wigoder brothers and their cadre of leftists heard what happened, they grabbed a stack of the "Enough" flyers and scurried down to Musrara. Within minutes, squad cars surrounded them. Everyone started running. Meir, the youngest, sprinted eastward through an open field at the edge of the neighborhood. He headed toward the transit station near the Old City's Damascus Gate. A bus was about to leave, and he hopped on, relieved because he believed he had gotten away. But then, only a few moments after the bus left the station, it stopped. A cop boarded the bus. He advanced toward Meir, grabbed him by his waistband, and dragged him out of the bus and into a police van. In lockup, Meir was surprised to see some familiar faces. The police were rounding up all of his friends. As he was booked and then processed for transfer to a remote detention center, Meir was overcome with a surreal feeling. *I am 16 years old*, he told himself. *What are they so afraid of? What are they hiding?*

Meanwhile, detectives scoured the city in search of other suspected activists. The sound of sirens and the sight of cops filing in and out of patrol cars disturbed urban life in downtown Jerusalem in a way that would have been more commonplace in Palestinian East Jerusalem. But for the genteel population of the city's western half, a manhunt produced an unfamiliar atmosphere. That's not to say that the hunted were hiding.

The police, for example, caught up with Haim Hanegbi, one of Matzpen's most familiar faces as he was sipping coffee at Café Ta'amon, where he spent a good chunk of every day regaling impromptu audiences with stories. An officer in plainclothes walked into the café and presented Hanegbi with an arrest warrant. *We have confidential information that for the past few weeks you have been inciting disturbances of the public order and preaching dangerous ideas,* he said. Hanegbi received the officer's charges as if they were a gift. For years, Matzpen tried to antagonize and subvert the establishment but were never successful at warranting a police crackdown. They held demonstrations that questioned the state's very legitimacy and still had never earned the privilege of being arrested in preemptive detention under the authority of obscure penal codes. Getting arrested, finally, made him feel like a revolutionary. It made him feel like he, too, was a Black Panther.

Hanegbi was the second to last arrested out of a total of 15 who found themselves locked up. In the first roundup, police captured the core of the Panthers: Saadia Marciano, Meir Levy, Charlie Biton, Eli Avichzer, and Haim Turgeman. Next up: the Wigoders, Yigal "The Goat" Noah, and Kaubilio; Dany Levit, the rebel son of a pre-state Zionist militia commander; and Rafael Ben Zaken, Yaakov Amuyal, and Uri Brock. Then, Hanegbi. For their last target, the police grabbed Bardugo, the man who claimed to have started it all.

The authorities tried to present the detentions as a routine matter of public safety. They fooled no one. Many Israelis did not need to be privy to government deliberations to read the situation as a standoff between disaffected Mizrahim and the political establishment. Faced with a challenge from a disorganized group of youths who somehow made it into the newspaper, the government chose repression. First, by targeting them with a domestic surveillance operation. Then, by answering the incendiary claims of the Panthers with condescending rhetoric, with one lawmaker, for example, dismissing the matter as a manifestation of hooliganism and many others describing the Musrara youths as puppets who were being controlled by other, more sophisticated actors. Finally, came the preemptive arrests. In full public view, Meir had presided over one of the most egregious and consequential denials of civil liberties in Israeli history.

Mayor Kollek loved the look of fresh grass and dedicated himself to planting acres and acres of it. In the years after the 1967 war, the portly mayor of Jerusalem embarked on a massive public works program that would earn him comparisons to King Herod, the ancient Roman ruler of the city and its most prolific builder. Kollek decided he would gift the city and its denizens with lush parks and gardens. With the help of his team of landscape architects, he persevered against the dry and rocky terrain of the Judaean Mountains. Soon, manicured lawns began cropping up throughout the ever-expanding urban footprint of Jerusalem. In the very middle of the city, a ring of green encircled the walls of the Old City. The lawns gave the city a sheen of affluence, an aesthetic that alluded to Europe—and for Kollek, to Vienna, the city of his childhood. But to Kollek's frustration, city dwellers did not immediately sync up their behavior with his vision. "We were desperately trying to teach Jerusalemites to respect the first few gardens that had been planted in the city," he later recalled.

On March 3, 1971, at around 3:30 in the afternoon, Kollek peered out of a window from the third story of city hall, looking down at the grass-filled courtyard out front. What he saw made him furious. A crowd swelling into the hundreds was gathering there, on the lawn. Outcasts and young people with attitudes, long-haired hippie types, a random assortment of onlookers, students, journalists: hundreds of insolent bodies stomping and sitting and squashing his precious blades of grass.

So began the inaugural demonstration of a group of youths from Musrara that had recently shocked the country by announcing, "We will be the Black Panthers of Israel." The turnout was beyond anything the youths could have imagined. More importantly, they drew some incredibly high-profile attention. Every national newspaper sent a reporter to the scene as did the radio and the country's sole television station. Even the *Washington Post* dispatched its local correspondent, who called the event an "unusual act of civil disobedience" for an Israeli society that tended to comply with state authority.

Rafi Marciano addresses the crowd outside Jerusalem's city hall at the first protest of the Black Panthers on March 3, 1971. Digital image of photograph by Steve (full name not provided by Israel Sun Inc.)/Israel Sun Ltd., from the Judaica Collection of the Harvard Library, Harvard University.

The arrival of several national celebrities fueled the hype. Haim Gouri, one of Israel's most prominent poets, appeared in the crowd. Two other major figures, who drove in from Tel Aviv, stepped up to deliver speeches. Dahn Ben-Amotz was a former combat soldier, playwright, satirist, and radio host who was known for trying to emulate the persona of his famous American friend Marlon Brando. When Israel was created, the country had symbols but no identity, ideology but no character. Ben-Amotz helped fill that void. His swagger and irreverence came to define the archetype of the new Israeli man.

"I don't know what the Panthers want," he told the crowd from atop a wall that came to serve as the demonstration's makeshift podium. "But I am here to protest against the police for taking away their basic right as citizens to demonstrate."

Amos Kenan, a literary figure, political critic, and Ben-Amotz's archrival, echoed the same sentiment. "Today, for the first time I realized: the police, which I thought protected the citizens, became a force that protects the government from its citizens," Kenan said.

Ben-Amotz and Kenan were two voices from deep within the Israeli cultural establishment, and they granted the Panthers a legitimacy they could hardly have garnered on their own. The mere presence of these figures served to make the Panthers fashionable. On that unseasonably mild afternoon in Jerusalem, it felt like everyone who was anyone had shown up to the first demonstration of the Israeli Black Panthers. Everyone—except for the Panthers themselves. They were locked up in the dark, dank holding cells of the Israeli police.

For all his glowering, Kollek should not have been surprised at the fact of the gathering. He knew perfectly well that a protest had been scheduled for that time and place, and the preemptive arrests had only fueled more interest in the group. But he couldn't help himself. His temper was taking over again, and he had long decided that it was better "to let it out than to have it eat away at my insides," as he later put it. Among the crowd, the atmosphere was calm and even cheerful. Cameras were being set up. Police were there but they remained composed. The mayor observed the scene from his perch until he couldn't hold back any longer. "Get off the grass!" he bellowed. "Protest or not—just get off the grass!" When Kollek finally came down to the courtyard, his cheeks were flushed with anger. He tried to nudge the crowd onto the paved pathways. Unsurprisingly, his efforts failed and he soon retreated into city hall.

The next thing to hold the crowd's attention was a middle-aged woman trampling the grass with the most potent of energy—that of a mother acting in defense of her child. The scarf on her head, her checkered dress rendering her body a shapeless mound, the way she gesticulated with outstretched arm and pinched-together fingers, the accent in her voice as she spoke—these were easily readable signs indicating she was an immigrant from North Africa. Aliza Marciano, crying out indignantly for the release of her son, Saadia, provided the perfect foil

Aliza Marciano protests the detention of her son Saadia and his friends during a demonstration outside Jerusalem's city hall. Digital image of photograph by Steve (full name not provided by Israel Sun Inc.)/Israel Sun Ltd., from the Judaica Collection of the Harvard Library, Harvard University.

for the haughty intemperance of the mayor. After he ensconced himself back inside she led the crowd in a charge of city hall doors. With uncharacteristic delicateness, the police repelled them away.

What the demonstration needed now was an authentic voice from one of Musrara's youths. But the core cadre of Panthers were locked up and so the crowd produced Reuven Abergel.

He didn't quite cut a Pantherly figure. At 28, Abergel did not belong to the same age group as Marciano's, though he had younger brothers who did. He was married and living with his wife and child in their own apartment, which was more of a shack. He wore his hair short. He didn't look fashionable in the American-inflected manner of the younger men in his neighborhood. Many in his neighborhood thought of him as an intimidating thug. He represented what was perhaps the only thing the younger guys could aspire to become: an outwardly tough and feared neighborhood character.

Perhaps contributing to that reputation, only four months earlier, his house had been raided by police and he'd been arrested as a suspected drug dealer. It started when police officers brought a sniffer dog named Loki to an empty area behind a few homes at the edge of Musrara. She followed her nose to a particular spot and dug into the ground until reaching a rock. Underneath was a plastic bag containing a black chunk of what turned out to be 263 grams of opium. A few feet away, Loki dug up another bag, this one with 56 grams of hashish in it. The police decided to search a nearby home, which turned out to be Abergel's, and reportedly found a pipe and other paraphernalia stashed on his roof. They put Abergel in jail on a 12-day detention order. Formal charges, however, were not brought against him and, without explanation, Abergel was released and the case remained open.

At the protest, urged ahead by a sudden calling of his name, Abergel climbed up to join Ben-Amotz and Kenan on the speakers' wall. What he saw from up there mesmerized him. Cops who had never hesitated to beat him up now stood back. Ashkenazi people held up protest placards scrawled with slogans that acknowledged the forces that shaped his life: "No more discrimination," "No more poverty," and "We are all Black Panthers." Everyone was expecting him to say something, but Abergel couldn't find his words. He stayed frozen until he heard Ben-Amotz speaking into his ear. Quoting a line from the Talmud, Ben-Amotz encouraged him: "Open your mouth and let your words illuminate." What Abergel said in his first public speech was not recorded. But the very act of delivering it would change his life forever. He would go on to describe this moment by comparing it to Moses's encounter with the burning bush.

After speaking to the crowd, Abergel led them off the mayor's precious lawn. The crowd marched a few hundred feet to reach the municipal police headquarters, which was known as the Russian Compound

Reuven Abergel delivers a speech at a Black Panther demonstration in Jerusalem. Digital image of photograph by Shalom Bar-Tal/Israel Sun Ltd., from the Judaica Collection of the Harvard Library, Harvard University.

because the underlying land belonged to the Russian Orthodox Church. Across from the police building stood a cathedral signifying the Russian presence, and priests in frocks peaked out of the Byzantine Revival structure, watching as the protesters reassembled outside. Abergel had been booked at this precinct countless times before, most recently over the drugs found in the vicinity of his home. Now, he was returning under different circumstances. At the head of a stream of bodies, Abergel came to demand the release of those detained. Only three of them were on the premises, behind the barred windows visible by the crowd. The rest of the detainees had been shipped off to other jails. But from the ground level where they were being held, the three could hear and just barely see the demonstration. The show of solidarity made their eyes tear up.

The police invited the crowd to send in a delegation. Joining Abergel were Ben-Amotz and Kenan, as well as Saadia Marciano's younger brother Rafi Marciano, who had spoken at the demonstration in front of city hall, and another teenager, Zion Buhbut. At any time prior to that day, the lowliest of officers never would have hesitated to harass Abergel or the other young Mizrahi men on the street. Now they were sitting at a table across from the precinct's top brass. The conversation concluded with a promise to begin releasing those detained that very night. The Panthers didn't know it yet, but in the eyes of some, Abergel had assumed a position of leadership in the movement. Once freed and reunited, the detained Panthers would have to contend with his involvement, while also figuring out how to cash in on all the publicity.

Some would come to revile Abergel over his supposed intrusion into the affairs of the Panthers, alleging that he only joined to extricate himself from legal jeopardy after being linked by police to a drug bust. Others would crown him as a hero of the people. Ultimately, his contributions to the movement would help transform both Israeli society and alter the course of his own life. He couldn't know the personal price he would pay for becoming a Panther, how it would turn him into a leader but also lead to his undoing. But speaking up didn't feel like a choice. It was the moment in which he began what he would call the "archaeological excavation of my life." Examining the ruins around him—broken-down families, poverty, pridelessness, rampant criminality, and drug abuse—he would attempt to reconstruct what had led his community astray.

9

CONFIDENTIAL INFORMANT P/51

THE NEXT DAY, Superintendent Avraham Tourgeman, the top intelligence officer in the Israeli police's Southern District, dispatched an order to all the investigators under his command. He asked them to contribute to a new mission. Labeled "secret," the memo detailing the order referred to the Panthers as mere criminals who had been encouraged to believe society had wronged them. Tourgeman congratulated the department on its vigorous response. He indicated that the threat had subsided. But, he warned, things could pick up again suddenly and escalate, as had happened 12 years earlier at Wadi Salib.

Whether ethnic discrimination was "real or imagined," it was the job of the police to detect and suppress political agitation. To that end, he explained, the intelligence apparatus would begin systematically infiltrating the "communities of the deprived." Officers were to quietly discover groups and places where conditions were ripe for ethnic conflagration.

Tourgeman recommended deploying officers of the "appropriate ethnic-ity" to such places. The objective of the mission would be to draw up a list of leaders and key people who might serve as informants for the police.

Tourgeman's jurisdiction extended over a large swath of Israel. The Southern District included the entirety of Jerusalem and stretched south across the Negev Desert all the way to the resort town of Eilat. The distances involved meant he had to delegate authority to dozens of police stations in this region. But when it came to the capital itself, Tourgeman trusted only himself. The initial informant on the Pan-thers, supplied by one of his subordinates, had proven a failure, bring-ing false intelligence that the Panthers were arming themselves. Indeed, when the first protest took place, in defiance of the preemptive arrests, none of the demonstrators brandished studded clubs. The weapons which the Panthers were alleged to have amassed didn't exist and the protest passed without violent confrontation. Tourgeman set out to recruit a more reliable informant. In a few weeks, he would suc-ceed in a way that would surprise even himself.

Tourgeman was the kind of immigrant from Morocco that Israel liked to parade in front of potential Jewish donors from the United States. Born poor in Morocco, he reached his teenage years during World War II just as Nazi Germany threatened to expand its genocide to North Africa. After the war, but before Israel was founded, a Zionist campaign called Youth Aliyah recruited him from the slums of Casa-blanca. The group taught him Hebrew, gave him a political education, and sent him to the Holy Land in time to enlist in a militia and fight in the war that created the State of Israel. After completing his service, he looked for work. There was none, so he joined the police force. At the academy, he studied some criminal law and excelled enough in his training to be selected for an advanced track. To judge by Tourgeman's story alone, Israel was a country that saved the least fortunate of Jews from the clutches of backwardness in Arab lands and then offered them a real shot at advancement.

Early on, police work brought Tourgeman into contact with other immigrants from Morocco who, for one reason or another, fared worse than he did. He encountered them in 1959 when he was dispatched to Wadi Salib. In the 1960s, he accepted a permanent assignment in Jerusalem. The city's delinquents came to know and fear Officer Tourgeman. Among those who became familiar with his boot and his baton were Marciano and the other youths of Musrara. In their minds, he came to be closely associated with the walkie-talkie he carried around—and not because he used it for communication. It was how he used the bulky device when you did something to vex him. He'd gleefully bash your skull in, the stories said.

After the war in 1967, money and drugs flooded the streets of the city. As head of the local Patrol and Operations Bureau, Tourgeman insinuated himself into the criminal crevices of the newly conquered Old City and Arab neighborhoods of East Jerusalem. Only two months after the war, he knew the seediest parts well enough, and felt safe enough roaming around them by foot, to bring along a reporter on a late-night patrol. The resulting newspaper vignette quoted heavily from Tourgeman's dispensations of street secrets. Near the historic Perfume Market: *Here's where crooks like to congregate.* On the young people rushing by: *They are either homosexuals or just out to score drugs.* About the woman searching for her friend: *A known prostitute.* Wherever he looked, Tourgeman seemed to encounter gambling halls, stolen goods on sale, cafés doubling as hashish dens—a veritable carnival of illicit activity.

Tourgeman's devotion to crime-fighting was handsomely rewarded. By the start of 1971, he had become one of the top officers in the city and probably the only Moroccan immigrant in such a senior position anywhere in the country. With the rank of superintendent and as head of the patrols and operations division in his police district, he was important enough to have a subordinate who read newspapers for him, flagging relevant articles for his review. Tourgeman was sitting at his desk at the Ras al-Amud police station looking over curated headlines one morning when the words "Black Panthers" popped out at him. Who were these slum youths speaking the American language of revolution? What came to his mind in that instant was his experience at Wadi Salib and the chaos he had helped suppress as a young cadet. So he did what his own subordinate did; Tourgeman took the news higher up the chain of command. Born in Romania but raised in British Palestine, David Ofer was the commander of a police district stretching across much of the country. Ofer responded with skepticism to Tourgeman's warning of the coming turmoil. "Turgie," he said, using his nickname. "Listen to me. It's just a tall tale." But within two weeks, after it became clear the Panthers were real after all, Ofer gave Tourgeman a shiny new job title: Head of Special Duties.

Tourgeman did not manage to conceal his attempt to land an informant. The Panthers sensed they were being spied on and spoke openly of police attempts to recruit among them. A few days after the first protest, the Panthers, now including Abergel, sat down with a reporter for their first major interview in which they allowed their real names to be published. In the interview, Abergel described how the police tried to pressure him into cooperating by bringing up his arrest for drug possession from months earlier. "They planted hashish to frame me and say they'll close the case if I agreed to snitch," he was quoted as saying.

Perhaps Tourgeman wasn't being sloppy and conspicuous, however. By making his intentions to buy informants known, he sowed suspicion among the Panthers, some of whom came to believe Abergel did make a deal. Meanwhile, other members of the Panthers gave the group reason to question their own loyalty. Some accepted placement in jobs or job training programs. A few were hired as production assistants at the state television station. Some left town for a while to train as professional cooks at a luxury hotel on the coast that had agreed to accept reformed delinquents. One Panther, Abergel's brother Eliezer, who had a criminal record, got the most curious of postings: he began working at the auto shop of the police department.

It was well understood among the Panthers that they were being bought off by the establishment—they knew the perks came with some strings attached. But who could blame someone with so few prospects in life for accepting an opportunity to break out of their circumstance? Or be surprised that someone facing a jail sentence would agree to tip off police in return for leniency?

As with any incipient social movement, the boundaries around who belonged to the Panthers grew somewhat permeable. The boys from Musrara could no longer jealously guard their clique. If they wanted more influence, they had no choice but to let people in, a fact which made them all the more vulnerable to Tourgeman's encroachments. After the Wigoders and Abergel, scores more pledged their solidarity to the Panthers. The support came from as far away as France, where someone telegrammed the Panthers to express their enthusiasm. In Egypt, a newspaper published an open call suggesting that "the Palestinian resistance movement would do well to enter a dialogue with these young people." Countless strangers showed up in Musrara seeking to become volunteers and activists. Some inevitably worked their way into positions of influence. But the growth of their ranks was not just the organic result of their publicity. Abergel, for example, organized a membership drive as one of his first acts. He had registration forms printed and led a canvassing effort across the city's poorest neighborhoods. At the end of a week's work, he announced 3,000 membership forms had been filled out. The number may have been exaggerated, but a skeptical journalist inspected some of the signed forms and verified that at least 600 were real.

The weeks after the first protest were a time to experiment, negotiate the identity of the group, and formulate a platform. In short order, they recruited university students to volunteer as tutors to children who were struggling with school. With little coordination, different members issued statements addressing the criticisms that had been leveled at them. On the matter of Matzpen, some Panthers denounced the leftist group and vowed to cut ties with them. However, Marciano and his lieutenant Charlie Biton maintained their personal relationships with members of the far left. The question of violence versus nonviolence also came up, and the Panthers' stance seemed to soften. Bardugo, for example, who entered the fold again after his absence for reserve duty, publicly said that "if our demands are not met, we will use every *legal and democratic* means at our disposal." They had yet to formalize a platform, but the Panthers did latch on to several policy issues. As they saw it, there existed in Israel a largely unspoken but pernicious regime of ethnic segregation. That schools must be integrated and "Oriental ghettos" would have to cease existing were consensus issues for the Panthers. Recalling their own experiences growing up, the Panthers also spoke of offering juvenile offenders avenues for rehabilitation and reforming prisons to reduce the abuse meted out by guards. In another sign of their growing sophistication—or pacification—the Panthers announced they had formed a task force called the War on Delinquency Committee. Made up entirely of Panthers, the committee promised to produce a survey on youths in distress and housing.

It was now mid-March, 1971, and the focus of attention was inside parliament. A group of about 20 Panthers was seated in the public viewing gallery. Through a sheet of bulletproof glass, they looked down at the lawmakers in Plenum Hall. As it happens, the glass had been installed as a security measure because of an act of desperation by a disaffected, and possibly mentally ill, Mizrahi man in 1957. Moshe Dwek, an immigrant from Syria, had an intestinal injury and couldn't get the public health system to treat him. One day, he ascended to the visitor's balcony at the old original parliament building and lobbed a grenade at the lawmakers below. Among those injured by the shrapnel were the prime minister, David Ben-Gurion, and his foreign minister, Golda Meir.

In the hall below the Panthers, there were 120 seats, one for each member of parliament, though not all were occupied. Lawmakers in Israel typically show up only for matters that interest them or require party-line voting. When the day started, the discussion revolved around topics that were sacred in Israel, such as national security and foreign relations. Foreign Minister Abba Eban gave a speech and more than 70 lawmakers were present for it. As the next discussion was announced, the Panthers looked down at a nearly empty room. They outnumbered the remaining lawmakers. The topic on the agenda was the Panthers themselves, and the discussion would touch on poverty, drug use, civil unrest, and police violence. But those words were too blunt for the parliament's chairman, who euphemistically listed the agenda item as "The Problem of Youth in Distress Throughout the Country and Jerusalem in Particular."

Sitting across in the public viewing gallery, the Panthers observed the dais. Its backdrop is a relief of stone, an abstract sculpture titled, "Pray for the Peace of Jerusalem." The title is derived from Psalms 122:6, a passage attributed to King David. With no mention of outside enemies or war in this psalm, the strife that King David seems to worry about is internal. "May there be peace within your walls," it reads.

His prayer for peace is a prayer for unity. The Panthers were hardly the cause of the current strife gripping Jerusalem. They were its symptom, and perhaps also its solution. Seated in the audience section, the Panthers listened quietly as a lineup of lawmakers delivered pleas for more funding for social services and proposed new policies. The first few speakers dismissed the Panthers as insignificant or even attacked them.

Then came the turn of Uri Avnery to speak. He was a fiery lawmaker unaffiliated with any of the major parties and an editor of *This World*, the muckraking magazine that was sympathetic to allegations of anti-Mizrahi discrimination. He was Ashkenazi like most of the law-makers but he didn't sound like them. The Panthers noticed how he opened his speech by giving them credit for the unexpected pivot in public attention from national security to domestic matters. And they appreciated how his speech didn't couch the problem of inequality in the jargon of social work. "Take a young person who grew up in Rehavia and one who grew up in Musrara," he said, using the names of two neighborhoods to stand in for two distinct ethnic groups in Israeli society. "They each have an equal level of intelligence, talent, and char-acter, but their opportunities in life are entirely different. . . . One will soon buy a Jaguar and the other will become a Panther." Avnery went on to castigate the police for how they hunted down the Panther activ-ists ahead of their first protest, and rejected the portrayal of the Pan-thers as puppets of ill-intentioned left-wing extremists.

At the conclusion of Avnery's polemic, the Panthers in the audience broke out in applause. In response, the parliament's chairman demanded silence, but Avnery egged them on. "I don't know who's up there but I thank them for their applause," he said into the microphone. Ushers arrived and ejected the Panthers from the gallery, citing the rules of par-liamentary decorum. The Panthers apologized. They said they didn't know about the prohibition on clapping. We thought it was like a movie theater, they explained as they left. Outside, in the hallway, someone came to intercept them. It was Avnery's former ally Shalom Cohen, who had recently turned on his now-rival. Cohen had an oversized and square-shaped head and a thick black mustache. His style seemed calcu-lated to emphasize his Mizrahi roots. Cohen was Iraqi-born and Egyp-tian-raised, but he was quite unlike the Panthers. He had grown up in a wealthy family of merchants. Now a creature of the left, Cohen fash-ioned himself a champion of the downtrodden. Cohen and Avnery had met while serving together during the war in 1948 and became best friends. As the co-editor with Avnery of *This World,* Cohen had pro-duced some of the best journalism on inequality in Israel. In addition to publishing the magazine together, the pair founded an eponymous political party. It remained small yet influential. By coincidence, as the Panthers got started two months earlier, the partnership between Cohen and Avnery came to an acrimonious end. Cohen now needed a new political home.

The reason he saw potential in the Panthers might be found in a book he would soon publish about Avnery, promising to expose him as a failure of a leader and guilty of deep-seated anti-Mizrahi bigotry. In the introduction to the book, Cohen lays out the litany of social ills afflicting the country. He asks whether Israel is doomed. The answer: "No. Beneath the surface are new forces. Seedlings are sprouting." He points to the youth revolt gripping the country and particularly to "the Black Panthers who are going against the grain." Cohen would remain involved with the Panthers for years, a fateful relationship whose first point of contact happened just outside the parliamentary hall. He gave the Panthers a quick tutorial on parliamentary etiquette, made a promise to the ushers they would behave, and showed them back inside.

The quaintness of the incident, and how harmlessly it was resolved, serves as a reminder of the stark contrast between the Israeli Panthers and their namesake American group. Four years earlier at the California State Capitol in Sacramento, a different kind of showdown took place in a similar setting. Members of the Black Panther Party walked into the state Assembly Hall mid-session while toting rifles and wearing dark sunglasses, berets, and bomber jackets. Some lawmakers ducked for cover when they saw the black militants. The Panthers came not to stage a violent attack but as part of a legal protest. They were opposing a bill that would eliminate the right of Californians to openly carry guns. Founded a few months earlier, the Panthers became famous for patrolling their communities in armed groups as a response to the often-violent policing that happened on the streets of Oakland. They would drive around, following police officers as they made arrests, implicitly threatening to intervene when black people's rights were being violated. What the Panthers were doing was completely legal; it wasn't a crime to brandish a shotgun in a moving vehicle. To make such an act illegal, lawmakers—incidentally, they were working in tandem with the National Rifle Association—proposed a bill to ban open carry.

No one stopped the Panthers from entering the legislature, but police soon ordered them to leave and arrested them on felony charges of conspiracy to disrupt a legislative session. The gun control bill, known as the Mulford Act, meanwhile, passed. The news coverage described the California-based Black Panthers as invaders and served to permanently brand them as violent extremists. By all accounts of their day in parliament, the Israeli Panthers were polite and amenable, and their visit could hardly be considered a protest. Because of the name they chose, they were being judged on the reputation garnered by actions far more confrontational than their own.

Perhaps this relative lack of militancy is why it was so easy and took so little time to infiltrate the Israeli Panthers. By March 23, Tourgeman had succeeded in his mission. Surveillance reports started pouring into police headquarters daily and sometimes several times a day. All of them cited a source identified as P/51, "someone close to the decisions being made." Only Tourgeman, and perhaps one or two other officers, knew the source's identity. Based on the breadth of information coming in, P/51 had to have been either one of the original Panthers or someone who had infiltrated the group's core leadership.

The rapidly available and detailed reports drew the attention of the omnipotent Shin Bet, Israel's domestic intelligence and internal security agency. Police memos on the Panthers were regularly delivered to the secretive agency, specifically to three units known by code names

675, 251 and 268. The first code refers to the Shin Bet's central data repository. But the other two were units whose mission was to keep track of Israelis suspected of working with foreign enemies. The Shin Bet told Tourgeman, he later recalled, that the intel from P/51 was so detailed and reliable that there was no need for the agency to establish its own undercover operation targeting the Panthers.

For the time being, at least, the kind of activities documented by P/51 would hardly seem to justify the level of attention trained on them. An early surveillance report from March 24, for example, relayed a sighting from the source of "red-colored ribbons made of cloth" with the words "Black Panthers" written on them in white. They were meant for "wearing around arms and foreheads" during protest marches. That same memo meticulously recorded P/51's areas of responsibility in the Black Panthers: guiding a film crew through the neighborhood and going door-to-door to sign up students for free tutoring.

Of more use to police were P/51's observations of feuds and other points of contention within the group. Publicly, the Panthers tried to project a sense of unity. But, internally, one of the problems they dealt with was that Panthers were accepting job offers, and such offers were materializing at an unprecedented rate for people who had rarely found work before. Should people who take jobs be considered quitters? Would having members who were employed—even working at government agencies—undermine the essential message of rebellion? Many Panthers seemed to believe they could take those jobs and continue with their political struggle, or quit without consequence when necessary. But the police learned, at least, that the dilemma did rouse debate within the group, generating tension between hardliners and moderates.

The Panthers were busy preparing for their second public action, the first since the protest that got their entire leadership was locked up. It was important for them to present a united front, especially considering all the people who now hoped either to assimilate into the organization—

or wrest control of it. The event was organized by the Student Union at Israel's flagship institution of higher learning, the Hebrew University of Jerusalem. Billed as a rally to demand action on "the problems of discrimination, poverty, and underachievement," the event would take place at Wise Auditorium with the Black Panthers forming a panel of speakers.

In the two days leading up to the university rally, P/51 witnessed just how disjointed the Panthers were as new members jockeyed for position. A newcomer to the group named Eddie Malka demanded that he speak on behalf of the Panthers. At 30 years of age, he was older, more educated, and considered more articulate than the others. Previously, he was mostly known for dabbling in hypnosis, claiming he could bend metal spoons with his mind. But his "greatest talent was his power of rhetoric," according to an ethnographer who studied the Panthers. "He could always be sure to attract a crowd and to hold them spellbound by his great pathos and emotion." Malka's alleged charisma failed to impress Abergel, who dismissed his demand to speak and told him to back off. "We'll beat the crap out of you," he told Malka.

Though P/51's identity was a guarded secret, anyone privy to the police memos on the Panthers could have carried out a process of elimination based on the details provided. The account of Malka and Abergel's confrontation, for example, would seem to eliminate the two of them. Another incident chronicled by P/51 involved an argument between Abergel and Marciano, adding another name to the list of people who were not Tourgeman's mole. In this case, Marciano got into a yelling match with Abergel one night and branded him "Hitler" for going at everything alone. The charge against Abergel came as he found himself consumed with the work of the Panthers. In his relentlessness, he could hardly accept any setbacks. When, for example, he failed to recruit enough volunteers to carry protest banners for a rally, P/51 heard Abergel lash out in frustration. He threatened to self-immolate like a Vietnamese monk: "I am willing to take gasoline and ignite myself at Zion Square," Abergel said. "Maybe that will stun the public."

"Well, we have finally made it to the university," Marciano quipped sardonically from the stage of Wise Auditorium as he appeared alongside Abergel, Malka, and several other Panthers. They were peaceable together, each personality now subsumed in the collective identity. An audience of 1,000 students and faculty sat down to listen and were enraptured with these exotic specimens from the Mizrahi ghetto. The Panthers enhanced this impression by apologizing profusely for their "poor Hebrew," even as they used language that hit many listeners as revelatory. Sitting among them in the front row, with his arms crossed, his head tilted up at the stage and his eyes transfixed, was P/51, displaying an attentiveness matching that of everyone else. There was no way for others in the room to guess that P/51 was focused because he knew he might be asked for a playback later.

Even among supporters, the question disturbing many people was why they had chosen such a name. "We chose the name 'Black Panthers,'" Marciano explained, "because nobody ever heard of an organization with a name like 'Katamon residents for Katamon.'" The fact they had to defend the name reaffirmed to Marciano that it was the right name to choose. It got people's attention. Banners and the speeches helped deliver the message:

> We are a majority that is a minority.
> Why are all the prostitutes Moroccan?
> Good enough for the army but not enough for decent housing?
> Abroad I was a Jew, here I am a Moroccan.

Only once that evening did the rally devolve into disorder. It happened after a family of ten was invited onto the stage. The father, a janitor working for the city, talked about his despair as he struggled to find adequate housing for his family. His teenage son read out the family's correspondence with unhelpful government agencies. The son's school teacher happened to be in the audience and he spoke up to corroborate the story. The teacher said the boy was gifted, a genius even, but that poverty had forced him to drop out.

The crowd appeared moved by this story of suffering and the hall was quiet and attentive. Then the voice of someone in the crowd yelled out: "Have you not heard of the pill?" Whoever it was cynically brought up the question of birth control, implying that people who had so many children should not complain about being poor. Incensed by this interruption, some of the Panthers jumped to their feet to search for the mysterious speaker. They too came from large families and knew there were reasons Mizrahi families tended to be so large. The Bible, for one, commanded the Jewish people to "be fruitful and multiply." Mass procreation of Jews was also official policy and a national priority, intended to correct the demographic imbalance with Arab countries. Families with more than ten children were given government commendations and were even visited by the prime minister in some cases. So a few of the Panthers dashed into the crowd, looking to punish the smug man. A fight broke out. But that didn't spoil the event because it quickly ended and news reports were mostly forgiving. Such public expressions of Mizrahi anger did not, yet, disqualify the Panthers in the eyes of the press.

As P/51 spied on the Panthers, he also necessarily spied on the journalists who covered them. He would be present when reporters arrived for interviews, keep tabs on who was visiting and who seemed sympathetic. He would tell his handlers about the journalists, whom they sought to interview, and what questions were asked. The police learned, for example, that *Jerusalem Post* reporter Susan Bellos began to frequent Panther hangouts in the wake of the Wise Auditorium event. The mole relayed the contents of an in-depth interview that Bellos conducted with Abergel. It would have come as no surprise when, four days later, the *Post* ran a sympathetic profile of Abergel, who was described as a "very articulate representative" and "very gifted political agitator." The story also described him as "a bombshell of energy who could never be described as lazy." It disturbed Bellos, she wrote, to meet a person of her same age whose life in poverty and lack of education represented "wasted potential."

Not everything Abergel said in his interviews made it into the papers. One afternoon around this time, a group of reporters arrived to interview him. He told them, according to P/51, about the police's cruel interrogation methods: "[Abergel] told them about the torture methods used by the police, saying that they are equal to the methods that were used by the Japanese." Abergel bombarded them with anecdotes in horrifying detail, calibrated to tantalize a journalist. Abergel knew a man, he had said to the reporters with P/51 listening in, whose head was bashed in with a stick so many times that his hair stopped growing afterward. He named two others who were hit in their genitals and a man who was beaten during an interrogation "and made to crawl on his knees to kiss the interrogator's feet." None of these anecdotes made it into print. Perhaps the reporters did not find Abergel's stories credible. Or maybe the police intervened somehow to keep them from being published. It is impossible to know, but the spying meant, at the very least, that the police knew of the allegations and had a chance to preempt their publication.

P/51 would continue to prove his usefulness. On the evening of March 31, close to 60 Panthers gathered at the Abergel home, a shack of wood and tin where he lived with his wife and their small child. In the room, there was a bed, a dining table, and a few other odd belongings. A picture of Elvis Presley hanging on the wall spruced up the spare environs. The size of the crowd reached the limit of the shack's capacity, and many people had to hang out by the doorway to listen in. Since his recruitment by police a few weeks earlier, P/51 had visited this house many times. Now, as he looked around the room, so many new people were present that he could recognize only a fraction of the faces.

The hierarchy within a group of so many loosely connected individuals was not well established. Hosting the meetings at his home afforded Abergel an advantage beyond what he earned through the sheer power of his personality. He moved to open the meeting, and everyone stopped what they were doing to listen.

"As the chairman of the Panthers—" Abergel began, per P/51's report.

He couldn't complete the sentence, however, because Marciano raised his voice to interrupt.

"Chairman . . . maybe until this point," Marciano said. "[But] now we want to distribute roles and responsibilities. You can't be everything."

It is not clear when exactly Abergel had been named chairman, but at some point the center of power had shifted far enough in his direction for that to happen.

Aiming to reclaim power from Abergel and delegitimize the title he had taken, Marciano demanded the group hold an election for leadership and do so by a secret ballot vote. "Please," Abergel responded. "Let's do it."

The two most dominant voices in the Panthers were signaling that they would agree to cede influence as part of an election. But with this rare harmony on the verge of an important moment—a first election, a move toward democratization—there was tension.

Bardugo, back from an absence, chimed in to assert his place. "As a Panther, I also say there must be an election."

Then, one of the Ashkenazi left-wing teenagers, Dany Levit, decided to give his opinion: "The vote doesn't have to be secret."

That set off Abergel.

"You're a Matzpen snitch!" Abergel said, "who's just angling to see how people cast their votes so he can go and snitch."

Then Abergel made explicit the power he derived from hosting the meeting at his house:

"Get out of my house!" he yelled.

Levit did not belong to Matzpen, though the press kept branding all the Ashkenazim orbiting the Panthers as Matzpen. Levit was more of an I'm-angry-at-my-parents rebel than any kind of party leftist. But simply being Ashkenazi incriminated him in Abergel's eyes.

The meeting could have devolved into a chaotic argument but something else happened. P/51 decided to intervene and stand up to Abergel. At least, that's what he later told police.

"I am opposed to using words such as 'get out of my house,'" P/51 said in Levit's defense.

Standing up to Abergel was risky. P/51 needed to maintain access to Abergel for his secret police duties.

"Who are you and what is your role here?" P/51 asked. "Because, as far as I know, we haven't started voting yet."

"He's with Matzpen!" Abergel said of Levit again.

"But who told you he's with Matzpen and how do you know?" P/51 asked.

From there, others found the courage to speak up and counter Abergel.

"I have friends who are communists," Bardugo said. "Does that mean I am communist, too?"

The argument ended with Abergel pacified and Levit remaining in the house.

De-escalation would not be the typical move expected of informants. The playbook tactic for moles is to trigger and exacerbate the worst tendencies within a social movement. But there was also an advantage to how P/51 handled the situation—he made himself stand out and earned the respect of the many in the group.

As soon as one fight ended, another broke out. The cause this time was Bardugo, who undermined the concept of the secret ballot by vocally endorsing a slate of three leaders. He proposed elevating Saadia Marciano and his brother Rafi, as well as David Levy, a member of the original clique. To calm things down, the gathering took a tea break. When they returned, the voting began. The top three candidates would share authority as chair and two deputies.

But when the ballots were counted, something strange happened. The second and third spots went to Levy and to Biton, who was not previously seen as a leader. He was more of Marciano's sidekick. But Marciano did not place first. Nor did Abergel. Somehow neither of them made the cut, having failed to muster enough votes.

The person elected as the head of the Panthers was P/51, per the informant's report to his police handler.

A majority of the Panthers, voting anonymously, were won over by P/51, who had just demonstrated his ability to bring the infighting under control. P/51 was not an unwise choice for chairman. But his election was a fluke and the most surprised person present was probably the P/51 himself. He had been assigned the role of infiltrating the group—not taking it over. So P/51 objected to the result. He wouldn't take advantage of this turn of events. *I am not the right person for the job,* he explained. *I see myself as a disinterested supporter, an adviser to whoever is elected.* He managed to persuade the group to carry out another round of voting. Like beads on an abacus, the votes realigned to produce a far more natural and digestible result. Charlie Biton maintained his support, placing first. Saadia Marciano took second, and Reuven Abergel third. A temporary détente.

For the most part, the Panthers managed to conceal from the public the feuds and suspicions that threatened to blow up the group before it managed to accomplish much. Marciano came the closest to revealing these internal dynamics. It happened shortly after the secret election during one of the only in-depth interviews he would ever give to a journalist. Describing the election—but omitting mention of the recount—he explained the group's unusual leadership structure. A "troika" with no single person at the helm, he said, ensures that the authorities "won't be able to just buy one of us off." He didn't get into specifics. But he did lay out the threats and temptations that abounded: criminal indictments hanging over their heads, offers of jobs with hefty salaries, large donations by shady businessmen with opaque interests.

Marciano did not mention, because he had not a clue, that the Panthers had aided in their own cooptation by nearly anointing a police plant as a member of the troika. Through P/51, the police became privy to just how unstable the Panthers really were. Late one night, about a dozen core members were huddled at Abergel's house. Someone raised the issue of money. There still wasn't a lot of it: Only a few thousand pounds from contributions by members and supporters. But the group couldn't agree on how to handle its finances. They argued for hours. Eddie Malka, the hypnotist and telekinetic who, as a newcomer, had tried to speak at the university event and was chewed out by Abergel, was present. He hadn't given up. In the middle of the argument, he leveled a barely veiled accusation against Abergel. "What's with the closeness between you and Bareli?" Malka asked him, referring to Jerusalem police chief Daniel Bareli. He was asking about a rumor of duplicity that started after Abergel and Bareli were seen talking to each other privately. The gathering dissolved without a solution to the money problem nor with a hashing out of the allegation against Abergel.

With all his angling, Malka himself could have been accused of harboring ulterior motives. He courted Marciano by providing him access to an office and phone. That soon led Marciano and a few others to agree to merge with Malka's own amorphous group, which he called the Second Israel. It was a catch-all phrase for people outside the Ashkenazi hegemony. But the merger turned out to be more of a split. Malka and Marciano made their agreement without so much as notifying most of the Panthers or even the rest of the troika leaders. And even the split wasn't really a split because, publicly, there was still only one Black Panther movement. When the press caught wind of an apparent divide, a few cursory stories were published and then the newspapers quickly dropped the narrative. Marciano's name never appeared among the breakaways in the press.

It was approaching mid-April, and the spirit of revolt still throbbed in the streets of Jerusalem. The phenomenon known as the Black Panthers had lodged itself thoroughly in the public's consciousness. Superintendent Tourgeman turned out to be wrong when he judged that the group would fizzle out following their first protest. Beleaguered by infighting, the Panthers were nevertheless busy writing revolutionary tracts, devising new confrontations, and building up their base. His own intel said so. The intel provided by the indomitable P/51. Now came time for Tourgeman to write to his commander a brief on the status of the group. In a seven-page report summarizing everything he had learned, Tourgeman didn't reveal the identity of the source. For obvious reasons, police protocol dictated that only handlers knew who their informants were. And yet the report did feature the name of the mole. It listed him casually among the other leaders of the Panthers: "Yacob Elbaz—38 years old, a native of Israel, a son of parents from Morocco, divorced, a father of 3, lives in Givat Shaul, a thief, a former burglar, and currently, a pimp."

This alleged pimp was born on the outskirts of Jerusalem to pious parents, immigrants from Morocco, who arrived in the Holy Land decades before the mass immigration of Moroccan Jews. The parents had seen many of their offspring die at birth or soon after. They named him Yacob after one of the dead, and, as a further precaution, they also gave him the middle name Chai, meaning "alive." The family was so poor that they didn't pay the *mohel* who performed the baby's *brit milah*.

Yacob Elbaz was a mole inside the Panthers, providing information on the group to the police.
Digital image of photograph by Shalom Bar-Tal/Israel Sun Ltd., from the Judaica Collection of the
Harvard Library, Harvard University.

Instead, the *mohel* gave the parents a few coins and said it was for the
honor of being chosen to carry out the circumcision ceremony. When
the baby grew into a boy, his parents sent him to a learned man who
lived nearby to study Torah and other Jewish texts. Elbaz saw that man
was old and sick and he did what he thought was the ethical thing to
do. Each morning, on his way out, Elbaz would sneak into his mom's
chicken coup and steal a few eggs and bring them to his hungry teacher.

Nothing fascinated Elbaz more than fire. He would regularly test
different objects—his sister's doll, a pair of wool pants, his brother's
curtains—for their degree of flammability. His reputation for pyroma-
nia and general mischief did not seem to ever get him in trouble. If anything, his family and friends found it charming. When he grew older,
Elbaz cycled through various jobs. He was a roving vendor of dubious
medicinal remedies, then a plumber, and finally a sailor, the last being
the only job in which he lasted for a while. Eventually, however, he left
seafaring behind, too, and turned to crime.

Despite their common lineage, at least a couple of Elbaz's brothers fared far better than he did. As teenagers in British Palestine, they got involved in the Zionist underground and, when Israel became a state, they made their way into the country's establishment. Whereas Yacob intermingled with the underworld, his brother Zion joined a group of upwardly mobile Moroccan Jews, called the Association of the Mughrabi Community. Members of this association referred to themselves as Mughrabis to differentiate themselves from the more recent riff-raff arriving from Morocco en masse and filling ghettos such as Musrara. Tourgeman knew the Elbaz family from the Mughrabi circles. When he needed to spy on the Panthers, Tourgeman turned to Yacob, the wayward Elbaz brother, whom he knew to be dashing and street-seasoned, someone sure to impress the young men from Musrara.

In return for infiltrating the Panthers and reporting back, Elbaz got cash payments but he also received something far more valuable: impunity for pimping.

10

PASSOVER, AN OCCASION FOR LIBERATION

IT WAS NOW EARLY April 1971, and the Jewish residents of Jerusalem were preparing for the coming of Passover. This meant heading to the souk in the center of town and purchasing eggs and perhaps fresh fish or beef tongue as finances allowed; counting seats at the table for all the distant cousins and friends who would show up; and scrambling to clear the kitchen and dining areas of all remnants of *chametz,* or leavened grains. The homemakers of Musrara carried out this Jewish custom of spring cleaning with special zeal, hunting for wayward crumbs in the deepest recesses of their floors and cabinets. The temporary elimination of bread and its derivatives compelled the community to remember the protracted desert wanderings of the ancient Israelites.

In the context of the mass migration of Mizrahim to Israel, Passover was especially resonant because the holiday's story promised freedom in a new land, memorialized in the blessing, "To Next Year in Jerusalem." Now, finding themselves in Jerusalem, these modern-day Israelites might have asked a question that the Passover story, as told in the Haggadah, doesn't answer. Exodus achieved, what exactly comes next? What might liberation look like?

Late on the night of April 5, five days before the holiday was set to begin, Abergel sought to answer the question. He told the handful of Panthers gathered around him to go home and each fetch a copy of the Haggadah. None of them had read Mao Zedong or Karl Marx or Frantz Fanon, but they were all deeply familiar with Moses. His radical demand—"Let my people go!"—and the story of his clash with Pharaoh offered as fertile a revolutionary template as any secular tract. With several Haggadahs for reference, the Panthers listened as Abergel read the incantations, and pinpointed the parallels between the textual afflictions of Egyptian slavery and their own life experiences. Hunched over a typewriter, they began composing the Panthers' version of the Haggadah, a manifesto for Mizrahi liberation.

Prime Minister Golda Meir steps in as Pharaoh, the Panthers play Moses, and the destitute masses are the weary Israelites. The story reads like a sequel of sorts. In the original, biblical installment, the protagonists had overcome all odds and escaped captivity. Taking place thousands of years later, the new Passover tale undercuts the happy ending suggested by the original. After having escaped Egypt, the Israelites are in the Promised Land, where they encounter a new challenge. The following passage lays out the drama:

> This is the bread of affliction that our fathers ate in the land of
> Morocco and Egypt.
> Little did we know, we'd have even less in Jerusalem.
> In Morocco, it was always: whoever is hungry come and feast,
> In Jerusalem, all such memories have ceased.
> In Morocco, they had promised us liberation,
> But instead, they gave us subjugation.

The Passover seder is composed of melodious, operatic songs and philosophical skits, a format reproduced in the seven-page Panther Haggadah to tell tales of the struggle for decent housing, gainful employment, and proper education. One of the most poignant uses of this narrative device is the Panthers' rendition of the song "Dayenu." It describes the modern exodus from Egypt (and other Arab countries) to Israel as a story of alienation and disillusionment, rather than deliverance.

Yet, there is still hope.

"And they shall ask our help and that of the people to achieve our august goals," the text reads in a pastiche of the Haggadah's style. "And the Black Panthers shall deliver us with a mighty hand and an outstretched arm, and with great awe, and with demonstrations and hunger strikes." God's "signs" and "wonders" are replaced with modern acts of protest.

In a section that imitates the original Haggadah's wrangling of rabbis over philosophical questions, a debate opens with the words of one Rabbi Golda Meir.

She posits that "a Jew who speaks no Yiddish is no Jew." A dialect of German, Yiddish is a specifically Ashkenazi language spoken by Jews who came from central and eastern Europe. There is no documentation of the prime minister ever making this inflammatory statement, but many believed she did say such a thing, and the Panthers were only glad to stoke the suspicions. A commonly photographed sign hoisted at the group's protests reads, "Golda, teach us Yiddish!" And while Meir may not have explicitly invalidated anyone's Jewishness, she did have a special fondness for *Yiddishkeit,* a word that describes an essentially Ashkenazi Jewishness. In speeches, she sometimes waxed nostalgically about the Yiddish-speaking community of her youth, and showed a yearning for a return to an imagined ideal, one that was by definition Ashkenazi.

The banner in the center reads, "Golda, teach us Yiddish," a sarcastic slogan accusing the prime minister, Golda Meir, of favoring Jews of Ashkenazi, Yiddish-speaking backgrounds. Digital image of photograph by Itzik (full name not provided by Israel Sun Inc.)/Israel Sun Ltd., from the Judaica Collection of the Harvard Library, Harvard University.

In rebuttal to Rabbi Golda Meir, the Haggadah's Panthers proclaim that "Sephardic culture is more rich and varied . . . more enlightening and civilized . . . Sephardic culture is culture."

One of the most dramatic moments in a Passover seder comes toward the end when the celebrants collectively enumerate the ten plagues. Each person dips a fingertip into their glass of syrupy red wine and flings a drop onto their plate for each of the plagues. It feels satisfying and perhaps a little righteous to ritually smite a mythical tormenter by delivering frog infestations, locusts, and hail. Recognizing the power of narrative as a tool for movement building, the new avengers in Musrara substituted the ten plagues with their own calamities. They inflicted plagues of people's power upon a wretched government. The group regarded its founding as the first plague—an infestation of Panthers. Then came the distribution of political pamphlets, followed by actions like the occupation of Kollek's lawn and the solidarity rally with all the university students at Wise Auditorium. And unlike the official Haggadah, which refers to a time and place beyond the scope of recorded history, this tract was being written in real time with some of the plagues scheduled for the future. In other words, it was a Haggadah in which deliverance was neither ordained nor guaranteed.

One of the enumerated plagues hadn't taken place yet. It spoke of a hunger strike on the first day of Passover to take place in the courtyard facing the Wailing Wall, copying a tactic popularized in the preceding months by the movement to free Soviet Jewry, whose endorsement by the media sparked the incipient Panthers' anger and rise to action. The Panther Haggadah doubled as a flyer inviting the public in a couple of days to join the Panthers at their next action. The group hawked copies to passersby on the streets of Jerusalem. Out of curiosity or solidarity, hundreds of people paid what they could for it.

The writing of an alternative Haggadah—and the recasting of the Passover story as a modern-day parable—placed the Israeli Panthers in conversation with the legacy of African Americans, who in turn had drawn inspiration from the original Jewish text. The selling of copies on the street ahead of the holiday to raise money for the revolution also neatly mirrored Bobby Seale and Huey Newton's early days selling Chairman Mao's *Little Red Book* to help fund the Black Panther Party. And in the same vein, by arguing that "Sephardic culture is culture," as one section of their Haggadah does, the Panthers inaugurated a Mizrahi version of the American slogan "Black Is Beautiful."

11

FACING PHARAOH

DAYS BEFORE THE PASSOVER HOLIDAY of 1971, Abergel typed out a letter of only two lines and carried it with him across Jerusalem. Leaving his crowded slum and heading due west he traversed the holy city's jagged terrain of ancient cobblestone alleyways and newly paved boulevards to reach the district where the top government offices were located. In his ragged yet fashionable clothes—probably the jeans, t-shirt, leather jacket, and white Chuck Taylors he wore daily—Abergel must have stood out to the officials who staffed the ministries. It was common for the 28-year-old street urchin to be stopped by police whenever he ventured out of his neighborhood. But perhaps now, after the transformation he had undergone, Abergel's characteristic impatience was interpreted by strangers as a sense of purpose, an air of legitimate urgency.

By force of habit, the former criminal scoped out the premises and, as far as he could tell, the only security at the

In the foreground, facing the camera are four Black Panthers, from left to right, Moshe Amuyal, Saadia Marciano, Ruben Belisha, and Charlie Biton, photographed in Jerusalem in 1971. © Meir Wigoder.

prime minister's office was a single sentry posted at the gate to the compound. The letter he handed the guard was addressed to Prime Minister Golda Meir. In the note, he asked for an audience with Meir on behalf of his fledging protest group. "Don't take this as an ultimatum," he wrote to Meir, but "we will stage a hunger strike in front of the Wailing Wall until you receive our delegation." The brazenness it took to demand an audience with the prime minister would prove characteristic of this group of young men with criminal records.

Unlike the American originals, the Israeli Panthers started out believing they could effect change from within the political system. Huey Newton and Bobby Seale studied Marxist texts from the beginning. Abergel, Marciano, and the others had not. Though they had a loose affinity with the ideas of the New Left, they were still far from a vanguard that rejects all cooperation with authority in service of radical politics. At their core, the American Panthers were revolutionary Marxists, while the Israelis hadn't, at least not yet, developed a political analysis that would lead them to attempt to overthrow capitalism or class structures.

Meir was an Ashkenazi Jew. She traced her ancestry to Europe, as did every one of her cabinet ministers except for the minister of police, which was the token seat informally reserved for Mizrahi politicians in those days. But Meir was also a woman in a political world dominated by men. She had gained her position by her grit and her wits—and by leveraging her American background. Having grown up in the United States, she returned there on an official visit in 1948 and was instrumental in swaying the American Jewish community to support and fund Zionism during an existential war. Crucially, in the era of television and mass media, Meir could speak, as an American, to the entire American public. She helped make the case for why the United States government should be Israel's most important ally.

The Panthers did not wait to get an answer from the prime minister. Within a few days, as the Passover holiday arrived, they followed through on their threat and staged a hunger strike in front of the Wailing Wall. They could not have picked a better target. Israel, still relishing their military victory of 1967, was showcasing Jerusalem's recently conquered holy sites for the entire world to see. Israelis and foreign tourists alike flocked to Jerusalem to touch the limestone bricks of the Old City, to visit the Church of the Holy Sepulcher where Jesus is said to have been buried, and to insert paper scraps scribbled with prayers between the ancient crevices of the Wailing Wall.

About a dozen of the young Panthers brought mats and blankets from their nearby homes and camped out in the plaza about a hundred feet away from the sacred wall. They did not pray. Though they grew up in observant Jewish households and knew the prayers well, the Panthers were determined to seek redress not from the divine but from the terrestrial authorities that ruled over their lives. On a sheet of white poster board, they painted their name in bold Hebrew letters and on another sign, they translated the name into English. "Blaks Panther" read the unfortunate sign, the one meant to attract the attention of foreign tourists and the international press. The long sunny day wore on and a crowd whirled around them. Some Panthers were interviewed on camera while others rested on the ground reading newspapers or grooming mop-top hairdos. News footage of the hunger strike shows that though the leadership of the group was all male, women were part of the movement as well.

A few days into the hunger strike, a uniformed police officer on a motorcycle rode up to the Wailing Wall plaza. He came to deliver a letter from the prime minister's office. Abergel's non-ultimatum had succeeded.

The group had to decide which Panthers, besides Abergel, would meet with Meir. Marciano, the earliest among the Panthers to develop a sense of politics and the first to rail against the "Ashkenazi establishment," could muster his entourage to ensure his selection. Then there was his younger brother Rafi, who also joined, and David Levy, another one of the core group of Panthers. All four young men shared the same background and the same grievances: unemployed parents whose spirits were felled by long-term dependency on charity and welfare; a childhood spent in streets torn up by war; and a poor employment outlook. In addition to these four Panthers, middle-aged Elbaz, the police informant who did not come from the slums, was also selected to join the delegation.

On the fourth day of Passover, April 13, 1971, Abergel woke up early, having barely slept the night before. He received the four other leaders for a brief meeting and by 7:30 a.m., they were on their way to the prime minister's office on the other side of Jerusalem.

It was a cool spring morning and at least some of the olive-skinned young men with long hair—Abergel always kept his hair short—wore brown leather jackets. A single guard received the group and, without patting them down or inspecting them, he led the Panthers into the prime minister's compound. Meir, two ministers, and a stenographer sat waiting at a wooden table when the five entered the conference room. With nine adults around the table, the room was so cramped that the interlocutors could not help brushing their feet against each other.

"Are all of you from Jerusalem?" Meir asked, opening the conversation.

"Yes," Abergel replied. Without waiting for her to say anything more, he continued speaking. "We request your forgiveness for the paucity of our language; we will not be able to express ourselves in formal Hebrew, but only as we were educated."

Abergel learned to read and write in Hebrew at home, using sacred and liturgical texts, but he was sensitive about having been denied formal schooling. So whether out of some sort of inferiority complex or out of a clever awareness of his unlikely oratorical gift, Abergel often apologized for possessing a "paucity" of language. By doing so now, during Passover, and in the presence of his modern-day pharaoh, Abergel was embodying the character of Moses. In the biblical story, God sends Moses to demand the liberation of his people, and Moses complains that he is not adequately articulate for such responsibility. "I have never been eloquent," Moses says, demurring before God. "I am slow of speech and tongue."

"Do you smoke?" Meir asked the Panthers, whose appearance likely did not carry any biblical gravitas in her eyes. Inspecting Abergel's features as they spoke, she thought he seemed like "a man who uses drugs and deals them, too," according to an impression she later shared in a closed government meeting.

The prime minister offered them a pack of filterless Chesterfields, and Abergel pulled out a cigarette. They had no matches left so he borrowed her already-lit smoke and used it to light cigarettes for himself and his four comrades. From early on, a socialist ethos permeated Israel, creating a blunt informality even among strangers or people of different class statuses. This flattening of personal relations can create warmth but it often serves to mask racial and ethnic tension.

"Were you born in Israel?" she asked. The prime minister had been born just before the turn of the century in Kyiv when that city was still part of the Russian Empire. At 72, she could have been a grandmother to several of the young men she was now facing.

"All of us are from Morocco," Abergel answered. "I am from Rabat."

That all of the Panthers present were from Morocco was not strictly true. At least Levy and one of the Marciano brothers were second-generation immigrants, whose parents arrived in the early 1950s. Elbaz, though ethnically Moroccan, hailed from a family that had been living in the Holy Land for more than a generation. Still, even if the Panthers were not exactly fresh off the boat, they had the dark features of their forbears and spoke Hebrew with a guttural Middle Eastern accent. Abergel's exaggeration served to accentuate the ethnic line dividing the room.

On his side of the dividing line, Elbaz stood apart from the other Panthers, and not just because he was a secret informant. The alleged pimp was nearly 40 when he joined the group of young hooligans shouting protest slogans. Perhaps it should have struck the Panthers as odd that a middle-aged man appeared all of a sudden, glad to be in their company all the time. Tattooed with a large knife on his forearm, a sinking ship elsewhere on his body, and an eagle with its wings spread out on his shoulder, he had managed to enchant the young men. It probably helped that he always offered to defray their bus fare and printing costs.

At this moment, he wasn't only fooling the Panthers about his allegiances. Meir, too, was apparently unaware of Elbaz's covert role. He was in essence spying on the prime minister on behalf of the police.

"Haven't you a job?" Meir asked Abergel.

"Yes, when I was able to," he said. "I used to work only in construction. I don't have the energy to work in construction anymore. I am married and have a child."

The 28-year-old was short and his small frame was not well suited for the hard labor he had been doing all his adult life; he was already developing a hunched back.

Through a series of questions about his family and his work, Abergel explained that the jobs available to him didn't pay. Not even the construction jobs.

"We didn't come here to talk about my personal business, because if this were my problem alone, that would be an excellent thing. This is a problem of the Sephardim," he said, using a common term for Mizrahi people at the time. "I wandered around the slums and I observed, though in the past I never used to wander like that. But this issue now interests me very much."

"Where did you get your name?" Meir asked, ceding for the first time that the nature of their meeting was political. Israeli leaders would have been aware of the American revolutionary group through media coverage that portrayed them as violent and antisemitic.

"On our own. We sat down and we thought and a couple of things brought us to the conclusion," Abergel said. Other, earlier groups championing Mizrahi causes, he pointedly added, used mild-mannered names and got nowhere.

"How did you arrive at this name, 'The Black Panthers?'" she repeated. Marciano now spoke up for the first time.

"This name was striking and galvanizing," Marciano said.

"Where did you get this name from?" Meir persisted.

"It's a name that makes an impact," Marciano repeated.

In total, Meir asked about the origin of the group's name five times. She accused the American group of being antisemites and supporting Palestinian terrorists.

The young Mizrahi men would relish her shock and horror at the group's name. The common racial slur against Mizrahim at the time came from Yiddish, *shvartse khaye,* meaning "black animal." By adopting the title Black Panthers, they unintentionally reclaimed a pejorative term.

Whatever their insurgent pretensions, the Israeli Panthers often clung to displays of loyalty and belonging.

"We are devoted to our country, and patriotic, and we love it," Abergel told Meir. "The very fact that we are aware of the problem that hinders our children and ourselves—and that we want a child who is healthy and fit to serve in the army and who needs to be nurtured accordingly—proves it."

Only 23 years old, Israel had already experienced three wars. In a state chiseled out of a utopian dream, with a population cocked for emergency, the collective eclipsed the individual. In the Israel of 1971, no institution surpassed the Israel Defense Forces in status. Deploying the rhetoric of patriotism, Abergel, who had evaded service after getting into a fight with an enlistment officer, trumped Meir's subtle condemnations. She dropped her prosecutorial tone.

The five Panthers and three ministers spoke and chain-smoked. They filled the small grey room with cigarette fumes that thickened into clouds.

Meir continued to play the role of social worker and asked the young men one by one about his education, employment, and family history. Each of the Panthers told her how having a criminal record from early on thwarted his efforts to advance in life. "A man who broke the law once and paid the price for it—does the mark of Cain need haunt him for the rest of his life?" Elbaz asked her. And Abergel added, "There are many boys who can be saved, who need only to be met halfway, given opportunities. We were never given such an opportunity."

Now, about an hour into the conversation, Abergel presented a list of 33 demands in the areas of housing, criminal justice, education, and youth delinquency. The list called for specific reforms to many government institutions and processes. Some of the changes were small and rather uncontroversial: for example, allowing individuals who are arrested to make a phone call and notify relatives. But the Panthers also presumed to suggest more fundamental reforms, such as the dismantling of the national housing corporations and integrating them into existing government ministries, a move that would place more democratic oversight over housing policy. Around half of the demands referred to programs and special rights that would shepherd poor youths from disadvantaged backgrounds to productive lives as adults. The focus on youths reflects the pain and regret Panthers felt about being maladjusted. "We want to erase the history of those who have a history," Abergel explained to Meir.

Whereas many demands centered on governance issues, others called for more social spending: housing subsidies, free preschool, free higher education, and special allocations for the poor. Together, this imagined welfare system would likely involve massive government expenditure for Israel, which was not a wealthy country at the time. Without using the term, the Panthers were calling for socialist-style reforms as a way to level Ashkenazi-Mizrahi relations. And by doing so they were pointing out the flimsiness of the socialism espoused by Israel's founding generation as well as the country's gradual adoption of a more capitalist economy. Would the Panthers, in championing the Mizrahi cause, curb the trend? That was yet to be seen, but the list presented to Meir in this historic meeting was the most comprehensive collection of demands the Panthers would make and a blueprint for future political struggles by Mizrahim.

As a founding mother of the Israeli state, Meir belonged to the echelon that built the institutions that the Panthers railed against and sought to reform. Being presented with an alternative political program, she was perhaps unprepared to treat the young Panthers as equals. She neglected to offer a response to the list and went on countering, and almost belittling, the complaints she heard from across the table.

Meir met every charge of racism and discrimination with a volley of anecdotes about her Moroccan colleagues and Mizrahi family members. Her own cousin, she said, was married to a Yemeni Jew. She

Prime Minister Golda Meir, May 1973. Dan Hadani Collection, The Pritzker Family National Photography Collection, The National Library of Israel.

argued that the prevalence of mixed marriages makes the Panthers' point moot. Besides, didn't she as a young woman have to work hard? Didn't her father in America once work in construction? He never complained. And so what if you have a Moroccan accent, she told Marciano. I have lived here for 50 years and I am told I still have an American accent, she told him. It doesn't make a difference, she said. Though it obviously did.

"I want to get it out of your heads that you have brought a revolution to the country," she said. "There is no issue of Ashkenazim and Sephardim here."

Meir's denial of domestic inequality echoed a statement she had infamously made in an interview with a British newspaper two years earlier. "There was no such thing as Palestinians," she said in response to an interview question. "It was not as though there was a Palestinian people in Palestine considering itself a Palestinian people and we came and threw them out and took their country away from them. They did not exist."

In that same article, the reporter asked Meir to respond to the charge that Arabs "look upon Israel and Israelis as Westernized intruders bent upon aggrandizement in a Muslim Middle East." The prime minister answered, "We are, I admit, an element which has taken this part of the Middle East that we are in control of; that is our country, Israel, and we have made of it a modern society which is based on more equality. We plead guilty to that." Meir justified her denial of Palestinian peoplehood with her illusions about Israel as an egalitarian utopia.

More than two hours into the meeting with the Panthers, Meir's deputy prime minister, Yigal Allon, began winding down the conversation. The Israeli parliament was scheduled to hold a discussion about the resurgent threats against Jews in Iraq under the Baathist regime. Less than 10,000 Jews remained in the country at the time and they faced harsh persecution: property confiscation, expulsion from social clubs and professional organizations, and an increase in official violence against members of the community. The government had recently executed 13 Jewish Iraqis over accusations of espionage.

"If we linger any longer, the Black Panthers will later claim that you failed to show up for the discussion on saving the Jews of Iraq," Allon quipped.

As the Panthers prepared to leave, Meir implored them to reveal nothing about their conversation to the gaggle of reporters who were waiting outside. "Be men and promise" not to say anything, she implored. The two sides agreed to schedule a follow-up meeting, with the Panthers asking to have the minister of police present. They wanted the man they had called a "black collaborator" to hear their complaints of police abuse.

The content of the conversation, including horrid tales of brutality, did end up leaking out but not to the press and not in a way those present would have expected. Questioned the very next day by Tourgeman, his police handler, Elbaz relayed a summary of what had been said. His account wound its way into a memo, which was circulated to various high-ranking officers, as well as the Shin Bet secret police. Eventually, a copy was delivered to the office of Minister of Police Hillel. That document presented, without comment and in the plainest of language, parts of the conversation that hadn't made it into the official transcript. The Panthers were said to have given an account of prison guards raping underage inmates and a story of being beaten up by police while under arrest. Meir had responded with bewilderment when she heard these stories, according to the memo.

"You mean to say this happens in our country?" she asked.

"Yes," the Panthers replied.

The provenance of the intel was as usual obscured with a reference to source P/51. Nevertheless, anyone reading the memo could have now deduced that Tourgeman's surveillance bonanzas were coming from one of five Panthers who had attended the meeting. That conclusion should have triggered a startling realization: Tourgeman had effectively spied on the prime minister, recording details from a closed-door conversation without her knowledge or consent. But in Israel, the integrity of the security forces went unquestioned. It is possible no one who read the memo had even the slightest notion that the police were in dangerous ethical territory. In fact, the feedback Tourgeman received from superiors suggested quite the opposite. Within two weeks of the incident, he was promoted.

Despite her deputy's warning, Meir did in the end miss the parliamentary discussion about saving the Jews of Iraq. Had she attended, she would have heard Foreign Minister Abba Eban express "full solidarity with the fate of the Jewish brothers and sisters in Iraq, Syria, and other Arab countries." He went on to say that these Jewish brothers and sisters suffered from compounding ills—not just life exiled from their ancestral land, Israel, but also enslavement. "There will be no solution until the gates are open for exodus and salvation," Eban said.

Eban's speech harked back to the story of Passover, in which the Israelites escape their enslavement under Pharaoh and migrate to the Holy

Land. He was now calling for a contemporary exodus of Jews from the Arab world. But Eban was glossing over the reality such Jews would face if they heeded his call. If the Holy Land once promised salvation, modern-day Israel was a land of oppression and inequality for many.

The condescension of promoting the rights of Mizrahi Jews far away while ignoring their plight at home was not lost on the Panthers. In the days following the meeting with Meir, the group was agitating to take action and strike back against the paternalistic attitude of the Ashkenazi elites. An opportunity soon presented itself.

On April 18, Moroccan Jews were preparing to celebrate Mimouna, a post-Passover holiday particular to their community. Tens of thousands were expected at Jerusalem's Sacher Park, where families would picnic, eating *mufleta,* a flat fried pancake, and listening to live performances. For the first time, both the prime minister and the president, Zalman Shazar, were planning to attend the festivities.

The Panthers, however, considered the announced visit by these Ashkenazi politicians a cynical act of pandering devoid of any real commitment to Mizrahi well-being. In the middle of the festivities, a few dozen Panthers showed up at the park. They began chanting loudly, "We are all Panthers!" and demanded to be allowed on stage to address the crowd. The police blocked them. A scuffle ensued. Shazar was whisked away, and Meir, who hadn't arrived yet, decided not to come because of the disruption. The group achieved its immediate goal of registering their protest against what they regarded as hypocrisy by Israel's top politicians, but the effect on the Mizrahi public gathered at the park is unclear. A month would pass before the Panthers made another major public appearance.

Just over a month had passed since Abergel's burning bush moment, when a phalanx of police officers with billy clubs ringed the mayor's precious lawn. The rules of his world prescribed that they should have charged ahead swinging and dislodged the crowd. Yet they didn't and their restraint defied logic. Abergel saw evidence in that implausible moment for the existence of a power beyond his comprehension. If Moses heard God speak to him from the undying flame, a voice telling him to go confront Pharaoh, then Abergel, too, felt a calling to help liberate his people. He authored his own version of the story of Exodus, demonstrating just how deeply engaged he had become in the promise of justice and deliverance.

On the cusp of confronting his present-day pharaoh, Abergel experienced self-doubt and complained that he lacked the necessary eloquence—Moses, of course, was a stutterer who usually had his brother speak in his stead. Meir, for her part, played an excellent queen of Egypt. The Panthers came to her to talk politics, but she swatted away their claims as if they were hollow pretensions and demanded repeatedly, "Why don't you have a job?" The fixation on that question evokes the word Pharaoh yells at Moses in Exodus 5:4–18: "Get back to work! Lazy, that's what you are—lazy! That is why you keep saying, 'Let us go and sacrifice to God.' Now get to work!" Pharaoh dismisses the Hebrew God as so much nonsense and condemns the Israelite slaves to additional hardship as a reminder to Moses of who is in power. In Meir's case, the nonsense was the noxious ideas the Panthers were spreading. But whereas Pharaoh justifies the fact of slavery, Meir denied its existence. In Israel, she held, all Jews were already free and equal. Mizrahim need not complain of racism and discrimination. They just needed to work.

The idea that Abergel cut the figure of a modern Moses would have been widely scoffed at. And not just by the prime minister. Superintendent Tourgeman, who pored over the raw intelligence that was quickly piling up about the man, believed Abergel only "wants to build himself up personally and that's what he's working toward." His assessment echoed the sentiments of at least some of the younger Panthers, who felt cast aside, perhaps justifiably so ever since Abergel appeared.

What encumbered Abergel and helped undercut confidence in his sincerity about fighting for communal liberation, was his preoccupation with his own legal jeopardy.

Abergel stood accused of trafficking in narcotics, a charge arising from the police sting five months prior that found a stash of hashish and opium in an empty lot by his house. He had brought up the matter in the meeting with Meir. He told her he had been framed. Shortly after the meeting, Abergel took Elbaz aside. He pulled out a folded piece of paper. It was a summons for an upcoming court appearance. "We have got to go to Tel Aviv," Abergel told Elbaz. There were some key allies to meet over there—folks with money. "In case I get jailed, I want to prepare you to become my successor," Abergel told the police informant. As if Tourgeman didn't have enough reasons to gloat over his success with this spy, it was now the second time that the Panthers had unwittingly offered to hand the reins over to his puppet.

12

NIGHT OF THE PANTHERS

THE WHITE ROTARY phone sitting on a rusty metal cabinet in the Abergel home broke out in a furious jangle. It was one of the least pleasant sounds that could greet a family early on a Saturday morning, but with public attention focused on the Panthers, such disturbances were now routine. A month had passed since the meeting with Meir. By now, the group had minted its own bumper stickers and two of them decorated the wall above the phone. One read, "Poverty must end," while the other offered a more coded message. "We, too, are national security," the sticker declared. Historically, demands for social change were silenced by raising the specter of war. National security demanded that divisive politics be set aside, authorities would always say. The Panthers rejected the logic that says the two realms were mutually exclusive. They argued that addressing inequality is imperative for national security.

The incoming phone call was patched through from out of town. On the line were comrades from what was being dubbed the Tel Aviv cell of the Panthers. A poster tacked to the wall above the phone warned callers: "Guard your tongue," the handwritten admonition said. "This line is being tapped." Wise to the real possibility of eavesdropping, the Tel Aviv crew called to coordinate an in-person visit for later that morning.

Once everyone was gathered at the makeshift headquarters a couple of hours later, the nine Panthers set out for the pine forest on the outskirts of the city. Jerusalem Forest was a favorite destination for weekend recreation among Israelis of all stripes and it was sure to be packed on the warm spring morning of May 15. The Panthers engaged the crowd of hikers and picnickers and asked for donations. A final ledger for the day showed $1,200 in contributions. The financial success and camaraderie of the fundraising efforts masked the cleavages that threatened to dissolve the group.

At a meeting held later that day, Dani Sa'il, one of the Panthers visiting from Tel Aviv, revealed the real reason he had come. In Tel Aviv, city officials were preparing to demolish an illegal structure belonging to two brothers. The Nagar brothers were Yemenite Jews and they had clout in the community of vendors at the Carmel souk, Tel Aviv's sprawling meat, vegetable, and spice market. Sa'il had promised to throw the weight of the Panthers behind the effort to block the demolition. He had made the promise, however, without consulting with the others. After the fact, Sa'il now argued that getting involved in the issue would help bolster their credibility. The Panthers' target audience included the Mizrahi vendors of the souk and others who found themselves entangled with the city's sometimes arbitrary code enforcement.

The Jerusalem Panthers found the proposal convincing. Their concern had to do with the Nagar brothers and their reputation as criminals. The taint of possible criminality made the Nagars unsympathetic victims, at least in a potential media campaign. The Panthers were in a dilemma: cave to Sa'il and work with the Nagars, or reject the idea and risk alienating the Tel Aviv Panthers. After arguing about it, the Jerusalem leaders finally agreed to meet with the Nagars. Fortunately for the Panthers, however, they didn't have to waste political capital on a showdown with city officials over the demolition—at the last minute, the Nagar brothers agreed to raze the illegal structure themselves.

Neither Marciano nor Abergel could credibly castigate Sa'il for speaking on behalf of the group without being authorized to do so. Amid all the wrangling for authority in the growing movement, Marciano had unilaterally asked the lawyer helping the group, Shlomo Segev, to draft an application to register the Panthers as a charity. The application included a list of founders and officers: "We, whose signatures are affixed below, [are] the representatives of the Black Panthers organization." Marciano's name appeared along with four other names: Eli Avichzer, Charlie Biton, Moshe Amuyal, and Meir Wigoder. Marciano and his closest friends were staking their claim as the true and original leaders of the Panthers. They were trying to use the government to formalize their position, to the exclusion of Abergel and others.

"Our war is directed against the authorities"—the application was submitted to those same authorities—"which for 23 years have implemented policies to amplify the socioeconomic divide, to exacerbate poverty," the application reads. "Our organization will act to fundamentally transform the structure of Israeli society—to eliminate the gaps and terminate poverty for the sake of equality for all residents."

The interior ministry was in charge of approving such requests and it returned a decision immediately, a rejection. But the reason was not a problem with the group's mission statement or an error in their application. The Panthers, it seemed, had already submitted a request to incorporate as a charity.

"Our office has received an earlier request to register an organization with an identical name," a clerk wrote to the lawyer. "I cannot process an application for another organization with that same name."

What happened was that Abergel had beaten Marciano to the act. A month earlier he had his own pro bono lawyer write up an application.

Abergel gave his name, and those of his confidants and supporters, a list of eight people that included two of Abergel's siblings and Marciano's younger brother Rafi. Abergel's mission statement said the Panthers would be devoted to "transforming the regime in Israel so that it would become a country for one people without regard to race and with no discrimination among the groups that constitute the Jewish nation." For all the talk of uniting the Jewish people, the two strongheaded young men had displayed a flagrant inability to unify their front.

When what each of them had done became known, the situation did not devolve into a crisis. As an ethnographer who witnessed the events unfold noted, "despite the growing factionalism, all wanted to avoid an outright split." Past experiences taught the Panthers that the best way for them to build unity was to stage an action in the streets.

May 18, 1971, would forever be known in Jerusalemite lore as the Night of the Panthers. Events started unfolding peaceably enough with a rally of several hundred Panthers at about 4:30 p.m. With a small squad of patrolmen off to the side, the protesters were gathered at what was called officially, and fittingly for this occasion, Liberation Square. Everyone referred to the plaza, though, as Davidka Square because of the war monument erected at its center, a makeshift mortar called a Davidka gun. The gun's name was meant to evoke David's defeat of Goliath as a symbol for the victory of Zionist militias over Arab forces in the War of 1948. Now, the Zionists had become the Goliaths. The Panthers moved through the crowd passing out leaflets with their demands and ideological positions written out in bullet points. Loudspeakers amplified speeches delivered by several of the leading activists. One particularly large sign held by the protesters read, "Join the Black Panther Rebellion, The Rebellion of the Sephardim."

As the rhetoric escalated, the crowd began to swell into the thousands. The Panthers had warned the authorities: continue to sideline us and we will explode in your faces. Forty minutes into the demonstration, Marciano decided to seize upon the momentum. He took the microphone and belted out a cry, "Down to Zion Square!"

The crowd didn't need much prodding. A mass of people started to march down Jaffa Street, Jerusalem's main thoroughfare, their bodies blocking traffic, their voices filling the air with the discordant sound of protest chants. There would be a debate about the exact conditions of the permit issued to the Panthers, but they knew they didn't have permission to take the route they picked. That act of defiance made the occasion feel all the more thrilling and urgent for those Panthers, like Marciano, who were focused on cultivating a radical and confrontational posture. A familiar face joined the front line of the rally. Elbaz, the person tasked with being the eyes and ears for the police, came to occupy a visible role at the helm of this unsanctioned gathering.

"*Ku-la-nu Pan-te-rim!*" shouted Elbaz, Marciano, and the throngs following behind. "We are all Panthers." And, "End the deprivation! End the discrimination!"

On the march from Davidka Square to Zion Square, a distance of just over a third of a mile, the Panthers passed through the city's shopping and dining district. Vendors folding up their wares at the end of the day paused to behold the spectacle. Shoppers poured out of the narrow storefronts, clutched their bags, and watched the parade of protesters. Some, magnetized and galvanized, joined in. There was no sign of the police.

A sliver of the square emerged in view and still, it seemed, the guards were absent and the palace was up for grabs. A young man with a mane of black hair split from the crowd. It was Rafi Marciano, Saadia's younger brother. He sprinted ahead and shouted over the general din: "We are going to change the name of Zion Square to the Square of Mizrahi Jewry!" The idea of symbolically renaming the square came from the Soviet Jewry movement, which had for a week declared it the "Square of the Silent Jewry" to protest the repression of Jewish dissidents behind the Iron Curtain; the Panthers hoped to draw a parallel between the two situations.

As the demonstrators filled the center of the square, a clump of police dressed in full riot gear suddenly appeared out of a nearby alleyway. The chief of the Jerusalem police district, Daniel Bareli, raised a bullhorn to his face. "This demonstration has been declared an unlawful assembly," he said. "I give you two minutes to disperse." Standing next to Bareli was Tourgeman, who studied the crowd calmly. His expression remained mute, professional. But perhaps his mind was busy trying to match the faces of Panthers to the names he collected in his intelligence memos. "Two minutes to disperse!" Bareli's bullhorn blared out again.

"Boo!" the Panthers yelled back. At the top of his lungs, Marciano ordered everyone, "Don't budge!" and the crowd obeyed. People stayed put even with the menace of cudgels, shields, and steel helmets only several feet away. For a moment, nothing happened; the chasm of asphalt between the protesters and the police remained empty. Then, a man of small stature and Middle Eastern features stepped forward. He flung himself to the ground in the space between the battle lines. "I am a disabled veteran!" he shouted over and over. The man's intention wasn't clear to either side but the police peeled him off the ground, bound him, and tossed him in the back of a van. He later recounted that he was beaten up in the vehicle. An immigrant from Iran, his name was Herzl, which, ironically, is the name of the father of modern Zionism. That evening at Zion Square, Herzl became one of countless individuals to risk police violence and declare that something had gone very wrong in the Zionist project.

The police chief sicced his phalanx of officers on the crowd and a rain of batons came down. The police captured territory quickly. They paused only to snatch those unfortunate few who failed to retreat in

Police deployed a truck equipped with water cannons to clear the protesters during the Night of the Panthers demonstration in Jerusalem's Zion Square, May 18, 1971. © Meir Wigoder.

time. Now, mounted police appeared in the square, and they were followed by an armored vehicle whose roof was adorned with water cannons. Within minutes the square was mostly cleared and traffic restored. That's when the confrontation began in earnest.

The demonstrators were pushed to the margins of the square and some disappeared into the alleyways. They did not disperse. The opposite happened as numbers only seemed to grow. Thousands of ordinary Israelis joined in against the police, with the Panthers themselves splitting into small units. Each group in turn nimbly darted out of hiding to hurl taunts and abuses at the cops, out for one second and withdrawing a moment later. The fury of the riot control squads was fully unleashed at this stage, and it made no apparent effort to distinguish between protesters and onlookers. The water cannons were even less discerning as they squirted high-pressure jets of liquid, dyed green, in every direction. At one point, the flailing torrents hit even police forces and later, also a baby carriage, whose tiny occupant had to be evacuated to the

The Night of the Panthers concluded with the mass arrests of protesters and numerous accounts of police brutality. Photograph taken on Jaffa St. in Jerusalem. © Meir Wigoder.

hospital. The aggressive crackdown inflamed the crowds, who yelled at police, "You're Nazis!"

Soon after the sun set, amid the chaos, Mizrahi teenagers began tearing down fences and preparing to overturn cars and burn them. This behavior caught the attention of Elbaz, who convinced the youths to stop. "Don't be violent because that will make us lose the public's sympathy," Elbaz told them. From a reporter's perspective, this anecdote added texture to the story of the protest and helped cast the Panthers as more than senseless rioters. But as the conduct of a secret police collaborator, Elbaz's intervention was somewhat baffling. Earlier in the evening, he had led the Panthers into Zion Square, an act he knew would provoke a police response. He was also the reason the police were so well prepared to ambush the protesters as they filed into the area—he had reported to his handler the day before that the Panthers had decided to occupy the square "no matter the price." He acted in

Meir Wigoder snapped this photo just before the police officer smashed his camera during the Night of the Panthers demonstration. © Meir Wigoder.

contradictory ways that in retrospect are hard to explain. Maybe he was trying to establish his credentials in the movement. Or maybe his loyalty to the police wasn't so complete that he was willing to accept the sight of youths acting out their anger by destroying property and fouling the Panthers' image in the process.

By now, the night had turned violent and the clashes were only ratcheting up. In one particularly cinematic street fight, a protester managed to knock a cop off his scooter and then proceeded to kick him in the head. Elsewhere in the square, Meir Wigoder decided to snap pictures in the middle of the melee, a few feet away from a mustached officer decked out in riot gear. The officer, meanwhile, saw the teenager with the camera and decided to lunge at him. With his left foot planted in front of him, the officer pulled back his left arm, to which was strapped a shield, as counter-leverage for his other arm, the one wielding a baton. From high above his head, the baton came crashing down on Wigoder—a split second after the closing click of the camera's shutter. The camera was smashed, but the film survived.

Behind an old movie theater, Marciano and a small contingent of protesters found a stockpile of empty bottles. They grabbed the improvised projectiles and passed them down the line to demonstrators at the front. Glass began hailing down on the police, shattering upon impact with their armor. The volley intensified. Bricks, pieces of wood, rocks, and garbage cans flew at the police. The smashing of windshields and display windows added more litter to the scene.

As the evening raged on, detectives in plainclothes blended into the crowd seeking out the Panthers among the throngs. After weeks of surveillance—and many years of street run-ins—they had become familiar with the faces of the activists. In small teams, the detectives infiltrated the mayhem, and their faces, too, were familiar to their targets. In some cases, the Panthers recognized their stealthy pursuers in time and got away, but in others, it was too late, and by the time they realized the danger, three or four cops were ready to snatch them away. Many were seized within the first few hours. Marciano managed to evade capture for a long while. At least twice, he spotted undercovers nearby, and each time he knocked them down from behind and ran away.

After five or six hours, the clashes were finally dying down. Marciano knew he was a prime target and he finally decided to escape the scene. He and Shimshon Wigoder, his constant companion that evening, darted toward the street, where, by total coincidence, a familiar car appeared and one of Marciano's brothers was behind the wheel. The two quickly jumped in. Before the vehicle could make it any distance, however, a patrol car doubled back toward them. Marciano and Wigoder jumped out of the car and took off in different directions. This was the last time Marciano was seen by any of his friends for a while.

Israel had never seen a civil disturbance of this magnitude and nature. Thousands of people, a majority of whom joined spontaneously, took part in physical clashes with the police on the Night of the Panthers. One of the closest approximations to that night was served up a few years prior by a group of haredi Orthodox Jews. They were protesting against secular encroachments, such as the flow of traffic through Jerusalem's inner streets during the Jewish day of Sabbath. But the wider public tended to regard the religious activists as parochial and antagonistic, and their frenzied standoffs with police as illegitimate attempts to impose religious observance on others. Newspapers casually referred to these protesters as the "Sabbath zealots." In another blip in the history of civic upheaval, students at Hebrew University demonstrated forcefully in 1966 against West Germany's chancellor, Konrad Adenauer, during his historic visit. Many Israelis, still shell-shocked by the Holocaust, shared in the outcry over the visit of a German premiere. Israel's Jews are divided by various cultural and religious sentiments; the Panthers stand out for managing to rally a movement against economic and social injustice.

As the Night of the Panthers was winding down, the police moved to sway the media narrative in their favor. In the late hours, with just enough time before the next's day morning editions went to print, Tourgeman called a press conference. He alone possessed the power to provide a coherent rundown of events from an authoritative, if one-sided, perspective. Reporters who had seen with their own eyes a riot squad violently remove protesters from a public square were told that the police had acted with all due restraint. The details and characterizations dispensed by Tourgeman—he shared a chronology that imputed blame on the Panthers, disclosed the number arrested, 74, and the number of injured police, 10, and alleged that subversive political actors were involved—made their way into the final news copy at the expense of most reporters' own eyewitness accounts. Because camera crews at Israel's sole television station happened to be on strike that night, the chaotic protest produced no iconic news footage as similar protests had in the United States of young people facing off against heavily equipped police forces. The Panthers, meanwhile, couldn't immediately provide their own version of events. Nearly all of them were locked up. The few who had escaped were in hiding.

Then, in the most tranquil moment of the night, after the unprecedented violence between Jewish citizens and the police officers sworn to protect them had ended, something else happened. It was an incident quiet enough to have gone almost unnoticed in the dead of night. At the same time, it was loud enough to change the whole conversation around the Panthers. The first Molotov cocktail hit a nearly empty area by the old central bus station. One person was lightly hurt. The next was hurled at a police vehicle but failed to explode. A third fire bomb flew over the wall enclosing the police's Russian Compound headquarters and landed intact in a yard. A sentry grabbed it and tossed it back over the wall where it burst upon hitting the pavement. What exactly happened that night and who was responsible for throwing the Molotov cocktails would be litigated in the arena of public opinion and among the Panthers for decades to come, but the impact of the fire-bombs was immediate.

13

NOT NICE BOYS

THAT EVENING, WHILE DOZENS of civilians were being
detained at Zion Square, another type of gathering took
place less than half a mile away. It was a ceremony at city
hall and the function drew an audience of military generals,
chief rabbis, government ministers, and cultural figures.
They trained their attention on a microphone-studded table
seating three of the country's most prominent figures. Meir,
the prime minister, was seated in the middle. To her right
sat Mayor Kollek, who was presiding over the event, and, to
her left, Israel's president, Zalman Shazar.

In the festive atmosphere, everyone appeared oblivious to
the clashes nearby; it profited them to have a police force
that kept disturbances at bay. The group's dominance in
Israeli society was underscored by the role of popular actress
Hanna Maron in the evening's proceedings. Maron was
marking a year since a terrifying and near-fatal experience.
She had been on her way to London to play the role of Golde

in *Fiddler on the Roof* when, midair, her flight was hijacked. She was wounded in the attack and her leg had to be amputated. With her appearance at this event, she was making her return to the public spotlight. Her role was to recite a passage from the diary of Theodor Herzl. The passage recounts Herzl's visit to Jerusalem in 1898 when the city was under the control of the Ottoman Empire. Herzl managed to score a meeting with German Kaiser Wilhelm II, who was conducting his own historic journey to the Holy Land at the time. Lacking any actual political power, Herzl resorted to pleading with the emperor. He begged him to support Zionist causes but the kaiser wouldn't commit. Forever after, the Zionist collective memory has logged this equivocation as proof that power only respects power. This particular recitation invited Herzl's successors atop the Zionist hierarchy to recall the limits of diplomatic endeavoring, to recall that military might was ulitmately what delivered Jerusalem into their hands.

After Maron finished her oration, the ceremony's central moment arrived. Kollek rose from his seat on the podium and looked at Meir, inviting her to stand up as well, so that he could present her with an award. Known as the Freedom of the City of Jerusalem, the award recognized Meir's role in shaping the city. Meir now gave a speech. She noted that she was about to mark the 50th anniversary of her arrival to the Holy Land. The thought led her to recall her first visit to the Wailing Wall in Jerusalem. A secular Jew, she was skeptical of the practice of scribbling prayers on slips of paper and stuffing them into cracks in the ancient stone. But she was changed by witnessing the scene of her fellow Jews praying at the wall. "It became clear to me that these Jews represent a rejection of what's given and their notes are an expression of their optimism," she told the audience. Meir then connected that memory to another poignant experience: right after the 1967 war, when Israeli forces invaded the Old City, she rushed in after them, aiming to see the wall after being kept away for so long. This time, she again encountered a romantic scene of worshippers—the conquering paratroopers had put their weapons down to pray. "One of the greatest things to have happened in my life was when one of the paratroopers detached himself from the wall, fell onto my neck, and cried," Meir said. "I felt as if I were his mother." She revealed that she was finally compelled to participate in the tradition of the wall, and slipped her own note between its cracked stones. She said the note had one word scrawled on it: "Peace."

Meir rounded off her speech with an account of her recent visit to the holy site. A few days earlier, she had encountered recent émigrés from the Soviet Union there. They told the prime minister about the many Jews who were stuck behind the Iron Curtain, yearning to be free in Zion. And while they suffer, they do not suffer passively, she said: "These are people who rise up and protest their abuse." In her mythologizing of this faraway struggle, Meir unintentionally underscored the hypocrisy and narrow-mindedness of the elite political class to which she belonged because, at that very moment, there were people protesting their abuse only a few hundred feet away.

When officers flashing pistols cornered Marciano, he finally stopped running and surrendered. It was late at night and he was one of the last delivered to the precinct. But he wasn't tossed in with the rest of the prisoners. Tourgeman ordered that Marciano be taken to a separate area. Marciano had tried to mentally prepare for what would come next. He knew there was a beating reserved for him.

About ten officers were now surrounding him. Four of the faces were familiar—moments ago he was sparring with them at Zion Square. More than the kicks and punches he sustained, what shocked Marciano was the sounds the cops made while delivering his punishment. Their shouts seemed to him animalistic, their ferocity disproportionate to the occasion. Escorted through the jail, another Panther,

Charlie Biton, saw a body tossed on the floor at the bottom of a staircase. He didn't recognize Marciano at first; his face was too bloody. He seemed dead. But then a cop kicked Marciano in the groin and Marciano flinched. A sign he was still alive.

Marciano found himself placed in a cell with a middle-aged man. The man helped lay him down on the filthy mattress on the floor and then he darted to the bars and shook them. He howled at whoever might be listening, his accent revealing that he was Palestinian: "Don't you feel any pity for this kid? He needs a doctor! He needs help!"

It took about three hours for a doctor to show up and he ordered Marciano to be taken to the hospital. A retinue of guards accompanied him and again Marciano felt the treatment he received was befitting someone accused of being a terrorist, not a protester. At Shaare Zedek Hospital, the medical staff stitched up the cut on his forehead to stop the blood from gushing out and flowing over his blackened right eye. A hospital report from a week later noted the stitches as well as injuries to Marciano's legs and a pain that made it nearly impossible for Marciano to make any major movement.

Marciano was probably the most badly wounded out of everyone, but dozens of other demonstrators at the jail sustained injuries as well. Those who didn't arrive looking very hurt took an extra beating while being questioned. In the basement of the Russian Compound, the Shin Bet secret police kept its own dungeon for interrogations. It was reserved for Palestinians, but the police would sometimes walk Jewish detainees downstairs to give them a glimpse of torture: a Palestinian man bound to a chair from his hands and feet in a contorted position meant to inflict pain, or what appeared to be a device for electrocuting the detained. Another method of intimidation and control, one that inmates were reluctant to speak about even 50 years later, involved sexual abuse. Specifically, officers would strap certain inmates to a bench face down and pants down. Then they'd take a bottle of soda, shake it vigorously, and uncap it for insertion into the rectum.

The repression toolkit also included the pitting of one class of inmates against another. The Russian Compound served as a place to hold people after they had been arrested, such as the demonstrators, but one of the cells was designated for felons, who were brought over temporarily from prison to appear for hearings at the nearby court-house. For the felons, a trip to the Russian Compound meant a chance to receive visitors and gifts. It was through these visits that inmates could obtain contraband, which they would smuggle back to prison, allowing them to play a role in the economy of the incarcerated. Manipulating the system of incentives, the guards would take away visitation privileges from the arriving felons and pin the blame on the Panthers. Incited, the felons would be released into the jail yard at the same time as the unsuspecting activists. This would lead to ferocious fights. The guards would intervene only too late, treating the incident as a routine altercation and reporting it as such to the press.

It's hard to tell exactly which abuses were meted out at the Russian Compound on May 19, 1971; the allegations were never publicly investigated or thoroughly documented. But the accounts of Panthers and others who got caught up in this Jerusalem dungeon tell a consistent story of deliberate violence.

As the day wore on, a relentless chill pervaded the air, and the activists grew more and more desperate. Panthers struck matches to two filth-soaked mattresses, igniting them on fire. Smoke filled the cell and escaped through a window in a thick dark plume that was caught on camera. The guards had to open the cells and drag out the suffocating protesters.

That same day, in a scheduling coincidence, Meir appeared in Jerusalem with an organization known as the Moroccan Immigrants Association. The event had been convened by the association in order to name her as an honorary member, and normally, these types of events were festive and unremarkable. But the event's host, Shaul Ben Sim-hon, a leader of the group, decided he couldn't ignore the previous night's unrest. Now in his 40s, Ben Simhon had in his youth been some-what of a labor rebel, fighting on behalf of the port workers of Ashdod. And so while he spoke against the use of violence by protesters, he could hardly dismiss them out of hand. Despite what had happened, he said, the Panthers were "basically nice fellows."

Then came Meir's turn to speak. She rose from her seat to a round of applause and addressed the microphone. The television camera flashed to her and Ben Simhon remained in the frame, sitting stiffly beside her in his suit and tie. He seemed uneasy as his eyes darted from some-where off-screen to Meir and then back toward the unseen point. As Meir spoke, Ben Simhon seemed to have forgotten he was holding a lit cigarette because he ashed it without having taken a puff.

"There is no more terrible disaster than a split among the people," Meir said in her usual tone of impatience and practiced overstatement. "Nothing will succeed if we let this poison settle among us."

She reminded the audience of her own humble origins and, once again, summarized the egalitarian narrative of Israeli history, in which all those who sacrificed were rewarded. She finished her speech by turning to face Ben Simhon. She wanted to rebut his softness toward the Panthers.

"My dear friend, these boys are not nice," she said while looking down at him and gesturing admonishment by repeatedly shaking her head. "I met with them."

Meir then spoke of her meeting with the Panthers a month earlier and said she was criticized for doing so. Her aides had warned her a meeting would only give them unearned publicity, but she told them she wanted to get to know the individuals in the group.

"They were once good boys," she said on the authority of having met with them for two hours. "Some of them still will be—but some won't anymore."

It was the first time the prime minister shared her thoughts publicly on the growing ethnic movement, and she used the opportunity to cast it as a violent threat to the sanctity of the Zionist cause: "How could it be that a Jewish hand in the State of Israel was raised to throw a Molotov cocktail at another Jew?" she asked.

"Whoever does that is not nice," she said, repeating the phrase "not nice," and directing it, this time, not toward particular Panthers, but toward whoever lobbed the firebomb. The phrase was immediately and widely criticized as an indication of Meir's condescending and derogatory attitude toward the Black Panthers and the segment of the population they represented.

The police had no suspects in the Molotov cocktail case. But she blamed the Panthers anyway, crafting a potent smear. Violence and the Panthers: the two would become inextricably linked, just as had happened with the namesake movement in the United States. Who had thrown the firebombs? Most of the Panthers were already locked up by that hour. The few others who had evaded capture could have. The police would in the coming weeks announce the arrest and interrogation of a handful of individuals suspected of the crime. Prosecutors, though, would never bring charges against anyone in the case.

In recent years, certain Panthers have said they know who the culprit was. Elbaz, some say, prepared the firebombs. He learned how from having participated in Zionist militia activity against the British in the 1940s. One former Panther, Yigal Bin-Nun, remembers practice-tossing Molotovs at a wall with Elbaz. It's impossible to verify any of this, and pinning Elbaz for the act is rather convenient now that he's dead and long exposed as a police informant. But there's another piece of evidence that suggests his culpability—the memoir published by Yacob Elbaz's elder brother, Zion Elbaz. The book makes no mention of Yacob's involvement in the Panthers, focusing instead on his life before and after. From the time he was a child, Yacob reportedly displayed a pyromaniac tendency to set dolls, curtains, and other belongings on fire. "The practice of testing objects with fire was typical with Yacob," the memoir says.

Meir refers to the Panthers in the masculine, as boys, or young men. Much of the discourse surrounding the Panthers has focused on the men of the group. In part, that's the result of the history: the youths of Musrara tended to form into gender-segregated groups so the original Panther gang was all male. The group's grievances centered on the disillusion of being young men who were expected by society to be soldiers and breadwinners but who were at the same time excluded from the institutions that would allow them to realize those roles. Photos from the Panthers' protests show that the crowds were made up overwhelmingly of men. And the leadership was indeed male. The media, meanwhile, amplified this gender dynamic by focusing almost exclusively on the men and their personalities.

Jerusalem's impoverished Mizrahi women didn't belong to the street gang scene that gave rise to the Panthers. They were more likely to be busy doing the work necessary to keep their homes and families functioning, be it domestic labor, working in laundries, or vending various goods. As the Panthers grew, however, they drew their sisters and mothers and female neighbors into the struggle. Their contributions went largely undocumented, but the women of the Panthers participated in protests and planning meetings and carried out critical community organizing jobs from crafting protest banners to bringing meals and cigarettes to those jailed as a result of protests. In his storytelling decades later, Abergel would praise women like his then-wife, Rachelle, or Mazal Sa'il, Louise Cohen, Shulamit Tsuberi, and Aliza Marciano as heroes of the movement.

The one woman who did receive significant recognition for her part in the Panthers was Ashkenazi and American. Freshly graduated from MIT as a political scientist, Naomi Kies immigrated to Israel after the 1967 war, fulfilling an aspiration of her Zionist upbringing that included studying at a Jewish school and learning Israeli folk dance. Her attrac-

Mazal Sa'il was known for her impassioned speeches. Digital image of photograph by Shalom Bar-Tal/Israel Sun Ltd., from the Judaica Collection of the Harvard Library, Harvard University.

tion to the cause of the Panthers stemmed from her prior participation in the U.S. civil rights movement—in both cases, she felt responsible to act as a privileged and politically minded young person. From an early point, she consistently showed up at meetings of the Panthers and gained their trust by providing office equipment for the headquarters, chauffeuring them around, and bailing them out of jail. Soon, Kies began acting as a spokesperson for the group, especially for the English-language press. She was such a fixture that police investigators considered her a leader of the group. Kies was prominent in the Israeli left until her death at age 43. Eventually, a small street in East Jerusalem was renamed in her memory. No other Panther has yet to earn that honor.

Whether the Panthers were nice boys or not, Ben Simhon had enough faith in the alleged Molotov throwers that, a few hours after meeting with Meir, while the protesters were still in jail, he attempted to broker a peace. He asked the government to be allowed to meet with the Panthers at the police precinct and offer them a deal: in return for an end to militant tactics, and a merger of the Panthers with his group, the Moroccan Immigrants Association, the Panthers would be granted immunity from criminal charges stemming from the Night of the Panthers. It was a classic attempt at co-opting a social movement. The government agreed to let Ben Simhon try to make a deal.

It was now about 9 p.m., some 24 hours after the big protest. Marciano had just arrived back at the jail from the hospital where his forehead got sewn up. An officer grabbed him and escorted him to the stairwell. Taking the flight down to the basement would mean entering the space usually reserved for interrogations of Palestinians, where the secret police reigned and inmates were broken. But the officer didn't take Marciano down. They climbed up to the second floor that housed the offices of the precinct's brass.

In the comfortably furnished room that he was brought to, Marciano noticed a large table with a spread of sandwiches, soft drinks, whiskey, cognac, and cigarettes. Out of anyone in the room, he probably looked the most ragged and distraught, but the four other Panthers who were there were also flustered. One moment they were being locked up, manhandled, and beaten up, and the next, they were invited to a feast by a group of cordial, smiling, and well-dressed men—senior police officers and members of the Moroccan-Israeli elite.

For the next eight hours—until five in the morning—Ben Simhon and his friends pleaded with the Panthers to change course. They exchanged personal stories, debated each other about racism, and argued about the merits of a deal between the two groups. The exchange was not documented, but according to an account from an ethnographer of the group, the Panthers at first "opposed the whole idea. Slowly throughout the night, they began to reconsider."

The back and forth that night produced a document. It stipulated the Panthers would agree to a merger as long as the joint group pursued "the just struggle for the improvement of the living standards of the backward sectors in the country, and will fight for the abolition of poverty and backwardness." But who would set the targets and milestones on this path toward justice? The parliament's Committee for Labor Affairs, according to the document. "We shall struggle for the acceptance of these decisions by the government and for their speedy implementation." The Panthers would further agree to abide by "the rule of law and democracy" and to deplore "any kind of violence which can disrupt law and public order." All actions would stem from a commitment to the country that remains "dear to them," and further, they averred that their struggle "has only patriotic motives."

More than any of the other Panthers present, Abergel believed that there was more to politics than protesting. Battling police in the streets would make the public listen, but for how long? Getting detained and then beaten in lockup would lend the Panthers some revolutionary sheen and even sympathy, but then what? He wanted the group to grow into a social movement that could shape policy.

Abergel had disappeared during the Night of the Panthers, making him one of the few Panthers who were not apprehended. In the morning, he appeared at the Russian Compound with a lawyer at his side to turn himself in. Since his name was printed on the permit for the demonstration, he was liable for the violations of the protesters. Another criminal charge now would be his third in six months. Even if he could beat the charge, he knew that court appearances consumed time and siphoned away money and attention. The discussion that night, in the second-floor office of the Russian Compound with the members of the Moroccan Immigrant Association, seemed to present an opportunity to disentangle from the law and, at the same time, redirect the group beyond their image as violent agitators.

The final version of the agreement had the initials of Abergel and enough of the others for the police to agree to their release without charges. Ben Simhon would later share in an interview that Abergel had sobbed during parts of the nightlong negotiations—"he cried out that he loves his country and that it's terrible to accuse him of actions that would lead to a civil war"—suggesting that Abergel's support for the deal was heartfelt. A headline on the front page of Israel's afternoon paper declared, "The Panthers joined the Moroccan Immigrants Association." But to complete a merger between the two organizations, the leadership of each would have to sell the idea to their general membership. It was hard to see how the Panthers would manage to do so because some of the signers shared their regrets almost immediately. Levy, for example, walking out of the Russian Compound that night, shared a message that did not bode well for the deal. "They bought us," he said to the supporters assembled outside. "We signed the agreement and they bought us." Then came the press conference called to announce the deal. Malka, who did not participate in the negotiations, shouted that the merger was a "fiction" and added that "the Panthers will get nowhere by joining other organizations." He said he was against violence but also warned that next time, "there will be grenades." Then came the most important withdrawal. Marciano and a group of his closest supporters denounced the merger deal in a statement they published later that day. This agreement "will humiliate the whole of the Moroccan community and Mr. Ben Simhon personally," the statement said. "The Immigrant Association is a social club which has nothing to do with a militant organization like the Panthers, who are fighting for the eradication of slums, poverty, and ignorance."

Abergel did not grandstand when he came out of prison. "I feel like I can be more useful outside jail than inside," was all he was quoted as saying by the press. For the moment, it seemed, the more militant voices had drowned out Abergel. Alone, perhaps, he believed that going along with the deal wouldn't stop the Panthers from fighting for change. The group held its first meeting after the release from jail of those who were detained, and Abergel was not present for it. They started brainstorming ideas for their next steps: to stage a public trial, charging the police with brutality; to squat in an apartment on behalf of a ten-child family; to help renovate dilapidated slums. The meeting left the Panthers with "a good feeling of 'getting on with things,'" the group's ethnographer later wrote. Meanwhile, the *Jerusalem Post* went so far as to report that Abergel had left the Panthers to become "apolitical."

But he hadn't left. He was simply searching for a way forward. On May 23, five days after the Night of the Panthers, Abergel went to city hall at the invitation of the mayor. Several Panthers joined him—Elbaz, Malka, and Levy—but none from Marciano's faction. The meeting took place in the office of Akiva Azoulay, one of the few Mizrahi high-ranking officials in city government. Ben Simhon was there, too, and the meeting opened with his new pitch to the few Panthers who were willing to listen. He offered to obtain medical treatment for the protesters who were injured—most of them were uninsured in a country that had yet to adopt universal health care—and to set up a summer camp for up to 200 slum youths. He said he could connect elderly people to welfare services and supply tutors to help struggling students. Finally, he dangled his connections, promising meetings with decision-makers and a direct line to the prime minister. But a merger remained out of reach. Abergel didn't have enough votes among members, and he said the only way to cooperate was as two independent groups. "Personally, I am with you," Abergel added. "I am sick of all the protests."

14

VOTE OF NO CONFIDENCE

WHEN THE SEVENTH PARLIAMENT of Israel convened for its 186th legislative session, Abergel was observing the lawmakers from the perch of the visitors' gallery. It was the afternoon of May 24, 1971, and the main item listed on the day's agenda had to do with his still-nascent movement. The Panthers had been mentioned in the plenum only a few times before, in discussions about poverty or juvenile delinquency, but never had they been at the center of debate. Now, one of Israel's two communist parties, known by its acronym Rakah, carried out a parliamentary maneuver that would make it impossible for the silence to continue. Using one of the few power plays available to small parties sitting outside the government coalition in parliament, Rakah submitted a motion of no confidence. The party was asking parliament to dissolve the Israeli government and plunge the country into a premature election.

The leader of Rakah rose to the podium. He was flanked by the Israeli flag, though he hardly recognized its authority.

Meir Vilner was a politician who had put his signature on Israel's declaration of independence while disavowing the country's founding ideology. A Jew, he led a party whose constituency came almost entirely from Israel's non-Jewish, Palestinian Arab citizenry. Fully aware of how unpopular he was among the majority of members of parliament, and for that matter, Israeli society, Vilner nevertheless spoke in all seriousness to try to compel forward his motion:

"We accuse the police, and the government officials that gave them the green light, of initiating and using violence, preparing all the tools to carry out the violence, mustering forces from around the country ahead of time, bringing horses, clubs, shields, and dyed water cannons—all this in an attempt to break the Black Panthers, to silence the cry of the poor and oppressed."

He argued that the government had disqualified itself by reacting so harshly to the Panthers, who, he said, justifiably raised an important social problem. He used his platform to publicize specific accusations of police abuse that occurred during the recent demonstration and afterward when the protesters were behind bars: a Panther who had been beaten in detention until he was unconscious, teeth that were broken during interrogations, a pregnant woman who was punched in the stomach. These allegations went on until Vilner finally concluded his speech by saying, "As long as there is poverty and discrimination, there will be a struggle against poverty and for civil rights."

Then came the government's turn to respond, and Hillel, the minister of police, was selected as its mouthpiece. He began with ad hominem attacks, painting Vilner as disloyal to his country and accusing him of merely imitating whatever emanated from Soviet, Egyptian, and Palestinian media. Moving on from the personal attacks on Vilner, Hillel defended Israel's record on economic development and social equality, arguing that the country had come a long way. He suggested that the current government didn't deserve the negative attention it was getting since these problems were common to all societies.

"And here," Hillel said, "I'd like to touch upon the problem known as the 'Black Panthers,' a miserable name imported from the United States."

"Of those arrested at least a quarter were neither Panther nor black," he claimed, faulting radical leftists for the recent mayhem during the Night of the Panthers. These outsiders corrupted the cause and made it impossible to set the Panthers on a path that would be acceptable in a democracy, he added.

Hillel mustered more and more criticisms: he said it was not the right time for such a movement—the country must unite to focus on freeing Soviet Jewry—and that the Panthers represented a threat to the rule of law.

"In response to the specific charges leveled by parliament member Vilner: we will not make parliament into a courtroom," Hillel said in his disdain for the communist lawmaker. "This here is not the national assembly of the country of Guinea."

The implication was that Vilner's politics would make Israel go the route of a Soviet-backed dictatorship in West Africa, whose leader was during that time fending off opposition by detaining and disappearing people. Hillel's own government stood accused of using violence against protesters—but he was claiming that what really threatened Israel and its democracy was Vilner's rhetoric.

Next, the speaker of the parliament, Reuven Barkat, invited each political party to the podium by turn to deliver their own statements. For nearly all of parliament's 13 parties, this was the first time they were speaking on the matter of the Panthers. The coalition of parties making up the government, including Hillel's Labor party, held the majority of seats and could be expected to parrot the official line. The real question was how the various opposition lawmakers would respond. Usually, they railed against Golda Meir's government, accusing it of folly, incompetence, or moral ineptitude.

The bulk of the opposition seats belonged to Likud and the right-wing stream of Zionism, organized under the banner of the Gahal list.

Increasingly supported by Mizrahi voters, these were dependable voices against Labor Zionism since before the founding of Israel. The representative of Gahal, Ya'akov Nehoshtan, took the podium. "Mizrahi communities bear the brunt of the problem of poverty, housing shortages, earning an income, the lack of educational opportunities," he said. "Why is it surprising that the despair engenders bitterness and indignation, especially among the youth?" The government must engage with the young men of Musrara "regardless of whether these boys are nice or not," he said, taking a dig at the prime minister for her gaffe. And he added that his party has "no faith" in the government. But Nehoshtan also condemned Rakah for bringing a motion to address "riots it had a significant hand in causing." He argued against bringing down the government over this issue. "A no-confidence vote will not solve the problem of poverty in Israel," he said.

Also in opposition was the party of the haredi Orthodox community, which used its influence more narrowly, obtaining resources for its constituents rather than competing for governing power. When his turn came, Shlomo Lorincz of the Agudat Yisrael party diagnosed the problem as one of declining religiosity. "The Black Panthers are the rotten fruit of a secular education system, which has methodically removed faith in God from the hearts of the young generation and destroyed their respect for their parents," he said. Ironically, many of the Panthers had attended an elementary school run by Lorincz's party. They were, if anything, the products of secularism's abandonment. Like the representative from Gahal, Lorincz said Israel should tackle its social issues, but that the problem didn't justify the behavior of the Panthers nor the toppling of the government.

Finally, there were some unaffiliated, independent lawmakers and each offered their own tailored indictment against the police and against the overall policy on social welfare. Uri Avnery, for example, who styled himself a progressive, said the police were at fault for the violence in the protest. "There's no debating this," he said. "It's good the Panthers forced us to confront the problem before it became too late. All those who came to speak today should recall who reminded them of the issue, who but the Panthers."

At the end of nearly two hours of discussion, the time came for a vote that would reveal just how divided parliament was. With a solid majority behind Labor, there was no chance of toppling the government, but would any of the dozens of opposition members from different parties decide to register their objections? The final tally was 83 for the government, and only four votes against. The four include three communists and one independent radical, Shalom Cohen. That the government easily defeated the no-confidence motion didn't come as a surprise. The communists were hugely unpopular. Even Avnery, who essentially agreed with them, abstained. "We won't vote with Rakah because we don't trust Rakah's motivations," he said. Whatever its motivations, the communist party helped expose something essential about Israeli politics: the rancor among the various parties—right, left, and religious—concealed a deeper consensus among them. In their speeches, all sides essentially said that national cohesion trumps the pursuit of social justice. They all presented the Panthers as a foreign import distorting the national culture.

Despite the rhetoric, the country's various political factions voted together to defeat the no-confidence motion, setting aside differences in the face of growing civil disobedience. The same couldn't be said about the Panthers themselves. To the ethnographer embedded with the group, the days after the release from detention seemed to spell a rupture in leadership. "Abergel was coming under ever greater attack," she wrote. The accusations against him were many: that he had jockeyed away authority from the younger founders, that he would speak on behalf of the group without getting approval to do so, and that he

Reuven Abergel's son sits on his father's lap while the Panthers hold a meeting at the Abergel family home, which doubled as the group's headquarters for a while in 1971. © Micha Bar-Am.

pushed out certain supporters—specifically the young Ashkenazi leftists who had been there since the beginning.

Abergel was and did all of those things. A big brother to two of the Panthers, and older than most of the rest, he sometimes dominated interactions in the group. Under normal, traditional circumstances, he would have been entitled to their deference. The social order in Musrara dictated that there was no equality among men of different ages. Younger brothers would not, for example, smoke cigarettes within view of their older brothers. To whatever extent that he did appease younger Panthers, Abergel was conceding power and privilege. Harder still for him was to share authority—or even be associated—with young Ashkenazi students and leftists who appeared at meetings and demonstrations. And though Abergel may have cast himself as the group's representative against the wishes of others, his public persona proved valuable.

Saadia Marciano catches a ride on a motor scooter to deliver banners to a demonstration in 1971. © Micha Bar-Am.

When the *New York Times* published its first story on the Mizrahi social movement on May 24, it was a profile of Abergel, titled "Israeli 'Panther.'" One of the few times the *Times* had broached the topic of Mizrahi-Ashkenazi relations, this sympathetic portrayal scored points for the Panthers in the critical arena of public opinion. Israeli leaders were acutely self-conscious about how the country was being portrayed abroad, and they came under pressure over the Mizrahi issue due to such coverage.

The next day, Abergel secured another win. Many of the Panthers were still badly injured from the Night of the Panthers a week earlier, and many among the injured were Abergel's biggest critics. Since universal health care hadn't arrived in Israel yet, they couldn't afford to pay for medical treatment for their broken bones, bruises, and concussions. Abergel persuaded the city to pay Hadassah Medical Center to treat the injured, including his critics and rivals in the Panthers. He did so by agreeing to meet with the well-connected Moroccan Immigrants Association, a group Marciano preferred to shun because he considered it corrupt and ineffectual.

Perhaps because of Abergel's success with obtaining medical care, Marciano and his closest allies did agree to come to a second meeting with the association and city officials. In any case, according to the minutes from that day, they didn't say much. Abergel spoke on behalf of the Panthers, proposing ideas Marciano's crew probably considered boring and conciliatory: to hold a study session and a conference; to do a neighborhood cleanup including hauling away junk and repainting exterior walls in Musrara; to take hundreds of children on a field trip on International Children's Day. "Each child will be sent home with a flower in their hand," Abergel suggested.

Group discussions like this one proliferated. Marciano's clique dismissed them as "committee work." The more meetings happened, the more they felt "that they were being forgotten on the streets," according to the ethnographer. In fact, the agitation among the young Panther core was worse than what the ethnographer may have realized. A subset of Panthers hatched a plan that would take the group in a starkly militant direction. They plotted to ambush a number of police officers at home and beat them up. Their main target was an officer named Amram Edry, who they felt deserved revenge because he had been particularly brutal to Marciano when he was locked up, kicking Marciano in the face. But before the idea could be executed, Elbaz, informant P/51, learned of the plan and went to debrief his police handler about it. According to an intelligence summary, Elbaz said that he managed to talk the Panthers down but that the officer should be warned just in case.

An ambush of sorts did take place, but not against any officer and not by Marciano. It happened on the night of May 31. The Panthers had called a meeting and a bloated roster of nearly 70 people showed up: the Abergel and Marciano factions, the Tel Aviv Panthers, Elbaz, and the Ashkenazi allies, including the Wigoder brothers, their friend Levit, and another friend, known as "Noah the Goat." It was a crowd too large to fit in their makeshift headquarters so they decided to leave Abergel's house and regroup at a different location downtown.

The door to the building the Panthers wanted to enter was locked. The place didn't belong to them—it was the property of another association of well-off Moroccan Jews, but it was big enough for the purposes of the meeting, and the Panthers broke in.

There are different versions of what happened inside, but the context is the same. Ten days earlier, most of the Panthers were locked up at the Russian Compound after the Night of the Panthers. One of the first to be released was the younger Marciano brother Rafi, who told the press, "We think Matzpen members threw the cocktails. The Panthers deplore the use of Molotov cocktails. We are opposed to violence as we are to delinquency." This message might have come from Abergel, who had brought Rafi under his wing. The next thing that happened came a week later, when Abergel attended a private meeting with Hillel and the top commanders of the police. According to the minutes recorded by police, Abergel demanded accountability for the use of violence against the Panthers. But he also placed some blame on "Matzpen people." Abergel complained about their influence on the Panthers and said he had warned them to stay away. Now he wanted help from the police to keep them off his back, but Hillel said he couldn't help: "We are a country of laws and cannot do anything to an individual just for belonging to Matzpen," Hillel responded. "Matzpen" became shorthand for the four or so Ashkenazi activists who had helped found the Panthers. Ironically, they did not actually belong to the far-left group. To Marciano, they were trusted allies and close friends. To Abergel, they were a liability on two fronts. Internally, he thought the Ashkenazi activists took up too much space in a movement that was supposed to be led by Mizrahi people. And in terms of public perception, their association with the Panthers made it easier to dismiss the group as a fringe left-wing phenomenon.

Now, after having broken in, the Panthers were ready to start the meeting. It would not last long. According to the recollections of Meir Wigoder, one of the first things that happened was that, in front of everyone, he accused Abergel of being a spy for the police. According to the information supplied to the police, it was Wigoder's friend Dany Levit who set Abergel off when Levit called another one of the Panthers a coward. Either way, Abergel and his clique physically attacked them and the Ashkenazi activists fled the scene. They stayed away from the movement for a while and returned only to a much-diminished role. In their desire to establish a broad-based movement, the Panthers continued to seek out alliances, but disagreements over who was trustworthy would only grow.

15

FIRE

THE INVITATIONS THAT ABERGEL printed out started with an expression of gratitude to "you who support our struggle" and "who have offered to render assistance." In a few weeks, there would be a special campaign by the Panthers to clean up the neighborhood of Musrara. The work would involve hauling away debris, plastering and painting exterior walls, and clearing brush that had overtaken the open space between housing blocks, creating fire hazards. At the top of the letter, under the word "Dear," were three dotted lines, a space to fill out a custom salutation for each recipient. For one particular recipient, Abergel reserved a special greeting:

> Dear
> Honorable lady
> Your honor prime minister
> Madam Meir

Making sure the snarkiness of saluting her as if she were aristocracy did not go unnoticed, Abergel scribbled a personal note on the back of the invitation: "Would you be so kind as to show up and prove just how nice the Panthers are," he wrote.

It was about two weeks since Meir uttered her condescending "not nice" line about the Panthers, and Abergel's note was plainly meant as a dig at her. His remark also revealed a desire for validation. Unlike some Panthers, Abergel was disturbed by the image of the group as unserious, violent, and unruly. According to Ben Simhon's account of a conversation between the two, Abergel broke into heartfelt tears when the Panthers' alleged lack of patriotism came up. Abergel reportedly pledged himself as a loyal citizen. Facing objections that such work was emasculating, Abergel now insisted the Panthers clean up Musrara and be seen doing it.

In the month before the campaign was slated to kick off, Abergel's internal conflict—his simultaneous urge to rebel and to belong—saw its fullest expression on eight pages of newsprint of a new publication called *Voice of the Panthers*. A stenciled image of a Panther, borrowed from the original that appeared in the official newspaper of the American Panthers, was stamped large on the front page.

Copies of the *Voice* went up for sale and the first readers could have bought one on June 14 during a demonstration in Jerusalem. They would have been leafing through the pages as speeches blurted out of a megaphone. And when the demo turned into a march they would have tucked the pages under their arm or rolled them into a cylinder and swayed with the crowd toward Zion Square.

At Zion Square, where hundreds of people now gathered once again, there was a bare flag pole in the center. Suddenly, a Panther latched onto it. As he began his ascent, someone handed him a banner. He climbed to the top, straddled his legs around the pole to free his hands, and hung up the banner like a flag. For a little while at least, Zion

Square had a new name. The banner declared it the "Square of Mizrahi Jewry," as had been the intention at the prior demonstration. Down below, activists were pleading with the protesters to remain orderly— and they complied. The march continued from the square and the crowd reassembled for a demonstration outside the police ministry. Hillel was served with a petition demanding a public inquiry into police brutality. To conclude the demonstration, the Panthers recited the national anthem, and then everyone dispersed peacefully. In virtually every way, the events of that day matched the spirit expressed in the *Voice* and embodied in Abergel. Though the paper listed no editorial staff—that was to subsume the individual in the collective—in reality, Abergel was the editor of the paper and he was also named as the chairman, not of the Panthers, but of a nonprofit he had set up in the group's name.

In the paper, there are fighting words worthy of an underground manifesto: "Our organization is an expression of Mizrahi resistance, a resistance whose history is as long as our acquaintance with the Jews of Ashkenaz."

And elsewhere: "We see no solution to this terrible situation other than a revolutionary solution . . . the revolution must come!"

But much of the text strikes a different tone. In the opening essay, the paper says the country is at risk of falling apart but that "we want to save it before it's too late." The Panthers are cast as "a Zionist party and perhaps the only one" and described as descendants of such towering figures of Sephardic Jewry as Maimonides, Judah Halevi, and Solomon ibn Gabirol. "What the hell makes us different from the giants of Sefarad?" the essay asks. "It's simple. We don't have any money."

One of the last items to appear in the edition is a letter to the Panthers signed by eight high school students from Tiberias whose names indicate they were Mizrahi. Only a few sentences long, the letter expresses "solidarity with your struggle to eliminate ethnic discrimination and poverty." But the support comes with one significant reservation: "Your struggle will garner more support if you avoid violence and act according to the law."

One government official hoping the Panthers could be nudged toward a subdued path was Uzi Narkis. A retired and venerated general, Narkis spent part of his post-military life as a senior executive at the Jewish Agency, which was in charge of promoting and facilitating Jewish immigration to Israel. As he would say a few weeks later in a press conference, the Panthers were threatening to scare away prospective immigrants from one of the most important sources: American Jewry. Some of the people contemplating a move from the United States to Israel were more worried about social upheaval than they were about the potential for regional conflict. "Americans were anxious to get away from their own social problems in the U.S. and were hardly eager to run into the same problems here," as a reporter for the *Jerusalem Post* put it. So Narkis concocted a plan. One of the main grievances that the Panthers tapped into was the lack of affordable housing. He would use his authority and connections to place young couples in empty apartments in the new towns that Israel was building on the country's periphery. "If they go to a development town, they'll keep quiet," he later said. "It will solve their problem as well as mine."

Abergel and a few other Panthers agreed to go along with the proposal and take a tour of the town of Maalot in Israel's Upper Galilee area. A few miles away from the border with Lebanon and a few hours' drive from Jerusalem, Maalot was one of the most remote towns in Israel. Only a few hundred families lived there and they were mostly poor. The group arrived by bus and visited the local schools and cultural centers, and the factories where they would presumably work. They had lunch at the health clinic where an official presented what incentives were available for those who came.

Late that night, the Panthers returned to Musrara and found a commotion outside Abergel's home. In their absence, part of his house, a wooden shack in the back, had been consumed by fire.

It was reported at 8:17 p.m., and a fire truck arrived about five minutes later, early enough to save a part of the Abergel home but not the stacks of documents, clothes, and other materials the Panthers had stored inside. Now, it seemed to many Panthers that the whole trip to Maalot was merely a ruse to get them away so that someone could set fire to the place while no one was looking. Among the Panthers, some even whispered that a member of their own group was responsible but they didn't dare say so out loud and risk revealing internal discord. So when the nightly news came on a little while later, the Panthers united in outrage over the coverage of the fire. They were angry that no footage was broadcast, even though a film crew had been dispatched to the scene, and also that the newscaster speculated that the Panthers had caused the fire themselves as some sort of ruse.

The news station became the common enemy. It was after midnight and a crowd of about a hundred began marching out of Musrara, chanting: "They burned our house, we'll burn their house!"

They crossed the city, arriving outside the gates of the television station in the Romema neighborhood. The building was empty, and a small retinue of police stood guard outside. The Panthers did not end up storming the compound because the station's influential news director, Dan Shilon, showed up to negotiate with the Panthers. By early morning, the two sides had settled on a solution: the next newscast would report on the Panthers' tour of Maalot as an example of the group's nonviolent, constructive side.

When the investigation into the fire concluded a few days later, police said arson was not the cause. The fire was ruled an accident. This should not have come as a surprise, a police spokesperson said, adding that "it was a hot day and thorny brush often catches fire." Meanwhile, the city engineer's office ruled the house structurally unsafe and ordered that the Abergel family be relocated.

Abergel didn't have much time to contend with the tragedy that had befallen his family: the long-awaited neighborhood cleanup day was about to arrive. The Panthers arranged for a delivery of rakes and shovels, paintbrushes and white paint, and municipal garbage trucks to haul away debris. For a few hours, young people in Musrara collected discarded rusted bedframes and soiled mattresses, and whacked weeds to clear the streets and sidewalks. They slathered walls, fences, and benches with white. A photo from that day captured Abergel and his wife, Rachelle, working on an area across from their half-scorched house, whose entrance was still marked with signs in English and Hebrew bearing the words "Headquarters of the Black Panthers."

Despite the personal invitation to the clean-up, the prime minister did not show up—she was busy that moment hosting CIA director Richard Helms. It was the height of the Cold War and Helms was touring the Middle East to assess the state of U.S. power in the region. Of particular concern was a "treaty of friendship and cooperation" signed a few months earlier by the Soviet Union and Egypt, Israel's enemy to the south. An important body of water separated Israel and Egypt: the Suez Canal. Normally, a massive amount of global maritime trade would be passing through the canal, but the Egyptians had been blocking it since the 1967 war. Getting the canal open again was a priority for both world powers. For her part, Meir had a different goal in meeting with Helms. She wanted the White House to approve the sale of fighter jets known as Phantoms to Israel to ensure the country's military supremacy in the air.

As Meir tried to work the Americans, and conditions on the Egyptian border remained volatile, the Panthers kept pressuring her on the streets of Jerusalem. The Panthers were refusing to be patient and wait their turn as the country's leaders had pleaded whenever organized Mizrahi discontent reared its head. They wouldn't be sidelined by concerns of national security anymore and insisted on challenging the notion that Israel's war needs should take precedence over their issues. So, when one of their largest demonstrations to date took place around this time, drawing thousands, one of the slogans chosen for the occasion was "less for the Phantoms and more for the Panthers." And when the demonstration turned into a march, a banner at the head of the crowd declared: "No ceasefire in the war on poverty." Saying that social and domestic concerns should not be subservient to national security was an audacious, radical message in a country constantly on the brink of war, and it was wholeheartedly embraced by the Panthers. In fact, as world leaders were engaged in talks, the group announced a plan to embark on its own diplomacy program to spread that message abroad.

The Panthers planned to go to the United States to increase awareness in the American Jewish community about inequality in Israel. This was meant to generate pressure on the Israeli government, which depended on support from the diaspora. As Abergel explained in a public panel about the trip, the Panthers intended to ask American Jewish donors, "Are you giving money to Jews in a State of Jews, or to Ashkenazim?" Naomi Kies, the American professor who had been helping the group, now agreed to act as the guide and translator for the delegation of four Panthers: Abergel, Marciano, Biton, and, marking the first time the Panthers elevated a woman to a visible leadership role, Shulamit Tsuberi.

Seventeen-year-old Tsuberi didn't come from Musrara, but her story was in many ways the same. Raised in a Yemenite family in the small town of Rosh HaAyin, she was the eldest of 11 siblings. After finishing elementary school, she had to support her family by working as a housecleaner. Skinny and very dark-skinned, she had stumbled her way into the Panthers, thinking they were a band of musicians at first. Her bona fides in the group were earned, in part, after police thrashed her so badly at a protest that she needed to be hospitalized for several weeks; she then returned to the movement still defiant.

Shlomo Segev was a lawyer from one of the Sephardic families that established themselves in the country long before Israel's founding, which set him apart from the Mizrahi immigrants as well as the Ashkenazi elites. He represented the Panthers pro bono and lined up anonymous donors to fund the trip to the United States. In advocating for her inclusion on the trip, he said Tsuberi possessed an intuitive understanding of legal philosophy exhibited during impromptu lectures to police officials and argued that Tsuberi's voice was so compelling she could emerge as a future Angela Davis or Helen Keller.

The announcement of a U.S. tour by the Panthers caught the Israeli government by the surprise—but it also triggered a reaction among officials at the American consulate in Jerusalem, who dispatched a message to the State Department saying they "can foresee being caught in a squeeze to issue visas promptly combined with the necessity to conduct careful and possibly time-consuming security checks, all to [be accompanied by] full publicity." Controlling the export of Phantom fighter jets was different from curbing the spread of American radicalism around the world; ideas did not require much in order to take root abroad. The memo noted that the Israeli group had "at present no more than loose ties of sympathy with the American Black Panthers." Indeed, the ties were so loose that it took until their fifth protest, on July 5, 1971, for the Israeli Panthers to start using the iconic clenched fist as a symbol and even then, they didn't credit the American Panthers for the image.

"We copied the fist from the Jewish Defense League," Panther leader Kochavi Shemesh told the *Jerusalem Post,* referring to the extremist movement led by American rabbi Meir Kahane.

16

GOLDA'S SPEECH

HAVING THE BIGGEST BULLY PULPIT allows a speaker to amplify their speech and gives them outsize influence, regardless of whether what they say is made up of disingenuous arguments, distortions, or outright falsehoods. Meir was guilty of all three in the speech she gave on the last day of the parliamentary session on July 28, 1971, just before lawmakers went on summer recess. It was her formal report on the performance of her office. Foreign papers covered her speech and several Israeli dailies printed it verbatim. Almost a year had passed since the ceasefire agreement with Egypt, and Israel was experiencing an unusually long period of calm on its borders. "I see no need to give an update on foreign affairs," Meir said in her opening. "I see the need to address issues of internal social character."

The subject matter for the annual address earned Meir praise from *Jerusalem Post* editor Lea Ben-Dor: "For once, it concerned only home affairs. Mrs. Meir was as outspoken, as direct, as uncynical as only she can be . . . [offering] a reassuring mixture of total confidence in our general approach and admission of error or failure on some points." In the following days, the foreign press corps, whose understanding of Israel often came directly from the pages of the *Post*, echoed the same sentiment. The *New York Times* reported about "her deep voice rising in incredulity" that the country should find itself divided. The *Baltimore Sun* described Meir as a "representative of dour, uncomplaining pioneers" who founded the country, and the *Los Angeles Times* noted the speech came as "Israel's wartime cohesion has loosened markedly."

In her speech, she never mentioned the Panthers by name but did open her remarks attacking the "exaggeration and unfairness" expressed by "some." It was "unfortunate statements" that were to blame for the decline in Israel's social cohesion—rather than festering inequality. Meir acknowledged the Ashkenazi-Mizrahi divide but added, "there can be no greater distortion of the truth than to say that the existing situation is the result of Israeli policy—not to mention discrimination, heaven forbid."

In Meir's eyes, rather than the fault of deliberate policies, the blame for inequality fell on the Mizrahi immigrants themselves.

"[They] brought deprivation and discrimination with them in their baggage from their countries of origin," she said.

She proceeded to explain that in the 1950s, these countries "had not yet developed intellectually, industrially, and culturally. The arrival of our brothers and sisters from the Islamic countries to Israel has brought an end to the conditions of backwardness they were stuck in for generations."

The prime minister's view of recent history and political geography was not only racist, it was also fundamentally untrue. The Jews of the Middle East had been concentrated in cities like Baghdad, Istanbul, Cairo, and Casablanca, which were all much more metropolitan and industrialized than Tel Aviv was at the time. As would be documented in later years, waves of immigrants from these places arrived in Israel and saw their average levels of education and income drop and their

Prime Minister Golda Meir addresses the crowd at the April 1972 Mimouna festival in Jerusalem. The Panthers had prevented her from attending the previous year. The man in the light-colored suit and tie on the far right is Minister of Police Shlomo Hillel, while the man second from the left, in a dark suit and tie, is Shaul Ben Simhon, head of the Moroccan Immigrants Association. Dan Hadani Collection, The Pritzker Family National Photography Collection, The National Library of Israel.

rates of incarceration spike. Abergel would point to the absurdity and tragedy of Mizrahi mass incarceration with a rhetorical refrain, "Who had ever heard of a Jewish criminal in Morocco?"

Around the same time Meir addressed parliament on the country's socioeconomic problem, Abergel delivered his own speech on the topic. He provided an alternative narrative of Mizrahi immigration and absorption in Israel, one that would be validated by later sociological and historical research. Abergel gave the speech over a bullhorn during a July 5 demonstration of the Panthers. Only snippets of Abergel's speech survive, recorded in writing by the ethnographer studying the Panthers:

"In the 1950s, the government, which was mainly East European, brought immigrants from Oriental countries. The parties divided them up between themselves as if they were their property. They were abandoned in huts, thrown into development towns. When the Romanians came in 1956, they were taken into the big cities and they were given everything they needed. They had it all coming to them—we had nothing. So the gap grew. . . . Large families with many children are crowded together in appalling living conditions. They supply labor at a very cheap price and they supply fighters for the army. Disparity and deprivation become ingrained in such families and will remain so for many generations."

Abergel was saying that the discriminatory policies that Mizrahi immigrants faced when they arrived served to keep them marginalized now. He felt that something in Zionism was broken if people so loyal to the notion of Jewish peoplehood were treated the way that they were. There usually wasn't room in Zionist history for people like Abergel, who pointed out internal injustices. That's because the state, born of socialist pretensions, claimed to have a monopoly over such discourse. Or as Meir put it in her speech, "Zionism has always been imbued with the aspiration and struggle for social justice."

At some point in the middle of her speech, Meir's tone took a turn from conceited but lofty to indignant and self-righteous.

"It is a gross distortion of the truth to allege that the state's initiative in dealing with the problem of the backward strata is a result of vocal demonstrations which have taken place recently," she said. "Progress in housing, education, and health services was achieved through the supreme effort of the people and government of Israel, although the country never had one day free of anxiety for its security and survival."

In the conclusion to her speech, Meir seemed to return to blaming the poor for the conditions of their lives. "Personal effort is needed by those among us who themselves suffer from poverty," she said. "They must not allow themselves to constitute passive objects."

She was about to see more clearly than ever before what happens when "those among us" decide to stop being passive.

17

EFFIGY

IN MID-AUGUST, U.S. President Richard Nixon announced sweeping economic changes meant to preserve the global power of the dollar, delivering what became known as the Nixon Shock. With the end of the American policy of converting dollars held abroad into gold, the international monetary system was upended. In anticipation of chaos in the economy, the U.S. government ordered a freeze on prices and wages and added a tax on imports, which made foreign goods more expensive to buy. For Israel, the Nixon tariff meant a massive hit to a critical industry—almost half of all Israeli exports were cut diamonds.

Like all governments around the world, the Israeli government was working on a response. Finance Minister Pinchas Sapir spoke on the radio to break the news just after midnight on a Saturday night: the Israeli government had decided to devalue its national currency by 20 percent. The devaluation was designed to protect exporters, foreign investors, and those Israelis who were receiving Holocaust restitution payments from Germany. What devaluation meant to the common consumer, however, was waking up that morning to encounter higher prices on basic commodities like butter, milk, eggs, and sugar, as well as gasoline and household appliances.

It was an easy pivot for the Panthers. On the day of the price hikes, they were gathered at their headquarters preparing for a major demonstration that had been scheduled for the next day. The flyers they had put out promoted the event as a response to the government's "Moscow-style show trials" of members of the group, who were facing charges of unlawful assembly from previous demonstrations, now moving through the courts. The tone of the flyers was combative with phrases such as Malcolm X's "by any means necessary" and instructions on how to protect oneself from tear gas. One flyer ended with an ominous teaser: "Prepare for a surprise." But while the Panthers couldn't have anticipated the price hikes, they realized Sapir's new economic measures would be their most galvanizing issue and they seized on it, making new banners, which bore slogans such as "Down with the Devaluation Regime!"

The atmosphere on Sunday evening before the demonstration surprised the Panthers' ethnographer. She noted a "strange, suspended calmness" that stood in contrast to what she had seen during the previous weeks. She thought the Panthers were buckling under the dual pressures of the spotlight and their own expectations. After repeatedly vowing in the press, for example, to deliver their message to Jewish communities in the United States, they had suddenly decided to call off their trip. That decision was made because of the increasingly loud accusations of disloyalty, warning that the Panthers would air the country's dirty laundry abroad. To make matters worse, there were rumors that their flights were being paid for by dubious forces like the Soviet Union or even the Palestine Liberation Organization.

One of the most impactful voices against the Panthers came from within the group. Malka, who had desperately tried to gain a leadership

Panthers prepare posters on the floor of the municipal youth club known as the Basement ahead of a demonstration in Jerusalem in 1971. © Micha Bar-Am.

Abergel delivers a speech during a demonstration in Jerusalem in 1971. Digital image of photograph by Itzik (full name not provided by Israel Sun Inc.)/Israel Sun Ltd., from the Judaica Collection of the Harvard Library, Harvard University.

position, broke off from the Panthers around this time—the Panthers would say he was ousted—and created a competing group. He called it the Blue and White Panthers, adopting Israel's national colors to signal his patriotism.

Meanwhile, Marciano and his faction, who promoted a macho environment for the Panthers, felt they were "disappearing" because weeks had gone by without a street demonstration. They believed that staging protests and confronting police were the goals of a muscular movement, and so they decided to plan a new one. As they loitered in their clubhouse one night, Marciano coined a refrain that would surface again and again in social justice struggles in Israel: "Either we'll have our share of the pie—or there will be no pie!"

The following day provided additional symbols and metaphors for the canon of radical Israeli politics. The backdrop was familiar by now: hundreds of people gathered at Davidka Square with the usual Panthers delivering speeches. Eager to provoke, the demonstrators made sure the television cameras captured their newest posters, which depicted the iconography of ramped-up militancy: the clenched black fist salute against a white background in the style of the American Panthers. The largest poster of all, positioned near the microphone, depicted a caricature of a naked, big-bellied Golda Meir. She had wings and an elongated nose like that of Pinocchio. Above her figure, the poster proclaimed, "Golda, Golda, Fly Away Already, Everyone is Sick of You."

Soon, the rally devolved into a traffic-stopping march zigzagging through downtown without regard to the route agreed upon with police. Amid the usual ruckus, the Panthers were carrying out their plan for a new surprise. A pickup truck slipped past the notice of police and slid into a side alley where several Panthers were standing by. In the bed of the truck, there were three long black boxes. They looked like coffins—they were coffins, a stark choice given the Israeli sensitivity around death and burial symbols.

The Panthers demonstrate in Jerusalem on August 23, 1971, carrying coffins that would later be lit on fire in a ritual funeral for discrimination. © Micha Bar-Am.

The Panthers in the alley unloaded the boxes, raised them high above their heads and joined back with the marching protesters, giving the crowd a distinct new silhouette. On one of the boxes floating above the swarm of heads was the word "discrimination" painted in white block letters. According to the Panthers' plans, the other two coffins were supposed to carry the words "ignorance" and "disparity," but for some reason that has been lost to time, they were sent out blank.

By the time the march reached Zion Square, the crowd had grown into the thousands. "Never had I seen, not even on Independence Day, so many people," Panther Kochavi Shemesh said sometime later. The police kept their distance and the energy of the crowd seemed to wane. To save the protest from dissipating aimlessly, Shemesh, a rising leader in the group, took the microphone and announced the Panthers would occupy the square until the finance minister arrived. "We will not move from here until Sapir himself comes and promises us a special

The effigy depicting Prime Minister Golda Meir was displayed during the August 23, 1971, demonstration of the Panthers and lit on fire as protestors clashed with police. Digital image of photograph by Itzik (full name not provided by Israel Sun Inc.)/Israel Sun Ltd., from the Judaica Collection of the Harvard Library, Harvard University.

cost of living allowance to poor families—and we'll determine the amount," he said. "We won't move until Sapir comes and gives an account to the people." After that, one of the Panthers lit a match. He held it to the banner displaying the caricature of Golda Meir, lighting it in effigy, until flames began consuming her image, naked belly, wings, elongated Pinocchio nose and all.

The fire grew as people fed it cardboard and any flammable thing they could find. The light emanating from the flames was a boon for photojournalists, an opportunity to capture the chaos after nightfall. The scene crystallized in one particularly enduring image from the era of the Panthers. On the right side of the frame is the fire, burning narrow and tall. In center frame, a stack of portable police barricades. Young men stand atop the barricades with their backs to the camera and their faces unseen. In the foreground, a figure of a Panther pops out. He's the only one facing the camera. His sideburns extend nearly to his mouth, framing furrowed eyebrows and a stern expression. This Panther is also holding a stick and wearing a necklace from which dangles a large Star of David.

He is no one famous, not Marciano or Abergel, but his identity is unmistakable: his black t-shirt is emblazoned with white letters spelling who and what he is: "Black Panther." Amram Cohen would largely be forgotten even though his militancy epitomized a certain image of the Panthers as violent thugs and arsonists, with one newspaper comparing the scene in the square to a European pogrom. But Cohen's moment of fame can also be read differently. In the photo, he is flanked by one of the caskets, and just barely visible is the word "discrimination." Moments after the camera shutter snapped, the crowd threw the casket into the pyre. For Cohen, this was supposed to be a funeral for discrimination.

Whatever image the Panthers hoped to project, what they managed to do is send Israeli decision-makers into further indignation and desperation. The morning after the protest, a parliamentary committee summoned police leaders for an "urgent" meeting. They wanted to know how the police had lost control of the crowd and what was being done to capture the activists and mete out punishment. "How do these boys make a living?" one lawmaker asked. "Who funds them? Is there someone driving them?" Another lawmaker said he was worried about the group expanding beyond Jerusalem. "This is spreading to every place with a concentration of Mizrahi Jews," he said. The meeting soon devolved into a chorus of condemnation:

"We must know that they represent nothing that is just. The group cares only for itself and has no right to exist. We must fight them."

"If there are citizens who want to bring a pogrom upon the public, we must punish them to the fullest extent of the law."

"We can no longer allow them to exist as a public presence."

The 23 people arrested during the demonstration were mostly minor figures or not part of the movement at all. The charges filed against them varied and included items such as violating the terms of the license to demonstrate, taking part in an illegal demonstration, and conspiring to take part in an illegal demonstration. Under pressure from parliament, the police now mounted a hunt for the leaders of the Panthers, who had all managed to evade the cops. It wasn't hard to get them. Abergel and Shemesh surrendered themselves within a day or two.

But three of the wanted Panthers, Marciano, Biton, Avichzer, plus their American friend, Ronny Horowitz, decided to run. Late at night, after the protest, they met on a soccer field and then dispersed, each passing the night by hiding on a roof or in some dark corner. In the morning, they met up again and took a car out of town. The next ten days would be spent at the homes of various girlfriends and allies, mostly in the Tel Aviv area. In an attempt to evoke or emulate revolutionary glamour, the Panthers called their escape "going underground." The Panthers' ethnographer didn't take this episode very seriously, writing that "the police could put an end to the whole escapade whenever they really wanted to." She was implying that detectives were able to track them. Whether that was true or not, the situation managed to entice the press. Journalists from nearly every paper found ways to rendezvous with the underground Panthers, scoring not-so-exclusive interviews. One reporter asked Marciano what he thought would be waiting for him when he finally resurfaced. Marciano responded, "violence and beatings from the police."

In the rhetoric of the left, the polemic released from prison is king. But a close runner-up is the missive smuggled from a place of hiding. And the Panthers leaned into the romanticism of the indignant political fugitive. "The real defendants should be those responsible for poverty, backwardness, and illiteracy—not us. They are the ones who

Several Panthers who had gone into hiding to evade arrest following the August 23, 1971, demonstration are interviewed by the press at an apartment serving as a secret refuge. Digital image of photograph by Uzi Keren/Israel Sun Ltd., from the Judaica Collection of the Harvard Library, Harvard University.

should be put on trial," Marciano was quoted as saying. And in a pamphlet written while in hiding, the Panthers threatened escalation: "If it becomes impossible to eradicate poverty under this regime of discrimination and racism, we will eradicate the regime."

After ten days, when they finally decided to turn themselves in, Marciano was seen wearing a black shirt with the words "By any means necessary—Malcolm X."

Quoting Malcolm X. Fighting riot squads in the streets. Burning an effigy of the prime minister. Making the police's most-wanted list. Issuing threats from the underground. The Panthers worked hard to hone their image as revolutionaries. In court, a few days after the last Panthers surrendered to police, the prosecutor asked the judge to extend the detention of the Panthers for five more days, and the judge agreed. The Panthers erupted into yelling, shouting at the judge and calling the prosecutor a liar.

For all their antics, the Panthers were rewarded with significant public support and recognition. A survey commissioned by the London newspaper *Jewish Chronicle* and published a day after the Panthers emerged from hiding provided rare empirical data on the Panthers' popularity. Only about 3 percent of respondents had not heard of the Panthers. Another 12 percent said they didn't know what the Panthers wanted or declined to express an opinion. The vast majority of Israelis, however, had a position on the Panthers, according to the survey. Support for the Panthers was at about 40 percent and opposition slightly higher, at 44 percent. Support among Mizrahim was higher, reaching about 50 percent compared to 33 percent among Ashkenazim.

The growing relevance of the Panthers was marked by a cover story in the magazine section of the September 12 edition of the *New York Times,* authored by Israeli journalist Amos Elon. An image of Marciano, pleading the Panthers' case on the street with a passerby, is featured under the marquee masthead of American journalism. The text is eloquent but provides little reporting about the Panthers themselves, focusing more on the complicated moral position of the Israeli establishment, who are said to be struggling to maintain Israel's egalitarian ethos. The increasingly visible rift between Ashkenazim and Mizrahim, Elon, himself Ashkenazi, writes, "[has] given birth to a crisis of consciousness" among the country's leading intellectuals and politicians. Who's to blame for the inequality? The Mizrahim themselves, according to Elon: "Though egalitarianism was deeply embedded in the ideology of the early Zionist pioneers, the importation of enormous poverty and ignorance with the massive immigration from such areas as Morocco, Tunisia, Libya, Iraq, Iran, and Kurdistan, seriously jeopardized some of the more utopian dreams."

Elon's disregard for the Panthers' actual arguments and his blindness to Israel's rampant racism also comes across in his disregard for basic facts. In the central anecdote of the article, Elon describes the scene of a televised protest in front of Jerusalem's city hall, the one that took place March 3, 1971. He describes seeing Marciano, "the young protest leader," who "stood in the blazing sun," his "smooth face twisted into a grimace of resentment and frustration." What's bizarre about these details is that Marciano was not at that protest. He was behind bars on administrative detention. The arrest of Marciano and his friends was the reason for the demonstration. It appears that Elon fabricated the event he described—perhaps by making a composite out of several disparate incidents—not caring to understand the Panthers' motivations even when ostensibly writing an article about the group.

A writer who concerned himself with the Panthers and not just with the headache they had caused Israel's establishment might have recognized an arc emerging. In the first protest in early 1971, the Panthers targeted city hall and the mayor in their attempt to hold someone accountable for the conditions of poverty in their communities. In the next major protest, they occupied Jerusalem's most central area, Zion Square, staking out a larger claim. There, they fought against police battalions under the command of Shlomo Hillel, the Iraqi-born minister of police. But neither the mayor nor the police were at the root of their grievances, and neither possessed the power to enact meaningful change. For their next target of scorn, they aimed higher—and deeper into the political system. Now occupying Zion Square for a second time, the Panthers demanded an immediate audience with Finance Minister Pinchas Sapir, whose policies, they had discovered, had pervasive consequences for Mizrahim and how they fared in the economy. By the end of that night, the Panthers graduated to targeting the prime minister, burning her effigy in protest.

This progression reflects not only a growing political savviness but also an enchantment with radicalism. It was no longer just the Israeli anti-Zionists of Matzpen who courted the Panthers. Now, the Panthers became the first port of call for left-wing radicals visiting from Europe and the United States. One such caller had arrived a few months earlier. His name was Massimo Pieri and he was a Jewish Italian activist.

After meeting the Panthers, he invited them to his country for an international summit, hosted by a group called Potere Operaio, or Workers' Power, that would soon take place with delegates from across the world. The Panthers were to represent the Israeli left; the conference's organizers offered to pay for one flight ticket. Abergel was selected as the group's representative but he ended up backing out, and Biton was chosen to replace him. Joining Biton were two Panthers who would pay their own fare, Eli Avichzer and Dani Sa'il.

The conclave took place at the Stensen Institute in Florence and was supposed to be a secret gathering with each delegate discussing the level of revolutionary potential in their country. The Israeli delegation betrayed their relative political moderation when they disclosed to a reporter the details of a trip that was supposed to be secret. On the day of departure, Biton was quoted making a promise that was at odds with the notion of young radicals venturing abroad for a secret meeting of revolutionaries. "We are not going to speak about foreign policy and security problems because we have no position on them," Biton said. "We are just going to talk about the problems of discrimination towards Oriental Jewry and poverty in Israel." In other words, he wouldn't talk about the Palestinians or Israel's conflicts with its neighbors.

The Panthers at times expressed this parochial view of politics for fear of alienating supporters among Israel's largely ultra-nationalist populace. The coalition that the Panthers were going to encounter in Florence would likely have regarded Biton's comments as a form of pandering given that the Italian coalition included hardcore radicals: a leftist offshoot of the Irish Republican Army, the Revolutionärer Kampf of Berlin, a Cuban-backed group from the Dominican Republic, and separatists from Switzerland and France. The gathering even featured a three-hour lecture by Irish revolutionary Seamus Costello on urban guerrilla warfare and sabotage.

The Israelis did, however, share something fundamental with one of the conference's delegations: their name. This was the first meeting between Panthers from Israel and those from the United States. It's hard to imagine what language they used to communicate and the only trace of the details of the exchange is a brief article in an Israeli newspaper a month after the meeting happened. Biton reportedly asked the Americans for moral support and told them that Israel faces a similar problem of "discrimination against the blacks." The Americans, he said, reported that they held a press conference to express support for the struggle of "the blacks" in Israel. It would be years before the Israelis and their namesake would meet again.

When Biton arrived in Europe, he was out of sync with his global leftist peers, but he returned to Israel transformed. "The meeting with activists had a great impact on [Biton], and he became a strong advocate of long-term organizational work among the poor and workers," the Panthers' ethnographer wrote. "He called for more ideological debates and greater ideological clarity. That included, for him, a clear stand against class exploitation and against Zionism, which he equated with the current social order."

Not many details of this period were recorded, and many of those who were there have either passed away or their memories have faded. Some documentation of the Panthers' increasing radicalization does exist, thanks, ironically, to a miscalculation by a venerated Zionist organization. Hadassah, a women's group based in New York City, was preparing to celebrate its 60th anniversary just as the Panthers were marking their first one. It was the winter of 1972, and Hadassah had commissioned a videographer to capture footage of modern Jerusalem, the Israeli capital where Hadassah had focused its philanthropic work for decades, feeding the hungry, establishing clinics, hospitals and a youth center, and sponsoring a stained-glass installation by famed Jewish painter Marc Chagall. In planning its anniversary exhibition party,

Hadassah was hoping for a stately and prideful reflection of the city on film. Given that goal, it was an odd choice to hire David Cort, the founder of a radical artist collective called Videofreex.

Videofreex grew out of a technological breakthrough in the late 1960s when Sony released the Portapak, a handheld video recorder that allowed instant playback. Until that moment, video production involved cumbersome equipment and required the resources of television and movie studios. A precursor to today's ubiquitous smartphone cameras, the Portapak was embraced by a movement of people who were part of the wider counterculture and thought of themselves as guerrilla videographers. Cort was the guerrilla leader. "I was overwhelmed by the lightness of the portable video camera, the intimacy of it, the way you could talk from behind the camera to people, and they could talk to you," Cort said years later.

Before landing in Jerusalem, he had captured Woodstock on film and interviewed iconic firebrand Abbie Hoffman. He also filmed an interview with the head of the Chicago branch of the Black Panthers, Fred Hampton, a month before police raided Hampton's apartment and fatally shot him. When Cort looked for scenes and subjects in Israel, he scanned the local zeitgeist. Alongside footage of the mayor, Wailing Wall worshippers, archeological digs, brain studies, and children playing soccer to satisfy Hadassah, Cort included intimate vignettes with Israeli draft dodgers and the Panthers of Musrara.

The 12 hours of video, which were screened in their entirety at the Jewish Museum in New York City, were titled, "The Word from Jerusalem." Hadassah's reaction was mixed, and the press largely ignored the event, with some of the only coverage appearing in the alternative newsweekly the *Village Voice*. Rather than depict the sheen of a triumphant Israel, Cort's work reveals how Zionism was being rocked by challenges from within. Young Israelis of privileged backgrounds were defying military conscription. Those of no privilege were accusing the whole system of being almost hopelessly unjust.

In the footage, Cort walks Jerusalem, guided by two young men from each side of the spectrum. There is Meir Wigoder, the Ashkenazi friend to the Panthers, who acts as an interpreter and explains the political role of hashish in bringing otherwise disconnected people together, and he is juxtaposed with Black Panther Moshe Amuyal, an introspective young man with long sideburns and Elvis-styled hair.

They take Cort on a tour of the poorest parts of Jerusalem, voyeurs into the homes of people who sleep three to a bed and cook on the floor. But it's not among the poor that Cort encounters Israel's ugliness. It's at a dinner party of the bourgeois. As the special guest of the evening, Cort tells the apparently Ashkenazi crowd about his visit to a family of two parents and ten children living in a cramped tenement-style apartment. The response is incredulous. He is told the family is faking its own poverty: "the trip was as framed up as could be," one of the dinner guests asserts, without explaining why someone would bother putting on a charade of suffering. In another scene of guerrilla television, Cort meets a young teenage boy hanging out on the street who says he is Panther. Amuyal asks him how the police treat him. "They grab us for no reason," the boy replies. "They beat us up, even on the balls. They grab you by the balls and take a small rubber tube and they hit you on the balls. So, you break and admit to having done things you didn't even do."

The footage lacks both editing and narration and the camera angles are as awkward as the image is grainy. Yet, the scenes do build up toward a moment of perceptible tension. In the final moments, the Panthers are preparing for a demonstration. Several Panthers predict a "strong response from the public" and 5,000 demonstrators. After lackluster attendance at the group's previous protest in Tel Aviv, these statements seem less like promises to Cort than their own attempt at self-assurances.

The following day, about 700 people gathered at Jerusalem's Menora Square, a smaller area than Zion Square but within easy walking distance of it. The protest was eventful enough, but what made Cort's footage significant was not the face-off with the police. Perhaps without even realizing it, Cort had captured a shift in the Panthers' rhetoric and their evolution toward a more radical political vision. This shift was led by Kochavi Shemesh, one of the few outside the Musrara set—he wasn't Moroccan, but Iraqi—to earn the group's confidence. Raised in a nearby slum, he had virtually no schooling. Even without a formal education, however, he had become literate enough to publish a community weekly newspaper in the late 1960s covering sports and human-interest stories. Under an Israeli law that remained in effect until 2017, Shemesh wasn't eligible for a permit that was required to operate a newspaper because he didn't have a high school diploma. And so, after only seven illegally published issues, the police arrested him and shut down the periodical. A judge gave Shemesh the choice of paying a small fine or serving a three-week prison sentence. On principle, he chose prison.

In Cort's footage, Shemesh speaks over a sea of faces, delivering a speech. "It's clear the Zionist Congress does not speak for all the Jews in the world," he says. "The Zionist Congress cares only about Russian Jewry."

A year earlier, the Panthers were a group of slum youths who were angry but because they were not exactly sure who to blame, they targeted the closest symbol of authority they could find. Now, the Panthers were confronting the Zionist movement as the root of their grievances. The organizers of the Zionist Congress had denied a request by the Panthers to testify few days earlier. Shemesh responded with a threat: "If they don't let the Panthers speak, no one will speak at the Congress."

18

KAHANISTS AND COMMUNISTS

ANOTHER RADICAL GROUP also demanded to speak at the Congress. It was the Jewish Defense League, led by the fanatical American rabbi Meir Kahane. At the time, the rabidly anti-Arab JDL was focused on getting the Soviet Union to allow its Jewish citizens to leave. But before Kahane started pressing Zionist leadership on the Soviet Jewry issue, he had fashioned himself a militant in a different context. He stylized himself as the defender of American Jews against what he regarded as widespread antisemitism among Black Americans. As Jewish-Black tensions flared up in Brooklyn in the late 1960s, he made the American Black Panthers his political enemy, and street fights between the two groups broke out on several occasions.

As Kahane's followers fought against the Panthers, they also mimicked their style. The JDL flashed clenched fists, vowed to defend Jews by "any means necessary," and sometimes referred to themselves as the "Jewish Panthers." They emulated the military discipline of the Panthers and even once consulted a Black Panther Party instruction manual to fabricate a small bomb. In Israel, Kahane's admiration for the aesthetics of Black Power did not translate into affinity with the Panthers of Musrara. Even though both groups felt sidelined by the institutions of mainstream Zionism, they did not turn to cooperation with each other. And soon they clashed.

It was mid-1972, and activists from the two groups would often run into each other in the city. There were only so many pinball arcades, late-night bars, and coffee shops that tolerated young men hanging out and arguing over politics for hours on end. The activists would trade insults, with JDL guys mocking the Panthers for spelling mistakes on their posters, deriding them as communist stooges, or calling them traitors for not showing up to demonstrations in solidarity with the Jews facing persecution in Syria or the Soviet Union

The barbs escalated as each side threatened the other. One night, a group of Panthers drove out to Rehavia, the wealthy district where the JDL had set up its new Israeli headquarters. But detectives were on their trail and eventually arrested four Panthers lurking outside the JDL headquarters. Police reported discovering two Molotov cocktails in the trunk of their car and said the Panthers were suspected of trying to break in and rampage through the JDL offices. That was hardly the end of the aggressions, but it's unclear from the historical record exactly what went on to happen. The Panthers would later boast that they did in the end raid the JDL offices, attacking the people inside and trashing the place. Perhaps to save face, the Kahanists never gave their own version of events, but simply retorted, "we have proven ourselves against greater threats."

As he established himself in Israel over the following years, Kahane carved out a home on the far right of Israeli politics and founded a new political party called Kach. Its flag was yellow, emblazoned with a fist set against the silhouette of the Jewish Star of David. He openly advocated for ethnic cleansing through the expulsion of the Palestinian population in Israel and its newly conquered territories. To stoke racial panic, he borrowed an American-tested tactic. Jewish women, he said repeatedly, must be protected from being seduced or raped by Arab men. In 1984, he would try to pass an anti-miscegenation law "for the preservation of the sanctity of the people of Israel." Kahane thought he would find a constituency among the impoverished Mizrahi classes so he borrowed from the rhetoric of the Panthers, blaming Ashkenazim (he himself was Ashkenazi) for their poverty and high rates of incarceration. Eventually, his party would be banned by Israel and listed by the U.S. State Department as a terrorist organization.

On the streets and in other venues, the Kahanists and the Panthers remained political enemies. In 1985, Marciano would try to curb the fanatic rabbi's influence among Mizrahim by producing a short film. In *Kahanism and the Cuckoo's Nest,* Kahane is a patient at a mental institution where the ghost of Adolf Hitler appears to give lectures to the other patients. Spellbound by Hitler, Kahane riles up the asylum and stages a mass escape. They all march on parliament to launch a campaign of racist destruction. "Kahanism is a social disease," Marciano said in an interview about the film, "and the sad part is that many Mizrahim don't realize they are infected."

While the Panthers consistently stood on the opposite end of the political spectrum from Kahanism, they didn't quite fit in with their own side—the left. In the 1970s, leftists in the West were splintering, and the most radical of them came to embrace spectacular and violent tactics. Marching and picketing were giving way to bombs and kidnappings. In the United States, for example, Students for a Democratic Society fell apart as some of its activists went on to found the Weather Underground. This group staged jailbreaks, issued a "Declaration of a State of War" against the United States, and set off explosives in government buildings. It was also the era of plane hijackings, with an average of three a month for more than a decade. With a name like the Panthers, the boys from Musrara sounded like local representatives of the global revolutionary vanguard, and they were sought out by foreign revolutionaries.

This revolution arrived in Israel in earnest on the night of May 30, 1972, in the form of three young Japanese radicals, members of the Japanese Red Army. They disembarked from an Air France flight from Rome with violin cases in their arms. Upon reaching the arrivals area of the Lod Airport near Tel Aviv, the three opened their violin cases and pulled out assault rifles. They sprayed the crowd with bullets. As they reloaded their rifles with fresh magazines, they pulled out grenades and tossed them. They murdered 26 people and injured 79. In the aftermath, the press found out that someone posing as a Japanese journalist had met with the Panthers a few months earlier. The suspicion was that he was a Red Army member who had come to Israel as part of the planning for the airport plot. Reached for comment, Shemesh, the emerging Panther leader, acknowledged that groups like the Red Army saw the Israeli Panthers as potential allies in violent activities. "If they only knew the truth, they would have never approached us," Shemesh said. "We do everything to avoid harm to human life. To this day, we have succeeded. We have managed to restrain hot-headed individuals who want to engage in terrorism, and try to explain that our struggle is political and not terroristic."

The distinction Shemesh tried to draw between terrorism and politics is one that Israelis have always emphasized—to better distinguish between the violence of the Israeli military and that of Palestinian militants. In those years, the Palestinian struggle was organized and armed and, increasingly, at the center of global attention. The apex came during the 1972 Summer Olympics in Munich. Before dawn on September 5, eight Palestinian militants organized by the Black September movement infiltrated the Olympic Village. Opening their duffel bags, they pulled out assault rifles, pistols, and grenades and made their way to the apartments where the Israeli delegation was staying. The attack turned into one of the most infamous hostage situations in history and ended 20 hours later with the deaths of 11 Olympic coaches and athletes. In Israel, the tragic event unfolded on television, touching every home. For the Panthers, it was especially personal because of their connection to one of the victims. Some months earlier, a few of the Panthers, including Abergel and Rafi Marciano, had taken a break from activism to train as sports educators at the prestigious Wingate Academy. There, they learned both pedagogy and fencing, studying under fencing master Andre Spitzer, who was killed in the Munich attack.

So when Shemesh pleaded for the Panthers to be seen as a political group but not an extremist one, he was trying to distance the group from any association with the Palestinian movement that Israelis saw as their enemy. It was not easy for the Panthers to assert a place in the global New Left and remain within the narrow confines of the sort of politics Israelis could tolerate. Shemesh was again caught in the middle a year later.

East Berlin was the host of the 1973 World Festival of Youth and Students, an event that became known as the Red Woodstock. The official motto uniting the 25,000 participants was "For Anti-Imperialist Solidarity, Peace and Friendship." From Israel came a delegation of Communist Party members, and Shemesh joined them. One of the headliners of the event was Angela Davis, who had been fashioned into a popular hero in East Germany, an iconic figure representing the American underclasses. In one of the only interactions between a figure of the U.S. Black Power movement and an Israeli Panther, Davis and Shemesh met on the sidelines of the Red Woodstock. The encounter was not documented but Shemesh relished meeting her and said so on many occasions, including to anyone who chatted with him at Café Ta'amon. Over a bottle of arak a few months after he returned from East Berlin, Shemesh and *New York Times* correspondent Victor Perera talked politics. In explaining his anti-Zionist bona fides, Shemesh mentioned that he had recently visited communist Europe and spoke "with obvious delight of a visit paid him by Angela Davis." According to an account of the encounter Shemesh shared many years later, he used the Israeli term "black labor" to describe the menial employment available to Mizrahim, and Davis chastised him for using the phrase.

Perhaps less comfortable for Shemesh's politics was another headline guest at the festival: Yasser Arafat. As chairman of the Palestine Liberation Organization, Arafat was the leading figure in the Palestinian struggle against Israel. He had condemned the Munich attack but the condemnation was tainted by the fact that the Black September faction, which carried out the attack, belonged to Arafat's PLO. Arafat and Shemesh didn't meet each other in East Berlin. But just by participating in the same conference, Shemesh got about as close as any Israeli at the time to recognizing the Palestinian cause as a legitimate one.

If Shemesh managed to remain at all within the Israeli pale, his friend and political fellow traveler Yehezkel Cohen did not. Cohen had been a Panther, joining early and participating in the first protests and meetings. But he soon found the Panthers to be too moderate and he faded out of view. His parents thought him depressed since he was 30 and a university graduate but seemingly resigned to working as a clerk at a Tel Aviv motel. In early December of 1972, the police came looking for Cohen and found him playing chess with friends. They arrested him, and, a few days later, the entire country learned why.

The police announced the discovery of a spy ring, operating on behalf of Syrian intelligence. The group called itself the Red Front cell and was described as the Arab-Jewish Network because it was made up of Palestinian Arabs as well as Jewish Israelis. Cohen was one of the four Jews. He was caught, reportedly, just before a planned flight to Damascus for training. Following the capture of the Red Front, much of the public attention focused on the figure of Udi Adiv. His act of treason came as a shock because he was not only a sabra, or born in

Israel, but the product of a kibbutz and a former paratrooper. In other words, he was an Ashkenazi who came from deep within the country's establishment. From an ethnic and ideological perspective, Cohen's identity was murkier. He blurred the dichotomy expressed by the hyphen in the "Arab-Jewish Network"—because Cohen could be said to occupy both ends. He was born in Iraq and raised there until he was nine. His disillusionment with Israel was the result not just of a left-wing worldview but of the barriers of racism that he encountered within Israeli institutions and society.

"Of the four Jewish members, I knew one well," Shemesh wrote at the time. "He is still considered a friend . . . [Cohen] blamed Israel for destroying his life." For Shemesh, it was senseless to call Cohen and the other Jews traitors since they didn't see themselves as part of the country. Prosecuting them for treason wouldn't solve the problem because others would follow suit after reaching the same political conclusion. But Shemesh also went further than just defending the group's Jewish members. "Jewish-Arab solidarity is a noble ideal," he wrote. "Those who genuinely strive for this solidarity must be involved in a struggle for it . . . and since there are two sides in this struggle, the Israeli and the Palestinian—the true believers of justice will find themselves on the Palestinian side and will have to aid in the struggle all the way, until the goal is achieved."

Shemesh formulated his polemic just as the Panthers themselves were facing an existential political question. The group's appetite for further demonstrations was low. Their numbers had swelled at first, but now, two years after the Panthers' emergence from Musrara, the crowds had dwindled, even as a core group remained convinced as ever of the need for fundamental change. They were inevitably headed toward a decision about their future.

19

A COUNTRY TRANSFORMED

ONLY ABOUT 80 PEOPLE showed up to the Israeli Black Panthers' first national conclave. Many in the room were Ashkenazi allies, some of the same radicals that helped start the group. "Even a few Panthers showed up, of course," a journalist quipped, mocking the group's diminished state. The gathering took place in the basement of a nightclub. A poster with stenciled images of a panther and a tightened fist was tacked onto the wall, and in front of it sat the group's core leadership. "It's sad to see that we are so few," one of the Panthers said.

It had been months since the last demonstration, and for that matter, since the group had done anything, on purpose, to garner publicity. The organizing activity had come to a standstill with few meetings and no new initiatives. Once-active members peeled off. The sociology student writing her dissertation on the Panthers considered the stalemate an appropriate point to conclude her ethnographic fieldwork—

her time with them, it seemed, had lent itself to a classic rise-and-fall narrative. The core organizers were saddled with criminal charges from their arrests after protests going back nearly two years. In addition to the repeated detentions of leaders, the legal system burdened the Panthers with fines and court fees. Summonses for new court dates kept arriving, followed by trials, which required the recruitment of pro bono lawyers or the raising of donations to hire legal representation.

Among themselves, some of the Panthers were blaming Abergel for sapping the group's energy. He didn't participate in this gathering and he had been gone much of the past year studying fencing at Wingate along with a handful of other Panthers. They were placed there with scholarships from a new welfare program that allowed them to bypass the institute's elite admission requirements. Abergel, with his third-grade education, was training to become a credentialed teacher of physical education.

The image of a Mizrahi slum dweller like Abergel clad in a white uniform and mesh mask partaking in an aristocratic sport provided the framing for breathless coverage in several newspapers on the rehabilitation of the backward classes. Abergel and the others also studied physiology, anatomy, and psychology, as well as pedagogical methods and theories of leadership. When he returned to Musrara, Abergel opened an after-school center with municipal funding where he mentored youths to get them off the streets. He saw no conflict between being a government worker and being a Panther. A reporter who found him one day at work described a crowd of ten-year-old boys clamoring for his attention. "Look," Abergel told the reporter, "demonstrations don't change anything. Oh, yes, there was a time when we needed to shout. But we don't need spontaneous demonstrations now. We need goals, we need to start solving problems. We are dealing here with a youth that is already half-broken by the conditions they've grown up in."

Abergel's critics, some of whom were now assembled in the dingy discotheque, considered him a sellout, but they, too, were facing the question of what should follow the spectacle of the protests. They wanted to sustain the movement and they needed to get organized. If delivering social services to the community wasn't the answer, what would be? Running for parliament, perhaps. The idea was brought up for a vote. It was not the obvious next step considering that the Panthers' rhetoric had centered on being outsiders to the political system. They had peppered their public statements with threats to overthrow the regime. The Panthers would be exposing themselves to charges of hypocrisy after denigrating Mizrahi politicians as ethnic traitors and lackeys.

There was also the issue of winning. The Panthers would have to earn the votes of tens of thousands of people to secure even a single seat in parliament. Winning would require full-time campaigning and organizational discipline; the Panthers had shown themselves to be improvisational, mercurial, and erratic. A lot would be at stake: losing would undercut one of the main ideas animating the movement, that the Panthers had the support of the impoverished and unheard-from Mizrahi masses. Meanwhile, the track record for parties that tried to court the ethnic vote was abysmal. In Israel's first two elections, parties claiming to represent Yemenite Jews and Sephardic Jews gained a handful of parliamentary seats, but those gains were fleeting, and in subsequent elections, no ethnic party had managed to win any seats.

Despite the long odds and risks, the group, which was whoever had decided to show up that day, voted 77 to 3 to run for office.

In the Israeli electoral system, whichever political party or coalition of parties secures a majority of seats in the country's 120-seat parliament has the right to form a government. Most of the population always voted for either of the two main Zionist parties, one on the left and one on the right. The dominant party could hope to form a majority by partnering with one or more of the niche factions in parliament, usually the religious bloc. The Panthers had no chance of upending the basic system, but they could, in theory, collect enough of a protest vote to make it past the electoral threshold, which was set at 1 percent of all votes. Any party failing to secure at least 1 percent was out and its votes were discarded. The goal of the threshold, common to parliamentary systems of government, was to keep the number of parties entering parliament at a reasonable level. So if the Panthers succeeded in conquering this hurdle, they would be putting themselves in a position to sway the parliamentary calculus.

The money the Panthers needed to run for office appeared about a month later, thanks, ironically, to a decision by the government they had been fighting against. A new law had just been passed entitling existing political parties to public funding for their campaigns. For lawmaker Shalom Cohen, this produced an opportunity. He was a party of one, an exile from his prior partnership with Uri Avnery. He now had money but no movement of people behind him. He proposed an alliance, and the Panthers accepted. The new party's name was the Black Panthers–Israeli Democrats, or Dai for short. The word "Dai" served both sides of the partnership nicely: it means "enough," which was the Panther's mantra, and it's also the Hebrew acronym for Cohen's "Israeli Democrats." Even in partnership, however, there was a hierarchy. Cohen's name topped the party list, Marciano's came second.

As the new figurehead, Cohen went about translating the rhetoric of "by any means necessary" into the register of conventional politics. For example, when asked if the party disavowed violence, he responded: "If an oppressed majority in some development town should take it into their own hands to secure their rights, we shall not regard that as violence but as an expression of the majority will." Dai's political platform didn't get much attention—but it should have. In it were universal health insurance, increased welfare support for the poor, and the abolition of a departure tax which made it prohibitively expensive for many working-class people to travel abroad. A few months into the campaign, Dai called on Israel's president to pardon all prisoners in the country. "With this significant official gesture, using your authority as the uniter of the nation, you could start to heal the wound afflicting all of Israeli society, not just the incarcerated," the party said.

This call for universal amnesty can be seen as a precursor to the prison abolition movement of recent years—to the extent that the Panthers were serious about it. That they would have supported the abolition is certain, but whether they believed in it as a tangible political goal is unclear. Their letter was sent to the president, who apparently ignored it. From Dai, there was no follow-up, at least not in those years, making it seem less like a principled position and more like the overall tone of their campaign, based as it was on headline-grabbing stunts. The group also produced a campaign film formatted as a documentary. Directed by Nissim Mossek, the 38-minute black-and-white film follows some Panthers as they enter the homes of the poorest people they could find, often while they were sleeping. Catching vulnerable people unaware on film for political propaganda is exploitative, but in those days, it also passed as provocative, especially under the ethical cover of the Panthers' own poverty. For another caper, the group unilaterally announced a flash sale at a supermarket chain located in one of Jerusalem's Mizrahi neighborhoods by pasting discounted price tags on staple items and inviting the locals to raid the store.

In one symbolic regard, the Central Elections Committee of Israel had no choice but to help Dai amplify its posturing and attitude. Each party running for office in Israel registers for the exclusive use of a letter (or two or three letters) as its election symbol. The letters appear on campaign posters and official candidate lists, and ultimately they are printed in large type on voting slips in the ballots on election day. When Cohen went to register the party, he picked the letter *zayin*. The word "zayin" translates as "weapon" but more commonly means "penis," or something like "fuck you." It was the first time a party had chosen the letter *zayin* as its symbol. As Cohen explained, "No one dared pick that letter all these years. We took it because this showed we were challenging Israeli society."

Almost three years had passed since Israel's last military confrontation, the so-called War of Attrition with Egypt. The start of the quiet period that followed corresponded with the early period of Meir's tenure as prime minister, and it was then she faced the dilemma of what to do about the Musrara boys who wanted to stage a protest. She bungled that decision, authorizing their detention and sparking an outcry that taught the budding activists an important lesson and launched their movement. But their subsequent efforts to portray her as a villain largely failed. In early 1973, polls showed that three-quarters of Israelis wanted her to run for office again. She initially said she would retire when her term ended, which made sense considering that at age 75, Meir was suffering from migraines, kidney stones, gallbladder attacks, and a relapse of lymphoma. But Meir loved serving as prime minister. It energized her; her young aides buckled under the pressure of the work schedule and she still did not. Moreover, the Labor Party needed her. By remaining at the helm, she could forestall the split emerging between two generations of Labor leadership.

When she finally announced her candidacy in the summer, Meir set the tone for the coming campaign season. Security concerns seemed to be fading somewhat, and Meir hoped to focus on poverty and social welfare during her next term. "Plans are taking shape in my head on domestic matters and I want to get things moving on the inside [of the country]," Meir said in a July 5 speech to a gathering of the national teachers' union. The results of a survey of Israeli voters suggested that this issue was the right one to run on. Only 43 percent of respondents said national security was their top concern. Domestic issues like housing for young families, economic inequality, and poverty alleviation collectively ranked higher.

For all their antics, the Panthers could have, and probably should have, pointed to the string of tangible gains for social justice achieved by their movement going back two years. As historians would later confirm—and political insiders later admit—systemic change in Israeli welfare policy started after and in response to the appearance of the Panthers.

In March 1971 alone, meaning in the days and weeks following their first protest, the state treasury started to jangle, releasing millions to fund social services. Welfare Minister Michael Hazani, for example, announced a plan to assume some of the responsibility for street youths from the education ministry and local governments with a new $900,000 program. As one newspaper headline put it, "The Panthers helped the government find the budget."

A few days later, Minister of Finance Pinchas Sapir announced $23 million for daycare programs to assist large families and bring children off the streets. Then, Sapir made last-minute amendments to the proposed government budget, adding $1.4 million in bread subsidies; $1.7 million in grants to development areas; $3.4 million for housing in the border area; $2.9 million for youths with special needs; and $2 million for new daycare centers for large families. In presenting these numbers, Sapir talked about the Panthers. He wanted the cabinet to know that the budget adjustments were devised months prior, before anybody had heard of the Panthers. But this hardly changed the fact that the plans only came out of the drawer and were presented to the cabinet for approval after the appearance of the Panthers.

Days later, on April 1, more funding was reported in the news. The Ministry of Social Welfare granted the city of Jerusalem $300,000 for social workers and after-school enrichment programs in poor areas. The city's social welfare budget shot up by 30 percent as a result.

Not all the achievements were financial. In May 1971, when the Panthers were still only beginning to press for change, the Israeli military made an announcement. It would no longer categorically deny enlistment to youths possessing criminal records. Now, instead of a blanket ban—even a kid caught once for stealing a piece of fruit would be rejected—the military would evaluate each youth on a case-by-case basis. The new screening policy mattered because the military offered one of the few vehicles for social advancement. The right to enlist was one of the first demands articulated by the Panthers.

In the same month, Education Minister Yigal Allon took a tour of schools in Jerusalem's poorest neighborhoods. This was his first visit to Musrara's schools, even though the ministry was located in Musrara, and Allon was 18 months into his term. After seeing the squalid conditions, the minister outlined his policy goals for the coming years. He said he would focus on integrating the elementary education system. There was no explicit policy of racial segregation, but in Jerusalem and elsewhere, Mizrahi and Ashkenazi communities were living in segregated neighborhoods, resulting in separate schools. Allon also planned to make education free through 12th grade and increase the number of kindergartens. Allon's chief adviser said that these educational policies were being devised in close coordination with the Panthers.

In the following year's budget season, when even more spending on social welfare was proposed, the finance minister allowed that there might be a link between the social fomentation and the funds. "There is nothing wrong in the government reacting instantaneously to the will of the public," Sapir said, before ultimately crediting the relative quiet on Israel's borders for the new budgetary focus.

Some observers, meanwhile, have taken to calling the 1972 spending bill "The Budget of the Panthers." It was the first time Israel ever cut defense spending in favor of other priorities.

The Ministry of Social Welfare saw its budget increase by 20 percent; the Ministry of Labor by about 20 percent; the National Insurance Institute by 42 percent; Ministry of Housing by 33 percent; and Ministry of Education by 24 percent. National funding for local cities and regional councils was up 88 percent. As a result, impoverished families received a

20 percent increase in monthly welfare payments. Twenty-two thousand students received stipends to pay for school uniforms, books, and other materials. And 2,575 impoverished families received household appliances like refrigerators, washing machines, and gas stoves. By early 1973, the welfare minister said juvenile delinquency rates were dropping.

Researchers would document a patchwork of hundreds of small and large policy decisions that were enacted at every level of government in these years. "In almost every relevant government agency and related institution, we saw a significant shift in consciousness," one study said, adding that "we have witnessed a brand-new landscape of services for youth and their various challenges." Later research concluded that the changes were not only correlated with the arrival of the Panthers but caused by it, citing interviews with dozens of government administrators across various agencies and ministries.

The parliament reorganized its committees, dedicating one to deal with youths by studying social problems, advising government agencies, and issuing general recommendations.

In the area of criminal justice and policing, the 1971 Youth Law established a separate court system with special probation officers and institutions designated to handle juvenile offenders. The length of pre-trial detention for youths was reduced. Officers started being trained in how to work with youths. The police carved out a budget for youth recreation and vocational training and added a new welfare unit.

"[The Panthers] can be credited with bringing the problem of poverty to the forefront of public opinion," Tourgeman, the police officer charged with suppressing the Panthers, said in 1973. "Many in the police identified with their struggle."

At the defense ministry, beyond the repeal of the ban on enlisting youths with criminal backgrounds, there was now permanent outreach to disadvantaged youths with specialized counseling made available. A new program was created to teach commanders about the challenges facing young people who were raised in poverty.

A housing ministry program was ramped up to support thousands of young couples, large families, and economically disadvantaged areas. The labor ministry began outreach to alienated youths through guidance counselors and training programs to increase employment. The welfare ministry shifted from passively receiving requests for social services to seeking out individuals who needed help. It established a task force on youths and inequality and created a new office devoted to long-term planning and research. Services were streamlined and scholarships funded. The National Center for Volunteer Services was created to jump-start community service with the explicit goal of narrowing the county's socioeconomic gap.

At the National Insurance Institute, which administers Israel's version of social security, the Panthers provided the cover needed for its director, Israel Katz, to overhaul the way benefits were calculated, resulting in increased funds for the poor starting in 1972. He changed the practice of pegging welfare support levels to the cost-of-living index, instead tying the benefits to the average wages, which meant a massive boost in payments at a time when Israel's economy was growing rapidly.

The money the government was throwing at the poverty crisis was substantial, but the proposals had not yet coalesced into a national welfare policy. That step would have to wait just a little longer.

It was June 27, 1973, about four months before the scheduled date of the national election, and Meir called a press conference to present the culmination of more than two years of work by a group of experts studying the problem of youth poverty in Israel. Known as the Prime Minister's Commission on Children and Adolescents in Distress, the initiative was more commonly referred to as the Katz commission because its head was Israel Katz, the National Insurance Institute director. The commission was made up of some 125 experts from academia and government, and they studied poverty more thoroughly than at any other time in the country's history. They produced a 750-page landmark report whose conclusions vindicated the claims championed by the Panthers. A quarter of all youths in the country were living in poverty and facing a variety of hardships, and a hundred thousand families were living in substandard conditions, the report found. The report also showed how poverty and Mizrahi origin nearly entirely overlapped.

Meir would maintain that the Katz report had nothing to do with the Panthers. But their imprint on the report was impossible to deny. Meir had commissioned a report from a new body of experts in February 1971, right as the Panthers were penetrating the public's consciousness. At first, the group was called the Commission on Youth Crime. In April, around the time the Panthers met with Meir, the name changed to reflect a new focus on poverty and its root causes. As time progressed, the commission decided to study not just youths but their family context. It continuously expanded its scope. Katz watched the Panthers and repeatedly credited them for bringing attention to inequality, without which his commission might have faltered. "When I sensed the growing momentum of the unrest and protests, of course, I took advantage of it and others did too," he later said in an interview. "When you are trying to make policy, you look for any hook to hang on to."

Even when they weren't mentioned at all, the Panthers were ubiquitous in discussions about the welfare revolution underway in Israel. For example, Israel's parliament was about to recess, holding its final meeting before the next parliamentary elections, when Meir took the podium. For the last speech of her term, Meir devoted more than an hour to the issue of poverty. In granular detail, she touted dozens of gains in education, employment, housing, and other areas. She never mentioned the Panthers and only alluded to the social upheaval by warning vaguely about the threat of "demagoguery." All the work of the past couple of years to alleviate poverty was "the natural next step of the Israeli government's continued efforts," she said. Nonetheless, her speech marked a fundamental transformation in the Israeli ethos. The country had been founded on the idea that suffering and sacrifice were patriotic. The constant state of war required each household to accept its lot, while giving cover to the hoarding of resources by a largely Ashkenazi layer of elites. Periodic panics over inequality and unrest would lead to the most minimal of concessions.

As they campaigned for the election, the Panthers did not know how to claim credit for it, but they had helped usher in the modern welfare state in Israel.

It was not only that the Panthers lacked the savviness to fully exploit the moment, they were also busy fighting among themselves. The split fell along the same fault lines that existed from the start. On the one side were Abergel and his supporters. Abergel opposed the pursuit of public office because he thought the moment wasn't ripe. "We have yet to convince this population that our ideology fits their needs," he said. "What we are lacking is intellectual and ideological leadership focused on the long-term and based on traditional Jewish values." Implicit in his stance was criticism of the radical posturing by the other Panthers, of picking, for example, *zayin* as their election letter. As an alternative path, he pointed to his work with youths as a manager of a neighborhood club and summer camp. "I teach not only sports, but also the love of the other, helping others, and how to find release from Mizrahi frustration," he said, describing his work at the time.

Marciano and his crew considered Abergel a sell-out for his acceptance of a government salary and his perceived capitulation to centrist politicians. His statements to the press cautioning against running for office undermined the efforts to do so, and at one point, Abergel's faction even threatened to petition to block the use of the name Black Panthers in election materials.

On August 26, with two months to go until the election, dozens of activists supporting the side of Marciano and Cohen arrived in Jerusalem. Yellow shirts emblazoned with the group's logo were handed out. Three trucks and a string of cars carried the activists through the city as part of a campaign rally. They honked horns and belted out their slogans from the windows. Finally, the cavalcade reached Musrara where speeches were scheduled to be delivered. But the rally also served to antagonize Abergel's faction who were already in Musrara, waiting. As soon as Cohen's group assembled, a fight broke out between the factions in the streets of the neighborhood. Rocks were thrown, knives brandished, and cars overturned. The police intervened after a delay and arrested 21 people. Some people were hospitalized for injuries. With all the decades that have passed since the incident, it has become impossible to parse exactly what happened. The animosity was both ideological and wrapped up in obscure personal grudges going back years and maybe generations. Each side accused the other of a carefully concocted ambush or of conspiring with police.

Following the fight, morale must have been low and the energy of the campaign dissipated by the negative attention it brought. Nothing much changed for the next two weeks until September 11, when the Histadrut, Israel's national labor federation, held its election. The Histadrut represented 1.2 million workers, a large chunk of the country's electorate, helped shape wages and conditions of employment for the country's workforce, and all but controlled many industries. As such, the Histadrut was, de facto, part of Israel's government structure, and the country's political parties vied to capture as much control of it as possible. With its roots in labor, Mapai dominated the Histadrut, but Herut, though a capitalist party, also ran for seats on the federation's executive council. In 1973, so did the Panthers. Elections for the Histadrut were closely watched as a political arena that could reveal possible outcomes in the national election that was to follow. The results began pouring in over several days as the ballots were counted, and they were immediately promising: some cities reported as much as 10 percent of the vote going to these ragged street brawlers.

In the final count, the Panthers won nearly 2 percent of the total vote and three seats on the Histadrut's council. The outcome of the election was not only a massive success on its own terms; it also portended a possible entry into parliament with Israeli voters going back to the ballot box in two months. An even better showing was likely in this next round, considering that the Panthers and their natural constituency didn't come from the traditional ranks of the Histadrut. Members of the Histadrut were employed in the formal economy and paid dues to belong. The urban poor, who made up the base of the Panthers, on the other hand, were more likely to be unemployed or work odd jobs like selling scrap metal or joining day crews on moving or construction gigs.

With this victory, the memories of conflict seemed to fade away. Some of those who had left came back. Soon, the Panthers were not only campaigning but also celebrating together, raising a toast to the eye of a news camera. The notion that Shalom Cohen would get to remain in parliament and have Marciano join him was so elating that some dared predict winning more than a seat or two, that a whole lot of Musrara boys would make it in. Some registered their excitement with political graffiti. In violation of campaign rules which allowed party materials pasted only on designated bulletin boards, they nailed posters to trees and spray-painted slogans on buildings throughout Tel Aviv. The mood among supporters was best captured in an interview given by Dudu Hezkiya. One of dozens of usually anonymous activists in the group, he envisioned how it would feel to have Marciano, with his broken Hebrew and rumpled shirts, be elected.

"I am dying to see Saadia Marciano serving in parliament. This would be the greatest sight of my life. When he sits there, it will be like we are all sitting there," he said. "Can you imagine a guy like Marciano, standing at the podium and the whole country is listening to him? Marciano with his shirts and his Hebrew. It will be amazing."

On October 5, with the election only three weeks away, the campaigning slowed down and then paused as the eve of Yom Kippur arrived. The Day of Atonement fell on a weekend, a 25-hour period starting Friday at sundown. The television and radio went on hiatus, all the stores were closed, and the roads were clear of vehicles. The many Israelis who spent the holiday fasting either crowded synagogues or stayed home. Children played in the streets, emboldened by the freedom of the uncharacteristic stillness.

By early Saturday morning, the first hint of disruption appeared in Jerusalem, as the sound of supersonic jets awakened the city. At the Wailing Wall, pre-dawn worshippers were wrenched out of their meditative praying by sonic booms. Through the morning, the atmosphere grew more discordant as military vehicles began rumbling through deserted streets and screeched to a halt in residential neighborhoods. Going from address to address, military messengers delivered orders calling reserve soldiers up for duty.

The mobilization told the public that fighting had broken out somewhere, but people were generally puzzled because the government had given no hint that war was imminent. Meanwhile, no new information was being delivered because of the news blackout of Yom Kippur. At 2 p.m., the air raid sirens came on and the eclipsing of the sacred day by the arrival of war was complete. Within minutes, the radio signal returned. In their bunkers, Israelis huddled around their receivers to learn that the country was under attack on two fronts. The Egyptians were invading from Suez and the Syrians from the Golan Heights. The Arab armies were intent on taking back the land Israel had conquered six years earlier.

News bulletins were broadcast once an hour and classical music was played in between. That evening, the prime minister took a break from her war meetings to address the public on the radio. Golda Meir tried to reassure the listeners. "The Israel Defense Forces are fighting and are repulsing the attack, and grave losses have been inflicted on the enemy," she said with a flat and somber voice. But it was clear that this confrontation was not a repeat of 1967 when the Israeli military pushed back enemy forces with ease. The country's much-heralded defensive lines had been breached, jets were shot down, and the fighting was bitter. The public would not know the full extent of the damage for a while, but even the little information that did trickle out of military command in the first few days was alarming.

All the political parties agreed to cease campaigning for the duration of the war. As the days dragged on, it became clear that the election itself, scheduled for October 30, would have to be postponed. Even after the tide of the war shifted and Israel began to prevail, an election remained an impossibility since so many voters were stationed on the battlefront and much of the country remained under emergency decree.

When the war finally ended in late October, Israel's casualties reached nearly 2,800 with about 8,800 people wounded. Hundreds of Israeli soldiers had been captured and were held as prisoners of war in Syria and Egypt. Territorially, nothing had changed. Sinai remained in Israeli hands and so did the Golan Heights. Nevertheless, leaders of the Arab world declared victory. They had punctured the image of invincibility that Israel had built up over more than two decades. Israelis, for their part, were stupefied. The existential danger of the past few weeks meant that their generals were fallible and that their superior air force was not enough to ward off adversaries. The country's intelligence apparatus was supposed to anticipate aggression and trigger preemptive action but it too seemed to have failed.

With the election now scheduled for December 31, Israelis were talking about what had gone wrong and what the geopolitical consequences would be; they were too preoccupied to focus much on the ballot. The assumption was that Meir's Mapai Party would win, as it had in every previous round, and continue its rule. The focus of the press, mirroring everyday conversations, was on the diplomatic jockeying over the terms of the ceasefire and the nature of the borders, negotiations that involved numerous governments including the world's two superpowers.

For the Panthers, the aftermath of the war spelled a break from past politics. "We have abandoned street demonstrations and anything likely to lead to clashes with the police," Cohen said. "The nation is mobilized and the old headline-grabbing techniques are not acceptable today." The activists turned their attention to the fate of the Israeli prisoners of war, many of whom were Mizrahi foot soldiers deployed to the frontline units that were overwhelmed by the surprise onslaught of October 6.

From Cairo, Egypt's Hebrew-language radio station broadcast interviews with Israeli captives. Among them was one Mizrahi prisoner who spoke about the ethnic stratification of the Israeli military. He said that Mizrahi soldiers were sent to the battlefront to die while Ashkenazim occupied positions of command. "What would you like to tell your friends in Israel?" the interviewer asked before concluding the segment. "Vote for the Black Panthers," he responded. As Israeli journalists noted with skepticism at the time, such statements were given under duress and could have been dictated by the captors. In any case, the statement was basically true. The military was ethnically divided, and the resulting loss of life and limb among Mizrahim belied the rhetoric of Israeli camaraderie and brotherhood.

The Panthers articulated a response to this reality in a pamphlet, trying to stake out space in the shell-shocked public discourse and perhaps garner enough votes to enter parliament. "Until this war started," they wrote, "we focused on our daily battle, the war for education, housing, and fair wages. We entrusted the establishment with national security. We believed in the promises from above until the Arab armies came and proved—with our blood and limbs—that we were wrong to give our trust. And so we come today, after the tally of dead and alive, to demand accountability."

A photograph from the war was printed above these words. It shows soldiers in an armored military vehicle. On a side panel, the soldiers wrote in white paint: "The Panthers to Damascus." The image reinforces the message that the government hadn't upheld its end of the bargain even as Mizrahim risked their life in battle.

Written in the style of Émile Zola's famous "J'Accuse" letter, the pamphlet criticizes the various elements of the Israeli establishment. "We will fight this regime, both the governing coalition and the opposition, until we topple it over," the pamphlet concludes. "We will fight in the name of our friends who died in battle because of its crimes; in the name of our children who were robbed of the fruits of peace and granted no security following the waging of war; in the name of all the soldiers who understand they were betrayed; in the name of the whole people, because this regime cannot bring peace just as it failed to prepare for war."

Finally, the day of the election arrived. It was a public holiday and nearly all commercial activity in Israel came to halt. Banks, offices, universities, schools, libraries, and stores were closed. There was some rain, which some feared would affect turnout. Adding to the uncertainty, polls showed that as many as 40 percent of voters were yet undecided.

At the ballot box, Israeli voters were faced with the choice of 21 party lists, and only 12 of those parties were represented in the previous parliament. Nine were brand new—including two, not one, bearing the Panther name.

That's because the chaos of the previous few months had brought one final and dramatic threat to the Panthers' prospects for crossing the votes threshold. Just before the deadline for parties to register for the election, the Blue and White Panthers headed by Eddie Malka suddenly announced it would also run for office. The group's name and colors not only signaled their patriotism but also served as an accusation of disloyalty and sedition against the original Panthers.

Malka knew he was diluting the strength of the protest vote but he argued that the Panthers had been hijacked by Cohen and had come to represent nothing substantial. He was joined by Elbaz, whose motive for causing a split can be explained by his role as a police plant, and by Shemesh, whose decision is harder to understand. A self-described anti-Zionist, Shemesh was oddly defecting to a faction that touted its Zionism with patriotic colors in its name.

Campaign ads for the Blue and White Panthers were appearing seemingly everywhere, from billboards to prominent newspaper placements. The source of the funding for the campaign was a mystery, and the sums that must have been spent were dumbfounding to Marciano, Cohen, and their supporters. They suspected that Israel's established parties or their donors were propping up Malka's faction to muddy the Panthers' image and split whatever voter base might exist for the group. A few years later, Cohen would feel vindicated in his suspicions when Israel's Industrial Development Bank published one of its annual disclosures. It showed that the bank had given a massive loan to Malka and that he had defaulted on it. That was proof enough for Cohen that a nefarious financial scheme was behind the Blue and White Panthers.

By the end of election day, 80 percent of Israeli voters turned out, and the vast number of undecideds had finally made their selections. Once again, Labor Zionism won. The Alignment list, an alliance of two parties led by Meir's Mapai, secured 51 seats, out of a total of 120. It was a drop of five seats from the previous election but still the highest number of any party by far. Mapai's counterpart on the right, Likud, gained seven seats for a total of 39. The shifts were significant—perhaps pointing to a new trajectory for the country—but they were not yet enough to change Israel's fundamental balance of power. Meir would remain prime minister. All she had to do now was to take her pick of allies from the smaller parties while granting minor concessions, thus obtaining a majority of seats in parliament for her side.

As it turned out, the Panthers did not earn the privilege of vying for a parliamentary deal with Meir. Both of the Panther factions had failed to cross the 16,000-vote barrier. The original Panther faction chalked up 13,332 votes. The Blue and White pretenders got 5,945.

Their combined votes would have been enough.

20

THE BALLOT REBELLION

THE WAR OF 1967 changed Israel and gave rise to the Panthers. It was the triumph that secured the quiet. And it was
the quiet that allowed the country to focus inward. With the
country's enemies pushed farther away and made weaker,
the din of internal dissent echoed louder. A movement for
social justice emerged. The ruling class appeared ready to
allow the country to change. Then, within six years, war
came again, as inevitably it would in a country with ambigu-
ous borders. The fighting didn't cost Israel in territory, but
all the gains in attention to domestic matters were reversed.
Social justice receded, and Israel's existential dread returned.

If the Panthers were never able to recover fully from their
defeat in the December 1973 election, that doesn't mean they
disappeared. They would operate as a group and then as
individuals for decades more, and the press continued to
document their protests and scandals. But the movement
never recovered its former appeal, vitality, or cohesion.

The camera catches a glance of Black Panther Amram Cohen, center foreground in black t-shirt and with long sideburns, surrounded by a crowd of fellow demonstrators. © Micha Bar-Am.

In the immediate aftermath of the 1973 war, the Panthers turned to the issue of prisoners of war. Many Mizrahi soldiers were on the front lines of the fighting and had been captured by Syria and Egypt, making the negotiations for their release a priority.

Israelis, emerging from the shock of their near defeat, reacted with indignation at the government's failures. Golda Meir was forced to resign as prime minister in 1974, only a few months into her second term, and her party replaced her with Yitzhak Rabin. A retired general, Rabin was abroad, serving as ambassador to the United States, when the Panthers emerged and had therefore avoided publicly commenting on the turmoil they caused. Since issues of poverty and inequality didn't disappear, but rather grew more acute with the economic downturn that followed the Yom Kippur War, the Panthers had good reason to carry on. They held occasional demonstrations and staged stunts like stealing cooking oil and distributing it to the poor. For a while, the Panthers were united as they rallied behind one of their longtime leaders, Charlie Biton. He had been found guilty of assaulting a police officer during a protest, and a court sentenced him to a seven-month prison term. The Panthers regarded the trial as an act of political persecution and campaigned to have Biton pardoned. They staged a hunger strike and lobbied various civic and political leaders. The Panthers even floated the idea of kidnapping a government official as leverage. The drastic measure became unnecessary because Israel's president did, in the end, grant Biton a pardon.

The united front began to fracture again in March 1975 when a delegation of three Panthers, including Biton and Abergel, flew across the Mediterranean to publicize their cause in Europe. In Paris, they decided to try to rendezvous with representatives of the Palestine Liberation Organization, considered a terrorist organization among Israelis but a liberation movement in Palestinian eyes. In announcing their intentions, the Panther delegates presented a vision of Mizrahi Jews as a bridge to peace, built on shared Arab heritage. "We believe that the

Palestinians are an integral part of the political landscape in the region and they must be included in all political processes," Abergel told an Israeli reporter at the time.

But some Panthers back home felt that the delegates had acted beyond their mandate and were worried about alienating supporters. An agreement was reached a few months later when the Black Panthers gathered for a national conference and voted to support the creation of a Palestinian state, a radical position for its time. In the language of the approved resolution, the Panthers declared that "a just peace is possible only on the basis of mutual recognition of Israel and the Palestinians, founded on the principle that this land is the common homeland of two peoples, each of which has the right to an independent country and sovereignty."

In the summer of 1975, Menaḥem Talmi, a correspondent for *Maariv,* decided it had been long enough since a journalist last descended on Musrara to survey its poverty. "What's up, Musrara?" reads the opening line of the resulting article. And the answer: "Nothing much." Amid the familiar prose about crowdedness and neglect, Talmi provides a snapshot of Abergel's life as the director of a municipal after-school program and summer camp centered on teaching fencing to local youths. "It used to be much worse around here," Abergel told Talmi. "A lot has improved. But only God and us know how much there is to do still, how far from acceptable things are."

Talmi goes on to describe a scene at a café in Musrara where he encounters Mizrahi locals hanging out with Palestinians from East Jerusalem, "as if nothing had happened." What had happened was that a few weeks prior, an explosive planted by a Palestinian militant in Jerusalem's Zion Square killed 15 Israelis and wounded 77, and afterward, residents of Musrara and other neighborhoods rioted in East Jerusalem.

According to Abergel's account in the article, he rushed to the scene with a bullhorn. Explaining to the crowd that violence would only serve the terrorists' interests, he managed to talk the rioters down. "If you grab innocent Arabs, and lynch them, you can certainly ask to draw a salary from Fatah," Abergel said, referring to the militant Palestinian faction. "It's exactly what they need from you."

Abergel was also asked about whether crime is a problem among Musrara youths. "Of course there is some," Abergel said. "For as long as the congestion and crowding continue, people aren't taken care of, the youth drop out of school, don't find work, collect police records, and are unwanted by the military—there will be crime."

Abergel also talked about drug addiction and its relationship to the problem: "There are folks who are addicted to drugs . . . there are no serious rehab facilities, and the problem is getting worse. And to get the drugs, they need a lot of money. Where can you get a lot of money and fast? Only through crime."

The portrait of Abergel proved ironic, given what happened next.

Less than six months after the interview, the same newspaper published another article about Abergel and put his photograph on the front page—but in the opposite context of the previous article.

The headline declared that Reuven Abergel and his two younger brothers, Eliezer and Yaakov, had been arrested overnight, and that they were "accused of armed threats, drug trafficking, political and financial blackmail, and terrorizing the neighborhood."

Authorities said that they had collected witness testimonies from dozens of Musrara residents indicating that the Abergels operated as a sort of mafia organization. The news became a sensation, with various outlets competing for scoops about the case over the ensuing days and weeks. They quoted the judge handling Eliezer's arraignment, who said in court to Eliezer that "if ten percent of what is said about you is true then you should be put away for ten years."

Over the next few months, the Abergels were dragged in for court appearances, where they listened as some of their own neighbors testified against them. Several Panthers and former Panthers testified in the trial, including Eddie Malka, Amram Cohen, Charlie Biton, and Saadia Marciano. The Abergels denied the allegations, arguing that some of the other Panthers had conspired against them to wrest control of the movement.

In the end, after all the initial and sensational publicity about the case, the allegations made in court testimony were somewhat underwhelming. Witnesses described a tendency to resort to threats of violence amid neighborly arguments; a rivalry that got out of hand; the dealing of a few grams of hashish; and a gambling operation that managed to generate only petty cash. It hardly sounded like the Abergels were behind a sophisticated drug and protection racket. The proceedings concluded with an eighteen-month prison sentence for Yaakov, while Eliezer received a much more significant sentence of eleven years. Reuven was acquitted after the prosecution failed to present enough witness testimony to implicate him.

This saga also produced a national hero. A young, ambitious member of parliament from the right-wing Likud party had spearheaded the effort to "clean up" Musrara, as the newspapers put it. He reportedly managed to disrupt the culture of silence among the terrorized residents of the neighborhood and prodded the police to take action. The name of the lionized politician was Ehud Olmert, the same man who, decades later, would become Israel's twelfth prime minister; exposing allegations of organized crime was how Olmert first made a name for himself.

Olmert's eventual fate would also prove ironic, given his start as a crime fighter. In 2006, months into his tenure as prime minister, he became embroiled in a series of criminal investigations over bribery and corruption. He resigned from his party and left office rather than seek reelection, and eventually, he was tried, convicted, and sentenced to prison.

In his first interview after being released, Olmert agreed in early 2018 to answer questions for this book about the Abergel episode and the Panthers. He conceded that it was "natural" and "human" for the Abergels to harbor anger against him. He also expressed skepticism that the outcome of their trial was entirely just. "Today, from my experience, I can tell you there is not always a basis when a court convicts," he said, alluding to his own claims of innocence.

Asked about the notion that the Abergels operated as a local mafia, Olmert responded, "Forget it, not at all."

He said, "Look, back then, when we started to talk about organized crime, it caused a halo effect. There was organized crime. There was a case in which two bodies were disposed of using a meat grinder. So we are not talking hashish, there was real crime. It could be that, unfairly, this generalization was projected onto [the Abergels]."

Fair or not, the episode devastated Reuven. In September 1976, nine months after his arrest and two weeks after his acquittal, he was reinstated as the director of the municipal program for youths in Musrara. But in his anguish over his brothers' verdicts and the betrayal by his fellow Panthers, he eventually developed a heroin habit. Abergel's tracks disappear from the public record for roughly the next 15 years, aside from a single interview in 1986 in a retrospective article about the Panthers. "Today, I am very bitter," Abergel said at that time. "I have no friends. I trust only my brothers. I got divorced. My children have scattered. The Panthers stripped away the happiness from my life. My life today contains no joy."

In 1977, with the Abergels out of the way, and a new election approaching, the remaining Panthers faced the decision of what to do. The previous election saw the group split into two parties, each vying separately for parliamentary representation and each failing to secure enough votes to cross the electoral threshold on their own, but getting enough votes that, if combined, would have meant victory.

Rather than learning a lesson and consolidating, the Panthers ended up doing the opposite. They scattered and spread out, making new political alliances and running for office as part of four different party lists.

None of the lists included Elbaz. His role as a police informant had played itself out, and he distanced himself from the group, fading into obscurity. He would die in 1996, taking his secret to the grave. The first person to discover Elbaz's duplicity was a graduate student named Hillel Cohen, a future historian of note. In 1999, Cohen found documents outlining the surveillance of the Panthers by police in the Israeli state archives. A journalist for a local Jerusalem newspaper wrote an article about Cohen's discovery but without naming Elbaz. "His identity will not be revealed here," wrote Vered Kellner. "He can no longer respond to the claims against him, and it's appropriate to be considerate of his family and friends." His identity was publicly revealed in the end when, about eight years later, investigative reporter Gidi Weitz found roughly the same set of documents and wrote an exposé for *Haaretz* about Elbaz's role.

Also absent from the ballot were the spoilers of the previous election, Malka and his Blue and White Panthers. Though they had disbanded by this point, a new faction styled in the same fashion and called the Zionist Panthers entered the 1977 race. Made up of relative newcomers, the party attracted barely any votes and placed second to last among 22 parties in the election.

Shalom Cohen, meanwhile, helped establish a party called Hofesh, or Freedom, an array of civic groups focused on socioeconomic issues. His party also failed to get enough votes, and Cohen left politics altogether. He returned to his roots as a newspaperman and became a Middle East correspondent for French newspapers, writing in a language he had learned during his days as a college student in Egypt. Following

Israel's 1979 peace treaty with Egypt, Cohen spent much of his time shuttling between the two countries and living in Paris. A 1992 newspaper profile noted that with Cohen's retreat from politics, he had been entirely forgotten by the Israeli public. He had intended to write a memoir about his time with the Panthers but didn't get to it before he died in 1993, just shy of the signing of the Oslo Accords, a historic breakthrough he had advocated for his entire life.

While the electoral efforts by the Zionist Panthers and Cohen's faction failed, 1977 was not a disappointment for every Panther. The splintering produced victories for Biton and—after a delay—Marciano.

They entered parliament with separate parties. Biton cut a deal with communists of the Rakah party to create the National Front for Peace and Equality. His name was third on a list that went on to win five seats. Two months into his term, an article in the *Jerusalem Post* described Biton as an "oddity" and a "freak" when juxtaposed with other lawmakers in the marbled halls of parliament. The article said that Biton was "tiny and looks as if he never had enough to eat as a child" and "might easily be confused with the extra help hired to do the washing-up." And while he may have looked that way to the newspaper reporter, his two parents were in fact custodial workers at the time, underscoring his improbable rise.

Marciano's win was a flimsier one. He had joined The Left Camp of Israel, also known as Sheli, a loose partnership of leftist groups that called for peace with the Palestinians. Since Sheli's vote total only translated into two parliamentary seats, party members bargained and bickered over who would get them. They eventually worked out a rotation agreement, and Marciano's turn came three years after the election.

On the day he was sworn in, Marciano started his morning by visiting the grave of his parents on the Mount of Olives, paying respects to a woman who had been a stalwart of the Panthers until she died six years earlier. He later stopped to pick up a new shirt that was tailored by his wife's cousin and matched it with a new pair of shoes and a new pair of pants that were grey but not quite slacks. He also spent part of the day visiting a local family that was being threatened with eviction from their asbestos-walled shanty. Not one to walk around alone, Marciano was accompanied by an entourage of nearly 50 friends, family members, and supporters when he finally reached parliament. "I am not going to disappear inside this building," he promised that day. "I am going to make my mark and that will give people a chance to judge." Greeting Marciano with a bear hug and a kiss at the podium was Biton, his former lieutenant in the Panthers.

Whatever their party affiliations, the rookie lawmakers saw themselves as spokespeople for the most disadvantaged segment of the Jewish population, the thousands of semi-delinquent young people who were neither employed nor enrolled in school. In mindset and values, they were of the streets, representing a population that had never been represented before—what some called "the non-respectable poor."

The irony of this milestone in Israeli political history is that the votes for Marciano and Biton didn't come from the people they championed. Sheli drew from a small number of disillusioned, mostly Ashkenazi leftists, while Rakah's base was made up of voters in Israel's Palestinian towns plus a few thousand diehard Jewish communists. Neither Panther managed to pull almost any Mizrahi support, not even in Musrara. The attention of the Mizrahi masses was focused elsewhere during the election of 1977, and a historic event of far greater significance came to overshadow Marciano's and Biton's successes.

As the results of the election were coming in on the evening of May 17, 1977, Haim Yavin, the ubiquitous anchor of Israel's sole evening news program, was brooding over how to describe the moment. He didn't want to frighten the millions of Israelis tuning in with the word "revolution," which might wrongly evoke the idea of violence or military action. But he also didn't want to avoid the word entirely, which would downplay the significance of what was happening. So while broadcasting live, he took the root of the Hebrew word for revolution and used it to coin a new term, *mahapach*. It means essentially the same thing: a reversal, an earthquake, an upheaval.

"We have then, nothing less than a *mahapach*," Yavin told viewers. "A revolution has taken place in Israel."

Yavin proclaimed the victory of Likud, the right-wing party led by Menachem Begin, over Mapai, which was headed by Shimon Peres, thus marking the downfall of the hegemonic Labor movement, which had dominated national politics since before Israel was founded.

The broadcast turned to the celebratory scene at the Likud party headquarters in Tel Aviv, where thousands had gathered, "swirling about in paroxysms of incredulity and ecstasy," as one observer put it. The crowd chanted, "Be-gin! Be-gin! Be-gin!" so loudly they drowned out the TV reporter, who eventually quit trying to describe the boisterous atmosphere. When Begin emerged, his face aglow with a wide grin, he had to squeeze through the swarm of his admirers to reach the stage. The bespectacled former guerrilla fighter, who had spent nearly his entire parliamentary career in the opposition, rose to the victor's podium and the audience greeted him like the king he had now become. They chanted, "Am Yisrael Hai!" which means "the people of Israel live!"

Begin commanded their silence by raising his palms in the air. From his pocket, he pulled out a yarmulke and recited the Jewish blessing of Shehecheyanu, a thank you to God for bringing about this moment. "Amen!" the adoring crowd yelled back. It may have been the Ashkenazi Begin who won the election, but the victory belonged to Mizrahi voters from Morocco, Iran, Yemen, Libya, and Iraq, rebelling at the ballot against the condescending elites of Labor.

After Begin's speech, the broadcast moved outside to the street for reactions from Begin supporters.

"You want to know why we voted Begin?" one supporter said. "We voted Begin because he's not a godless socialist like Peres and his lot. He's not ashamed to say 'God.' He speaks with a Jewish heart. That's why Labor always ridiculed him, and treated him the way they always treated us—like scum."

"Are you saying that Peres and his crowd are not really Jews?" asked the interviewer.

"They may be Jews, but they behave like goyim," the supporter responded. "Have you ever seen one of them inside a synagogue? What's a Jew without a synagogue? Where's their self-respect, their pride?"

Another Likud supporter butted in. "Those Labor bigwigs duped us," he said. "They brought us here telling us this was the redemption. Cheap labor, that's what they brought us here for. In Casablanca, my father was a respected member of the community. He was the patriarch of our family. He had honor."

"Honor!" the crowd repeated in unison.

"My honor has been trampled upon," the interviewee said. "Menachem Begin has given me back my honor."

On that empathic note, the group broke into song, chanting, "Begin, King of Israel."

History would validate Yavin's proclamation of a political revolution. The election has led to more than 45 years of Likud rule with only a handful of interruptions.

A debate among scholars, journalists, and politicians about what exactly caused the transformation of 1977 has gone on ever since. All sides of the debate will point to the series of corruption scandals in the years leading up to the election as a factor that grated on many voters; leaders of Mapai were acting like they could get away with anything. Another point of consensus is that Israelis grew increasingly angry at the establishment as they learned about the failures that led to the Israeli military's humiliation and near-defeat in the war of 1973.

A more complicated factor in Likud's rise is the role of Mizrahi voters. A demographic majority of Israeli Jews, Mizrahim had begun their migration to Likud in prior elections. Voting data says they helped tip the scales in 1977 and then again, more decisively, in the election of 1981, inaugurating a new political reality in Israel.

The question, then, is how an Ashkenazi-led party with a conservative economic platform, including a plan to slash welfare spending, managed to forge an enduring alliance with an impoverished Mizrahi public.

Some explanations resort to racism to depict Mizrahim as innately prone to authoritarianism and to the primal hatred of Arabs, tendencies that Likud managed to exploit by portraying Begin as a modern-day king and by embracing anti-Arab rhetoric. In this analysis, Mizrahim were susceptible to Begin's rabid nationalism and paternalist gestures because of ignorance, cultural backwardness, and an unhealthy fealty to tradition. Bernard Avishai, a contributor to the *New Yorker* and other prestigious publications, provided an example of this thinking in a 1981 essay about Israel's changing political landscape, writing that "[Mizrahim] refused to shed their cultural traditions and warmhearted patriarchal families for the sake of Labor Zionist theories they could barely understand."

Others, meanwhile, have shown how mutual self-interest helped drive the two groups together. In 1973, Likud enacted internal reforms that democratized its power structure. Instead of appointing local leadership from above, as Mapai continued to do, Likud now allowed its chapters to pick their own representatives. Moroccan-born organizers ascended the party ranks on merit and popularity, creating a genuine grassroots movement. Part of what propelled the movement was a shared experience of victimization. If the Israeli establishment were followers of Labor Zionism, Likud traced its roots to Revisionist Zionism, a competing ideology dedicated to maximal Jewish territorial expansion in the Holy Land. From the early period of settlement in

British Palestine through the establishment of the Israeli state, Laborites acted to exclude and marginalize the Revisionists, whom they regarded as reckless and dangerous. The Ashkenazim of Likud and the Mizrahi immigrants whose honor had been stolen were natural allies against a common tormenter.

Begin capitalized on the political opportunity by emphasizing Jewish pride and identity in a way that wouldn't have been comfortable in the secular environment of the Labor movement. For example, when, in 1981, a television host used a racist slur to refer to Likud supporters, Begin held his own rally and delivered what became one of the most famous political speeches in Israeli history. He dismissed the slur as an ignorant comment and recalled how he fought against the British shoulder-to-shoulder with Mizrahi Jews in the lead-up to Israel's founding.

"Our Mizrahi brothers were heroic warriors, even back in the underground," Begin bellowed in a slow, deliberate cadence to the tens of thousands gathered before him at Zion Square.

The climax of the speech came with an anecdote about an Ashkenazi Jew and an Iraqi Jew who died together as martyrs fighting the British for Israel's independence. "Ashkenazi ... Iraqi ... " Begin said. He paused and, then, with his fists shaking, and his voice a thundering howl, he dismissed these categories, yelling, "Jews! Warriors! Brothers!"

Mizrahim were ripe for a message that brought them into the Zionist fold, argues scholar Sami Shalom Chetrit, who has dubbed the 1977 election The Ballot Rebellion. What enabled the rebellion, according to Chetrit, was the collapse of several popular myths and the subsequent emancipation of the Mizrahi population. After the 1973 war, for example, it was much harder to trust "the few clever European Jews" to defeat the "backward Arabs" that far outnumbered them. The corruption of Mapai, meanwhile, undermined the promise of an Israel based on socialism and partnership. Finally came the uprising of the Black Panthers, puncturing the myth known as the ingathering of exiles, a utopian idea of what Jewish immigration to Israel would look like.

The idea that the Panthers inadvertently paved the way for the Israeli right to take over isn't new. This scenario was anticipated as early as June 1971, only months after the movement emerged. "The Panthers could bring the Likud to power," was the prophetic headline of an article by a high school social sciences teacher.

"When the typical Panther is in front of the ballot box, they will express their dissatisfaction with the government's treatment of their problems by voting for the opposition party. But this will be a right-wing party, not a socialist one," the article reads. "If the Black Panther movement manages to sweep the silent majority of the Mizrahi community . . . this demographic will become more than ever before the pillar of Likud."

To whatever extent the Panthers helped the Likud, the outcome is painfully ironic for many Panthers. They led a distinctly left-wing movement on behalf of Mizrahi Israelis. The Likud was led by Ashkenazi Jews, who, the Panthers believed, had no intention of relieving the economic plight of their Mizrahi constituency. A handful of lesser-known Panthers had always been Begin supporters, and some ended up as Likud voters. But most of the Panthers, and certainly the leaders, were lifelong, committed leftists. While they have been eager to take credit for playing an important role in redirecting Israeli history, they also lament how things turned out. The alliance between Likud and a significant portion of the Mizrahi public holds to this day, which is a factor in the repeated electoral victories of Israel's current and longest-serving prime minister, Benjamin Netanyahu, and in continued expressions of anti-Mizrahi racism in political discourse. Abergel, for one, likes to say, "In every revolution, the dreamers sow the seeds, the courageous carry it forward, and the bastards reap the fruits of the struggle."

Likud's takeover in 1977 was a political earthquake but it didn't change the basic ethos of the Panthers. They continued to defy, shock, and entertain as they had under Labor. The need for the Panthers as an accountability mechanism didn't go away with the new government, even if all they could do now was mount individual and symbolic acts.

Within Biton's first two months as a parliamentarian, he exposed a system of cheating in university admissions and jolted education authorities who had ignored the widespread sale of examination materials. He also publicized a prison strike against poor conditions and mistreatment, which was being led from behind bars by incarcerated Panthers. He invited a group of wives and mothers of inmates to join him as he stormed a parliamentary committee meeting. Later, he famously handcuffed himself to the speaker's podium in parliament in protest, which earned him a suspension. For another stunt, he delivered a speech on social issues with his back to other lawmakers "since talking to them is no better than talking to the wall."

Marciano was just as creative. He seemed to relish being provocative. In 1979, he led a group of Panthers to the home of the minister for social affairs, Israel Katz, while Katz was away giving a speech. They knocked on the door and when his wife opened it, the Panthers released a cage full of rabbits into the house. They said it was because Katz was a *shafan*, a word in Hebrew that means both "rabbit" and "coward." The following year, as the city of Tel Aviv was preparing to cut funding to a meal program for the elderly, Marciano set up an impromptu kitchen outside city hall, which he dubbed "Hardship Café." He and a few fellow Panthers cooked a four-course meal and delivered it to the mayor and his aides. And later on, to call attention to government inaction on the growing drug abuse problem, Marciano sent every member of parliament an envelope containing a hypodermic needle and a plastic bag filled with an unidentified white substance.

The Panthers didn't confine themselves to internal issues. They also intervened in national debates concerning Israel's expanding footprint in the West Bank. Israeli settlement of Palestinian lands had begun soon after the 1967 war under a Labor government and only accelerated under

Likud. The Panthers criticized Israel's settlement policy and demanded negotiations toward a peace deal with the Palestinians. In the late 1970s, this advocacy took the form of protests in West Bank settlements. The Panthers pointed out that limited public funding was being used to prop up settlements instead of to support established towns and neighborhoods with high poverty rates and housing shortages.

In 1980, Biton met with Palestinian leader Yasser Arafat on the sidelines of a conference in Bulgaria in possible violation of a new Israeli law against such encounters. The meeting represents a milestone on Israel's path to recognizing Arafat and the PLO as legitimate representatives of the Palestinian people, which culminated with the signing of the Oslo Accords 13 years later. An article in *This World* reported that it was Arafat's first-ever meeting with Israelis, calling the moment a "first-rate breakthrough." In an odd twist, *This World*'s editor, Uri Avnery, would later falsely claim that he was the first Israeli to meet with Arafat, a claim that was repeated in some of his obituaries when he died in 2018.

For all the headlines that the Panthers made through the 1970s and '80s, they failed to siphon Mizrahi support from Likud or any other party. But starting in the mid-1980s, a different force in Mizrahi politics emerged and quickly managed to do just that.

The founding activists of the movement later known as Shas were unlike the Panthers in one fundamental way: they were religiously observant, and some were even rabbis. The Orthodox world they inhabited was dominated by Ashkenazi rabbis who had little regard for the religious customs of Mizrahi Jews. Sick of everyday condescension as well as discrimination against their children in admissions to Orthodox schools, the activists launched a movement.

Shas built support among the same demographic the Panthers had come from, the urban Mizrahi youths who were deemed delinquents, by offering them a framework of religious education and social services. In November 1983, *Haaretz* labeled Shas "the Black Panthers from

Agudat Yisrael," using the name of the Agudat Yisrael political party as a stand-in for the Ashkenazi-dominated Orthodox world.

The rhetoric of Shas centered on the quest to restore lost Mizrahi honor, and it was backed by the kind of organizational discipline and unity that the Panthers failed to sustain. What also helped was that Shas didn't demand structural reforms to address Israeli inequality, which meant they were not a direct threat to the establishment. Shas went on to become a major political party in Israel, reaching its peak in the election of 1999 when it won about 14 percent of Israel's parliamentary seats. Striking deals with larger parties, Shas traded its votes to get public funding for programs.

For Chetrit, the scholar of Mizrahi history, Shas represents just one of many rebellions the Panthers ushered in by inaugurating the "era of radical awareness." The breaking of the taboo against talking about ethnic grievances liberated Mizrahim to process trauma and demand participation in the institutions of Israeli society. As part of this liberation, an entire generation of Mizrahi poets, musicians, writers, and scholars emerged in the late 1970s and during the 1980s, producing enduring works of art and scholarship. Chetrit is both a product and chronicler of this change. In his groundbreaking 2004 study of the Mizrahi experience in Israel, he describes this era as "a mass workshop for rehabilitating an oppressed identity, where participants open up their hearts, cry out freely, and undo the knots of indignity, helplessness, and isolation that characterized the life of submission and cultural humiliation in their encounter with European Zionism."

Abergel's hiatus from the Israeli revolution he helped launch lasted for more than 15 years following his trial and subsequent heroin addiction. In September 1989—by then, he had become homeless—Abergel ran into an old friend on the street. David Meiri, the Jerusalem social worker who had mentored many of the Panthers, hardly recognized Abergel at first. Drug use had claimed Abergel's teeth, turned his face gaunt and sunk his eyes, according to notes Meiri scribbled following their encounter. Abergel was frail and had lost 48 pounds. He told Meiri that he was "crying out for help" but that he didn't think anyone would care for him. "Despondent, he fears that if he doesn't get treatment for his addiction, he will die," Meiri wrote.

Addiction was rampant in Israel, but the country had almost no treatment infrastructure. Meiri, whose casework increasingly involved drug abuse, had found help abroad. He arranged to have Abergel fly to France and check in to a rehabilitation center in the Alps. The treatment worked, and several months later, Abergel returned to Israel. He also managed to forgive the Panthers who testified against him and his brothers. With his return, Abergel began helping others who had gotten caught up in Israel's addiction epidemic. To scale up his efforts, he was even willing to team up with Marciano. In 1990, the two set aside their old rivalry and mutual animosity to establish Zoharim, one of Israel's first drug rehabilitation centers, outside Jerusalem.

Abergel would later partner with Biton and Shemesh, with whom he also shared a similar history. They led a campaign demanding clemency for all Israeli prisoners, citing the high proportion of them who were incarcerated on drug possession charges. The three Panthers would also partner up in 1998 after the head of Israel's Labor party, Ehud Barak, issued a formal apology for his party's role in harming Mizrahim in Israel's early years by severing people from their roots and sending them to live in remote locales. "I ask for forgiveness on behalf of the Labor Party and Mapai of all past generations," Barak said. In response, Abergel, Biton, and Shemesh wrote a letter to Israel's prime minister, Benjamin Netanyahu, of the right-wing Likud party. "Even if we didn't mean to do so, we were one of the reasons that Likud found voters among the Mizrahim," the Panthers wrote. "Since the various leaders of the Likud have been known to enjoy Mizrahi votes and have not solved the problems of desperation and poverty in the poor neighborhoods and development towns, we call on you to follow in the footsteps of the head of the Labor party and ask for forgiveness from the second and third generation of Mizrahi immigrants."

No such apology has been issued by Netanyahu, who is now in his sixth term as prime minister. Nor did these alliances between Abergel and the other Panthers last very long. By 2000, as various journalists and documentarians set out to examine the legacy of the Panthers, old tensions resurfaced. Amid jealous bickering over the spotlight, Abergel found himself ostracized by many of his fellow Panthers again. But this time around, Abergel didn't sink into a depression. He was still invigorated by his recovery from drug addiction and busy with his renewed commitment to left-wing activism.

Abergel dedicated himself to cause after cause as he pursued social justice and human rights in Israel and Palestine. One day, he would be attending a hunger strike of Mizrahi women who were protesting the government's sudden slashing of income assurances for single mothers, and the next he was en route to Ramallah, where he and other Israeli Jews acted as human shields to protect Palestinian leader Yasser Arafat from Israeli bombardments. Over the years, he spearheaded a successful effort to preserve a valley in Jerusalem from being paved over by developers; helped submit a petition to the Israeli Supreme Court against land grabs by Ashkenazi-dominated rural communities known as kibbutzim; and campaigned to support the passage of a law that would allow residents of public housing to purchase their homes at a discount. Later, he was one of the first Israelis to endorse the Palestinian campaign calling on the world to boycott Israel, and in recent years he has marched with Ethiopian Jews demanding an end to discriminatory and violent policing and has delivered speeches at Israel's version of the Occupy movement.

In 2009, Abergel returned to Morocco for the first time since he left as a little boy. He traveled alone, and in the city of Rabat, he navigated by memory to his childhood home in the Jewish quarter. He met with the neighbors and sat down to talk with them in Moroccan Arabic. They remembered fondly his family and the other Jews who had left. Three years later, Abergel experienced another homecoming of sorts when he was invited by New York University to participate in a symposium on the global influence of the Black Panther Party. On the panel with him sat an Aboriginal Panther from Australia, a Dalit Panther from India, a British Panther, and an American from the original group.

"I am a Black Panther in my heart and soul and I am here today to tell you how I and an entire generation became Black Panthers," Abergel told the audience. The text of the speech he prepared was divided into 36 numbered bullet points, probably because the energetic 69-year-old tended to forget to pace himself, sometimes neglecting to give his audience enough pause to process, especially when he was emotionally overwhelmed. "My struggle taught me that regardless of whether a struggle succeeds or not, the most profound changes happen inside those people who fight for their rights and their dignity," he said. "It is through the struggle that people discover they are made of something they didn't know they had inside."

Years after the symposium, Abergel never stopped talking about the time he finally met his comrades in New York. It was an honor that he felt was denied him for his entire life: being recognized outside of the local context of Israeli politics.

In biology, there is no such species as a black panther. The term refers to any jaguar or leopard with excess melanin. Black panthers, then, are the black sheep of the feline world. For Abergel, there was a sublime sense of comfort in finally finding his own kind. In truth, in his old age, Abergel is surrounded by his own kind. They are not aging Panthers. They are the young Mizrahi artists and activists who flock to him to be near a venerable elder of the left, a token of a fading past, and a warm, embracing grandfather figure who calls them his friends.

Acknowledgments

For helping transform my ideas into the beginnings of a book, I am grateful to Sam Freedman and his tough love. It would be inappropriate to acknowledge Sam without also honoring "the ancestors," his moniker for the hundreds of alumni of his book writing seminar at Columbia Journalism School. Thanks to my agent Anna Ghosh for finding this project a home at University of California Press, to my ever-patient editor there, Niels Hooper, and the professors, anonymous and otherwise, who peer-reviewed my manuscript. Thanks also to Joshua Hunt, an early reader of my writings on the Panthers, for modeling how to be a journalist; Keren Simons and her father, Alan, for advice and support during the start of this book; Edo Konrad for being my springboard and for sharing in my delights and frustrations; Itamar Haritan for introducing me to Reuven Abergel and aiding in the excavation of Abergel's memory; Simon Bouvier for French assistance; Elisha Baskin for help obtaining many of the images in the book; Tom Pessah, Mirit Mizrahi, and Smadar Lavie for their insights on Mizrahi politics and Israeli history; Avi Sabag and Avi Dabach for archival help and parsing the history of Musrara; and Esty and Dani Shaul for the hospitality that enabled my research. And thanks to Deborah Bernstein, Sami Shalom Chetrit, and Gidi Weitz for answering my questions and for other contributions detailed in the source notes. I owe a special debt to my brother Roee Ali-Shalev and dear friends Clayton Hartmann and Benjamin Sales, who accompanied me on the long journey that culminated in this book and provided invaluable advice on the manuscript. Five of the people I interviewed for the book have since died: Morris Kaubilio, Avner Amiel, David Meiri, Kochavi Shemesh, and Avraham Tourgeman. May their memory be for a blessing.

The generosity and spirit of Reuven Abergel made this book possible, and I hope I have done justice to the parts of his remarkable life story that I have recounted. His brilliant partner Marcelle Edery deserves immense credit for preserving his papers, helping tell his story, and sustaining and nurturing him.

For sustaining and nurturing me since long before I started working on this book, I thank my parents, Etty and Yosi Shalev. They taught me ambition, hard work, and integrity. I recently lost two of my grandparents: Yaakov Shalev, who instilled in me a sense of pride and connected me to the Mizrahi story in its many nuances and contradictions, and Shelly Avidor, who tried to compensate for dropping out of school at a young age by reading voraciously, passing on to me on a passion for books. May their memory be for a blessing.

Above all, I am grateful to my wife, Shelly Elia-Shaul, for putting up with the book's demands on my time and attention, for advising and challenging me, and for her courage of heart and mind; and to our daughter, Carmel. This book is dedicated to them.

Notes on Sources

These notes provide sources central to my work in this book as well as citations for each chapter, whether described in general or linked to specific phrases and quotations in the chapters.

Throughout this book, observations attributed to the ethnographer documenting the Panthers are drawn from the dissertation of Deborah Bernstein, "The Black Panthers of Israel, 1971–1972: Contradictions and Protest in the Process of Nation-Building" (University of Sussex, Department of Sociology, 1976). Bernstein's contributions are much deeper than these citations alone. Her scholarly analysis and characterizations were invaluable to almost every aspect of my work.

Just as important to this book is the scholarship of Sami Shalom Chetrit, who produced the first and most comprehensive chronicle of the Mizrahi struggle in Israel, devoting a chapter to the Black Panthers. Originally in Hebrew, the translated edition of Chetrit's magnum opus is *Intra-Jewish Conflict in Israel: White Jews, Black Jews* (London: Routledge, 2013).

The police surveillance files regarding the Panthers cited throughout this book come from the Israel State Archives, but they are not currently available to the public. Journalists and academics made use of the files in the 1990s and early 2000s. When I turned to the State Archives seeking the same materials, archivists told me that the files had been released in error and that they were now sealed. I was directed to a dedicated web page featuring a small selection of these files, which were presented with redactions. The archivists said they could not process my request to unseal the files because the police official authorized to handle such requests had died in a motorcycle accident two years prior and no one had been assigned to replace him.

I did end up obtaining copies of the files thanks to a journalist named Gidi Weitz, who published a major investigation into police surveillance of the Panthers in 2007. He burrowed through stacks of boxes in the basement of his newspaper, *Haaretz*, to retrieve an inch-thick binder of copies he had made from the files in the State Archives a decade earlier. All references to police files in this book are from Weitz's binder. In 2018, the State Archives released a catalog of the classified files in its possession, and the listings indicate that there are far more files on the Panthers than what has been obtained by the public.

The thousands of news articles I collected while researching the Panthers come primarily from the Historical Jewish Press online archive maintained by Tel Aviv University and the National Library of Israel and from the archive of the *Jerusalem Post* accessed online through the New York Public Library. I accessed *Haaretz* through the newspaper's physical archive and *Yedioth Ahronoth* through an online database available at Beit Ariela Shaar Zion Library in Tel Aviv.

PREFACE

The account of Operation Milk draws from news articles in *Yedioth Ahronoth* on March 14, 1972, and the *Jerusalem Post* on March 15, 1972, as well as interviews, press photographs, and Bernstein's dissertation, "The Black Panthers of Israel, 1971–1972."

"*We must educate the young man who has come here from these countries*": Quoted in Hillel Cohen, *Haters, a Love Story: On Mizrahim and Arabs (and Ashkenazim, Too) from the Birth of Zionism to the Events of 1929* (Tel Aviv: Ivrit, 2022).

1. GOLDA'S DILEMMA

Details of the meeting convened by Golda Meir on February 28, 1971, are drawn from a six-page police memo dated March 10, 1971, and authored by a senior commander, Aharon Chelouche. Additional details are from articles published in the newspapers *Maariv* on March 1, 1971, and *Haaretz* on August 4, 1973.

Shlomo Hillel's encounter with the protesters in 1957 is described in Esther Meir-Glitzenstein, *Between Baghdad and Ramat Gan: Iraqi Jews in Israel* [in Hebrew] (Jerusalem: Yad Ben Zvi Publishers, 2009).

"The public must have confidence": From minutes of the Israeli parliament on July 3, 1957.

Sources on Matzpen's significance include Nitza Erel, *Matzpen: Conscience and Fantasy* [in Hebrew] (Tel Aviv: Resling, 2010); Tali Lev and Yehuda Shenhav, "'Call us not workers—but Panthers!': The Black Panthers and the Identity Politics of the Early Seventies," *Theory and Criticism* [*Te'oria Vebikoret*] 35 (Fall 2009): 141–64; Tali Lev and Yehuda Shenhav, "The Social Construction of the Enemy from Within: Israeli Black Panthers as a Target of Moral Panic," *Israeli Sociology* 12, no. 1 (2010): 135–58; and Eran Torbiner's documentary, *Matzpen: Anti-Zionist Israelis* (2003).

"good families": From *Yedioth Ahronoth*, March 2, 1971.

2. 1948: THEY PROMISED US JERUSALEM

The narrative of the Abergel family's migration from Morocco to Israel and their lives in Musrara is derived primarily from my interviews with Reuven Abergel, which began soon after we were introduced by a mutual friend, the activist and scholar Itamar Haritan, in early 2013. I checked Abergel's recollections against dozens of other written and oral interviews he gave over the decades. I also interviewed three of his siblings, Madlen, Yaakov, and Eliezer on various occasions in 2017 and 2018, and others who grew up in Musrara around the same time. Additional details about life in Musrara in the 1950s come from oral history interviews gathered in the Musrara Collection at the Naggar School of Art and Society in Jerusalem.

The historical circumstances of Moroccan Jewish immigration are from Yaron Tsur, *A Torn Community: The Jews of Morocco and Nationalism, 1943–1954* (Tel Aviv: Am Oved, 2001). The policy of screening people to prevent the immigration of the sick and unfit to Israel is described on page 287.

Details on the War of 1948 and its aftermath in Jerusalem include Salim Tamari, *1948: The Arab Neighborhoods and Their Fate in the War* (Jerusalem: Institute of Jerusalem Studies, 2002); Tom Segev, *1949: The First Israelis* (New York: Free Press, 1986); and Meron Benvenisti, *City of Stone: The Hidden History of Jerusalem* (Berkeley: University of California Press, 2000).

"Among the Africans living in the camps, you will find filth": From Aryeh Gleblum's series published in April 1949 in *Haaretz*.

The number of Jewish immigrants who left Israel is found in Bryan K. Roby, *The Mizrahi Era of Rebellion: Israel's Forgotten Civil Rights Struggle, 1948–1966* (Syracuse, NY: Syracuse University Press, 2015). More about the controversy of Moroccan Jews returning to Morocco can be found in Shay Hazkani, *Dear Palestine: A Social History of the 1948 War* (Stanford, CA: Stanford University Press, 2021).

The anecdote about communists who took over the ship is from a May 2, 1950, article in the newspaper *Herut*. The one about the Spanish Civil War veterans is from a February 4, 1949, article in *Davar*. And the article describing "an ethnic group of complainers and whiners" was published by *Hatzofe* on September 15, 1949.

For the history of political organizing by Mizrahim in the 1950s and '60s and for details about the particular case of the Pardes Hanna transit camp, see Roby, *The Mizrahi Era of Rebellion*.

The communist newspaper's account of the death of Avraham Harush was published by *Kol Ha'am* on August 23, 1950. More on radicalism among Moroccan immigrants to Israel is found in Alma Rachel Heckman, *The Sultan's Communists: Moroccan Jews and the Politics of Belonging* (Stanford, CA: Stanford University Press, 2020).

Efforts to block immigrants from leaving transit camps and heading to cities are discussed in Chetrit, *Intra-Jewish Conflict in Israel*. Firsthand accounts by transit camp residents and staff about these efforts and their impact are found in the documentary film *The Ancestral Sin* by David Deri (D.D. Productions, 2017).

For details about the Moroccan Jews who volunteered to fight in the War of 1948 as part of Machal, see the website commemorating their sacrifices: https://www.machal.org.il.

"a cartographer's nightmare and a geographer's catastrophe": From Benvenisti, *City of Stone*, 57.

"There's a new iron curtain going up in Jerusalem" . . . *"It was an atmosphere reminiscent of a South African or California gold rush"*: From *Palestine Post,* May 20, 1949.

"In 1948, [Sirhan] saw many things . . . woundings and sufferings": From *Los Angeles Times,* January 5, 1969.

"I am a German Jew from Hungary and I can never be anything but a German": From Theodor Herzl, *Complete Diaries* (New York: Herzl Press, 1960), 171.

"to expand the frontiers of Europe to the Euphrates River": Quoted in Cohen, *Haters, a Love Story,* 109.

The summary of policies and practices that discriminated against Mizrahim is drawn from Chetrit, *Intra-Jewish Conflict in Israel.*

"It's because I am Sephardic": From the newspaper *Haboker,* September 17, 1950.

"We became friends through our eyes": From an interview with Abergel in Jerusalem in June 2014.

"unique in her generation and perhaps in all generations": The episode involving Amalia Ben-Harush and David Ben-Gurion is described in Tom Segev, *1967: Israel, the War, and the Year That Transformed the Middle East* (New York: Metropolitan Books, 2006).

"What do you want to be when you grow up?": The account of Ben-Gurion's visit to Musrara is drawn from the *Jerusalem Post,* August 8, 1962.

"hundreds of families living in conditions reminiscent of the Middle Ages": From *Jerusalem Post,* January 17, 1958.

The lack of supervision over the Orthodox school in Musrara by educational authorities was reported by the *Jerusalem Post* on July 29, 1977, in an article by Susan Bellos, a veteran education and social issues correspondent for the newspaper.

"educational escapism . . . have no thirst for true learning": From *Jerusalem Post,* February 7, 1958.

Abergel has shared the anecdote many times about how he got kicked out of class for cracking a joke, including in an interview with me. The earliest instance I found is in the newspaper *Maariv* on June 25, 1971.

The account of Abergel's time on the kibbutz and its dramatic conclusion are from my interviews with him.

"No one ever came to look for me": From my interview with Abergel in Ashdod in March 2013.

3. 1959: THE REBELLION OF WADI SALIB

The police surveillance files regarding Wadi Salib that are cited throughout this chapter were made available to me by Renen Yezersky and Talia Aloni, who obtained them while working as researchers for the documentary *The Ancestral Sin* by David Deri (D.D. Productions, 2017).

The account of how the uprising at Wadi Salib began is drawn from journalist Gidi Weitz's article published in *Haaretz* on February 13, 2014, and from the archival documents upon which he based his article. The documents, which include testimonies, meeting minutes, and official reports, were produced as part of the work of the Inquiry Commission into the Events of Wadi Salib, also known as the Etzioni commission, and can be found in the Israel State Archives.

An officer snapped a photo of the moment . . . "Where is the justice?": The photograph appears in Roby, *The Mizrahi Era of Rebellion,* 200.

Mindful of the public spotlight . . . officers of Mizrahi backgrounds: From Roby, *The Mizrahi Era of Rebellion.*

One of the Mizrahi officers dispatched . . . Avraham Tourgeman: From my interview with Tourgeman in Rehovot, Israel, November 3, 2017. *In the 1950s and '60s, both men were implicated:* From articles in *Herut,* July 7, 1952, and November 20, 1961, and *Lamerhav,* November 20, 1961.

Evidence for Biton's dissidence . . ."This family refused to answer": The population survey is found in the files on Musrara at the Jerusalem Municipal Archive.

One Saturday after service, the adults gathered Abergel: From my interviews with Abergel.

But before it could materialize . . . 200 officers descended on the neighborhood: From *Jerusalem Post,* July 24, 1959.

The testimonies of Gabay and Cohen are from the Etzioni commission materials at the Israel State Archives.

On orders from the commission . . . "reconnaissance missions" and involved "state-sponsored": From Roby, *The Mizrahi Era of Rebellion,* 143.

For more on the letters of the disillusioned, see Hazkani, *Dear Palestine.*

The account of the clashes in Wadi Salib on the night of July 31 comes from Etzioni commission materials, police memos, and news reporting from the scene, particularly an article published by the *Jerusalem Post,* August 2, 1959.

He was pale and unshaven . . . Overnight, Ben-Haroush had torn: From *Jerusalem Post,* August 3, 1959.

He called them "political hacks, persons of degraded morality": From the minutes of a cabinet meeting on July 12, 1959, found in the Israel State Archives.

Now, faced with a manifestation . . . "a riot that must be crushed": From the minutes of a cabinet meeting on August 2, 1959, found in the Israel State Archives.

"Any man who comes to me" . . . "You are dividing the people": From *Yedioth Ahronoth,* August 16, 1959.

Speaking to the cabinet . . . "there is an important thing": Quoted in Weitz's article on Wadi Salib in *Haaretz,* February 13, 2014.

By the late 1950s, Amiel . . . "foster father and father confessor": From *Jerusalem Post,* September 25, 1959.

A reporter shadowing Amiel . . . "The boy imputed him guilty" . . . In response, Amiel simply laughed: From *Jerusalem Post,* January 30, 1958.

4. 1967: THE FALL OF THE WALL

The personal accounts of the war are based on my interviews with Reuven Abergel and Koko Deri, which took place primarily in Jerusalem from 2013 through 2018, and with Ayala Marciano in Jerusalem in January 2017, all of whom provide a Mizrahi perspective; Meir Wigoder in Tel Aviv in January and February 2018, with an Ashkenazi vantage point; and Philip Farah, who is Palestinian, on the phone on August 4, 2017. Quoted statements attributed to them were made in interviews unless otherwise noted.

Sources on the war and its aftermath include Segev's *1967*; Yossi Klein Halevi, *Like Dreamers: The Story of the Israeli Paratroopers Who Reunited Jerusalem and Divided a Nation* (New York: Harper Perennial, 2014); Anita Shapira, *Israel: A History* (Waltham, MA: Brandeis University Press, 2012); and Benvenisti, *City of Stone.*

"Certain deliberate calm" . . . "both ultra-Orthodox and militantly liberal Jews": From *New York Times,* June 5, 1967.

For narrative and analysis of the encounter between Mizrahim and Palestinians after the war, see, for example, Dana Hercbergs, *Overlooking the Border: Narratives of Divided Jerusalem* (Detroit: Wayne State University Press, 2018).

"Offbeat, unusual characters who came to Jerusalem" . . . "It was cut off": From an interview with Susan Bellos in Jerusalem in November 2017.

"Any reference to police violence or alleged brutality": From an essay by Susan Bellos in the *Jerusalem Post* on December 1, 1982.

Avraham Tourgeman agreed to be interviewed despite being in poor health. We spoke at his apartment in Rehovot in November 2017, less than a year before his death.

"declaration regarding the expansion of the jurisdictional area": From Benvenisti, *City of Stone,* 66.

5. ORIGIN STORIES

Itzhak Shorr recounted his reporting on the Panthers in his self-published memoir *We All* [in Hebrew] (Tel Aviv: Mendele Electronic Books, 2014).

Marciano, who served in parliament in 1980–81, was born May 1, 1950, in Oujda, Morocco, according to his official profile on the parliament's website. But other sources, such as articles published in *This World,* January 27, 1971; *Maariv,* April 15, 1971; *Jerusalem Post,* May 23, 1980; and his obituaries contain various and contradictory claims about his age and place of birth, suggesting, for example, that he was born in 1949 in Jerusalem.

Details about Marciano's upbringing are from various newspaper accounts and from my interviews with three of his siblings, Ayala Sabag, Yehudit Marciano, and Rafi Marciano, which took place in Jerusalem in 2017.

On one occasion, for example . . . A city inspector present for the reading lesson: From Bernstein, "The Black Panthers of Israel, 1971–1972."

It was during these sessions that Marciano first learned: From *This World,* January 27, 1971.

"American Jewry faces a terrible peril": From *Hachazit,* December 15, 1970.

Panthers Plan Anti-Israeli Propaganda Campaign: From *Maariv,* October 27, 1970.

The Terrorists—Idols of the New Left: From *Davar,* October 29, 1970.

The Challenge: How to Tame Panthers?: From *Maariv,* November 23, 1970.

The Black Panthers: Violent Revolutionism: From *Davar,* December 4, 1970.

Marciano read these stories . . . "We're going to be like the American Black Panthers": From Bernstein, "The Black Panthers of Israel, 1971–1972."

Inspired by the act, someone in Marciano's . . . "Tupamarconos": Cited in Mony Elkaïm, *Panthères Noires d'Israël* [in French] (Paris: François Maspero, 1972), 27; and in Bernstein, "The Black Panthers of Israel, 1971–1972."

The account of Bardugo's chance encounter with the future Panthers in Musrara is drawn from my interviews with him in Jerusalem in 2017. He also provided details about his upbringing and the rationale for changing his name. Additional details are from an article about Bardugo's Yellow Tea House in *Yedioth Ahronoth,* March 5, 1971.

The most famous one . . . "Middle Eastern psychedelic": From *Jerusalem Post,* April 2, 1969.

The account of sheepskin-jacketed Steve and his impact on Marciano and Biton is drawn from Liel Leibovitz, *Aliya: Three Generations of American-Jewish Immigration to Israel* (New York: St. Martin's Griffin, 2007).

The account of Meiri's life is from my interviews with Meiri in Jerusalem in 2016-2017 and with his son, Gilad, on the phone in 2017. Additional details are from Meiri's personal archive of writings, news clips, and correspondences.

A critic described . . . "forcefully carved, and stylized": From Karl Katz, *The Exhibitionist: Living Museums, Loving Museums* (New York: Abrams Books, 2016).

The account of Menashe Kadishman's rage at the young future Panthers is from my interviews with Avner Amiel, in Jerusalem in 2017.

The account of Meiri's first encounter with Marciano and the other future Panthers is from my interviews with Meiri.

Meiri described what he found in a letter . . . "I am working as a community worker": From an article describing the letter. The article was clipped out of an unknown newspaper; I found it in Meiri's personal papers.

"They want peace. And when they are happy": From an article clipped from an unknown newspaper and kept among Meiri's papers.

6. THE DEBUT OF THE PANTHERS

Sources on the role of street gang workers in the emergence of the Panthers and on the history of street gang work in Israel include interviews with former street gang workers David Meiri, Avner Amiel, Shabtai Amedi (Jerusalem, July 23, 2017), and Jimmy Torczyner (phone, August 9, 2017). Additional insights are from John Forester, Raphael Fischler, and Deborah Shmueli, *Israeli Planners and Designers: Profiles of Community Builders* (Albany: State University of New York Press, 2001); Jimmy Torczyner, "The Political Context of Social Change: A Case Study of Innovation in Adversity in Jerusalem," *Journal of Applied Behavioral Science* 8, no. 3 (1972); and unpublished research by Roni Kaufman, a professor of social work at Ben-Gurion University of the Negev. For a journalistic source about social work, social welfare, and inequality in Israel from the late 1960s through the 1990s, see Susan Bellos's corpus of work in the *Jerusalem Post*.

Yosef Meyuhas . . . "the only Jew who was ever born in Silwan" . . . "Black Is Beautiful": From *Jerusalem Post*, February 5, 1971.

They vowed that the next funeral . . . On another occasion, Amiel's unit used the press: From Forester, Fischler, and Shmueli, *Israeli Planners and Designers: Profiles of Community Builders,* 105.

This sentiment is encapsulated . . . "an archetypal street gang worker" . . . "They are fighting": From *Jerusalem Post*, February 5, 1971.

Many fellow municipal employees . . . "communists," "right-wing fascists," "homosexuals": From Torczyner, "The Political Context of Social Change."

Rabbi Moshe Porush . . . "Street gang workers!": From *Jerusalem Post*, April 8, 1969.

"One of the counselors was made to witness sexual intercourse between the boys": From *Al Hamishmar*, April 8, 1969.

But in this instance . . . including his ironclad backing from the public employees' union: From my interview with Amiel.

A correspondent . . . When the story was published . . . "Why bury a man?": From *Yedioth Ahronoth*, January 20, 1971.

"Why must we have street gangs threatening violence?": From *Yedioth Ahronoth*, January 20, 1971.

When asked about the talk of Black Panthers . . . "Here, among us, no such thing": Quoted in Bernstein's dissertation, "The Black Panthers of Israel, 1971–1972."

At first, he had only thought of the American Black Panthers as a frame of reference: Insight into Marciano's thinking at this time is drawn from the few contemporaneous press interviews; Bernstein's dissertation, "The Black Panthers of Israel, 1971–1972"; and the extended interview with Marciano in Elkaïm, *Panthères Noires d'Israël.*

Representatives from their neighborhood had only recently campaigned: From *Yedioth Ahronoth*, September 9, 1970.

Yes, there was a street gang . . . "they only become that way": From *This World*, January 27, 1971.

"These boys, unlike black people in America": From *Jerusalem Post*, February 5, 1971.

7. MAKING SULHA

The account of the burglary and subsequent reconciliation is from my interviews with Shimshon Wigoder (Tel Aviv, January 15, 2017), Meir Wigoder (Tel Aviv, 2017-2018), Morris Kaubilio (Jerusalem, 2017), and Charlie Biton (Mevaseret Zion, 2016-2017). Additional details come from police surveillance memos and news coverage.

"People from the bourgeois families and people from poverty areas came to parties": From Videofreex, *The Jerusalem Tapes* (1971), accessed through the Video Data Bank at the School of the Art Institute of Chicago.

The story of the Wigoder family is drawn from interviews with the brothers Shimshon and Meir, and from Devorah Wigoder's memoir, *Hope Is My House* (Englewood Cliffs, NJ: Prentice-Hall, 1967), as well as personal writings in her cookbook, *The Garden of Eden Cookbook: Recipes in the Biblical Tradition* (San Francisco: Harper & Row, 1988).

"By meddling in the matter": From a police memo dated March 10, 1971, detailing the government's attitude regarding the nascent Panthers.

The account of the left-wing protest outside parliament and fight with the JDL are from my interview with Shimshon Wigoder and from news articles published February 2, 1971, in *Davar, Yedioth Ahronoth, Maariv,* and the *Jerusalem Post*.

"Panthers in Yarmulkes": *Davar,* May 29, 1970.

Whoever he was, the police informant referred to in a police memo at this initial phase of the Panthers is not the same as the infamous police informant P/51, who would emerge later and eventually be exposed as Yacob Elbaz.

8. GET OFF THE LAWN!

The sequence of events from the initial arrests and ensuing manhunt for the other wanted activists to the protest over those arrests is stitched together from dozens of sources, including numerous accounts published in newspapers at the time and since. It also draws from my interviews with Avraham Tourgeman, Reuven Abergel, Charlie Biton, Meir Wigoder, and Avi Bardugo. Additional details come from an interview with Charlie Biton and Saadia Marciano in Elkaïm, *Panthères Noires d'Israël*. Haim Hanegbi's perspective is from a May 9, 1997, article in the periodical *Bamahane*. Another useful account of events is in a 1999 essay by Shimshon Wigoder in the Hebrew-language journal *Theory and Criticism [Te'oria Vebikoret]*. The police documented additional details in an internal memorandum dated March 10, 1971. I also consulted news photographs in the archives of *Haaretz* and *Yedioth Ahronoth,* and a short video clip from a news broadcast from the archives of Israel Broadcast Authority in Jerusalem.

Copies of "Enough!" and "Open Letter to a Black Collaborator" can be found in a nearly comprehensive collection of Black Panther leaflets, flyers, posters, and publications on the website of the Israeli Left Archives at Amsterdam's International Institute of Social History, thanks to a donation from Reuven and Dafna Kaminer, who painstakingly collected the materials.

Meir's involvement in the decision to preemptively arrest the Panthers and their supporters before their first demonstration was scheduled to take place was reported in articles published by *Haaretz* on March 4 and 16, 1971, and August 4, 1973.

The claim that police in Jerusalem had never carried out preemptive arrests before the detention of the Panthers was made by the late police commander Avraham Tourgeman, first in a statement to *Yedioth Ahronoth* on March 5, 1971, and then, decades later, in an interview with me in November 2017.

"Calling a demonstration without a permit constitutes incitement": From *Washington Post,* March 4, 1971.

That the police's decision to publish the names of those detained was irregular was reported in *Yedioth Ahronoth* on March 5, 1971.

The full list of names of those arrested is from *Haaretz,* March 3, 1971.

"We were desperately trying to teach Jerusalemites": From Teddy Kollek's autobiography (written with the help of his son, Amos), *For Jerusalem: A Life* (London: Futura, 1979), 254.

"I don't know what the Panthers want": The statements by Dahn Ben-Amotz and Amos Kenan are from *Yedioth Ahronoth,* March 4, 1971.

"to let it out than to have it eat away at my insides": From Kollek's autobiography, *For Jerusalem,* 254.

"Get off the grass!": From *Yedioth Ahronoth,* March 4, 1971.

Aliza Marciano's appearance and conduct are from several newspaper articles, press photographs, and a recording of a news broadcast from the archive of the Israel Broadcast Authority.

Accounts of the drug bust near Abergel's house appeared in *Davar* and *Yedioth Ahronoth* on November 11, 1970.

9. CONFIDENTIAL INFORMANT P/51

The biographical sketch of Tourgeman's early life is from my interview with him, supplemented by various news articles.

Shabtai Amedi, who worked so closely with Panthers as a social worker that he ended up considering himself one, told me that Tourgeman hit him in the head with his radio device. Tourgeman's reputation for violence was legendary, and Tourgeman himself admitted to me that he would beat up youths without hesitation if only to project his power.

An account of Tourgeman's late-night patrol was published on August 18, 1967, by the newspaper *Al Hamishmar*.

"Turgie . . . Listen to me. It's just a tall tale": From my interview with Tourgeman.

"They planted hashish to frame me": From *Yedioth Ahronoth*, March 12, 1971.

It was well understood among the Panthers: From Bernstein, "The Black Panthers of Israel, 1971–1972."

"the Palestinian resistance movement would do well": The police recorded these expressions of solidarity in a memo dated March 10, 1971.

At the end of a week's work, he announced 3,000 . . . verified that at least 600 were real: From *Jerusalem Post*, March 22, 1971.

"if our demands are not met": From *Yedioth Ahronoth*, March 12, 1971.

In another sign of their growing sophistication . . . War on Delinquency Committee: From *Jerusalem Post*, March 12, 1971.

"Take a young person" . . . At the conclusion of Avnery's polemic . . . "I don't know who's up there": From minutes of parliament, March 10, 1971.

Details about the Panthers' visit to parliament are from articles published on March 11, 1971, in *Al Hamishmar, Davar, Haaretz, Maariv,* and *Yedioth Ahronoth*.

book he would soon publish about Avnery. . . "No. Beneath the surface are new forces": From Shalom Cohen, *This World* [in Hebrew] (Tel Aviv: Tefahot, 1972).

Shin Bet . . . code names 675, 251, 268: Information on the function of these Shin Bet units comes from Yossi Melman, a veteran national security reporter for *Haaretz*.

The Shin Bet told Tourgeman, he later recalled: From my interview with Tourgeman.

Previously, he was mostly known for dabbling in hypnosis: From *This World,* June 2, 1971.

The account of the gathering at Wise Auditorium comes from police memos and from *Maariv, Davar,* and the *Jerusalem Post,* March 25, 1971, and *Al Hamishmar,* March 31, 1971.

"very articulate representative": From Bellos's profile of Abergel, published in the *Jerusalem Post,* April 2, 1971.

A writer who visited Abergel's house in May 1971 described what it looked like, including the photo of Elvis, in an article published in the June–July 1971 edition of *New Outlook Middle East.*

A "troika" with no single person at the helm: From a profile of Marciano in *Maariv,* April 15, 1971.

"Yacob" (instead of Yaakov) is an unusual spelling of the name, but it was apparently Elbaz's preferred spelling. In the Jerusalem Municipal Archive, I found two letters he wrote to Mayor Kollek, both dated April 14, 1972, that were stamped with official insignia of the Black Panthers, featuring Elbaz's name and title in both Hebrew and English.

Biographical details about Elbaz are from the memoir *In My Life's Path,* written and self-published in 1997 by his brother Zion, a copy of which is available at Israel's National Library.

The first person to discover the identity of P/51 and publicly name him was Gidi Weitz, an investigative reporter with *Haaretz* whose exposé on the matter was published December 4, 2007.

Police memos identified Elbaz as a pimp. In an interview, Tourgeman told me that he turned a blind eye to Elbaz's criminal activities in exchange for cooperation.

10. PASSOVER, AN OCCASION FOR LIBERATION

The account of the writing of the Panther Haggadah is drawn from my interviews with Abergel, with additional details from Bernstein, "The Black Panthers of Israel, 1971–1972," and a police memo tracking its sale.

A complete and original copy of the Panther Haggadah can be found in the Jerusalem Municipal Archive. In 2022, Jewish Currents Press released a new edition of the Haggadah with a translation in English and extensive commentary.

Meir gave a speech in which she lamented the decline of Yiddish right around when the Panthers were founded, and it might be the source of the often-repeated but apocryphal line. An article documenting the speech can be found in *Maariv* on January 28, 1971.

11. FACING PHARAOH

The sequence opening the chapter is from my interviews with Abergel.

"Don't take this as an ultimatum": From the Israel State Archives, April 7, 1971.

"Blaks Panther": The spelling on the sign, and the details of the scene at the hunger strike, are from *Yedioth Ahronoth* and *Haaretz,* April 12, 1971, and from a newsclip of the scene available through Reuters' online video archive.

The exchange between Meir and the Panthers is drawn from a 29-page transcript of the meeting. The transcript is widely available on the internet but without page 16, which is thought to be missing. I found the transcript, including the missing page, in the Israel State Archives. For a scholarly annotation of the transcript, see Tali Lev, "'We Want to Erase the History of Those Who Have a History': The Full Transcript of the Meeting between the Panthers and Israel's Prime Minister, April 1971" [in Hebrew], *Theory and Criticism* [*Te'oria Vebikoret*] 32 (Spring 2008).

"a man who uses drugs and deals them, too": From minutes of a meeting of the Israeli government, April 18, 1971, in the Israel State Archives.

Chesterfields: The particular brand of cigarettes is according to Abergel's recollection and a contemporaneous news article in *Yedioth Ahronoth,* April 14, 1971.

Descriptions of Elbaz's tattoos are from *Maariv,* October 29, 1971.

Intermarriage rates between Mizrahim and Ashkenazim never reached a level that would eliminate distinctions between the groups. Recent research by sociologist Yinon Cohen shows that only about 15 percent of Israeli Jews ages 25–43 are of mixed heritage. The proportion of Israelis of mixed backgrounds appears to be rising, but it could take decades for them to become a majority.

"There was no such thing as Palestinians": From *The [London] Sunday Times,* June 15, 1969.

"You mean to say this happens in our country?": From a police memo dated April 14, 1971.

"full solidarity with the fate of the Jewish brothers and sisters": From minutes of parliament, April 13, 1971.

In the middle of the festivities . . . "We are all Panthers!": From a police memo dated April 19, 1971, and news articles in the *Jerusalem Post* and *Yedioth Ahronoth* on the same date.

Sources on the cultural and political significance of Mimouna include Jacqueline Kahanoff, "The Maimona Festival: North African Jews Hold Their Post-Passover 'Woodstock,'" *Israel Magazine* 4, no. 3 (March 1972); and André Levy, "Happy Mimouna: On a Mechanism for Marginalizing Moroccan Israelis," *Israel Studies* 23, no. 2 (Summer 2018).

12. NIGHT OF THE PANTHERS

The description of the phone and its place in Abergel's home is drawn from a photograph in Abergel's personal archive capturing Abergel speaking on the phone in early 1971. The phone call itself is described in a police memo dated May 16, 1971, as is the fundraising drive and the debate about the Nagar brothers.

Charity applications and related correspondence are found in the Black Panthers files at the Israel Registrar of Associations.

"Don't be violent": From *Jerusalem Post,* May 19, 1971.

The account of the protest is drawn from Bernstein, "The Black Panthers of Israel, 1971–1972," as well as news coverage, published interviews, police memos, and the minutes of the Israel parliament's Internal Affairs Committee from May 26, 1971. Additional details are from interviews with the Wigoders and various Panthers, and from an indictment filed by prosecutors in connection with that night.

13. NOT NICE BOYS

The account of the award ceremony is drawn from articles in *Maariv* and the *Jerusalem Post* published May 19, 1971.

"Don't you feel any pity for this kid?": From Elkaïm, *Panthères Noires d'Israël*, 42.

Hospital notes describing the condition of injured protesters are in the Black Panthers files at the Jerusalem Municipal Archive.

Similar accounts of torture or the sight of torture were shared by multiple people I interviewed.

The pitting of prisoners against each other was described to me by Meir Wigoder. One such fight was reported by *Haaretz* on May 20, 1971.

With the release of protesters following the Night of the Panthers, the Panthers held a press conference in which various protesters spoke about the beatings and abuse they suffered while being detained. Minutes of the press conference are in the Black Panthers file at the Yad Ya'ari Research and Documentation Center in Givat Haviva. An article in the newspaper published by the Panthers in June 1971 provides additional details from the press conference. Letters to Golda Meir found in the Israel State Archive also detail allegations of police brutality.

Details about the press conference are drawn from news footage capturing part of the event and from Bernstein's dissertation, "The Black Panthers of Israel, 1971–1972," which features a transcript of Meir's speech—the only unabridged record of what she said regarding the Panthers at the event. Additional details come from articles in *Maariv, Yedioth,* and the *Jerusalem Post,* May 20, 1971. Meir would later complain that her words were taken out of context and that she didn't call the Panthers "not nice" but, rather, was referring to whoever threw the Molotov cocktails. Bernstein's transcript indicates that Meir was indeed talking about the Panthers and specifically the ones she had met at her office a month earlier.

Biographical details about Naomi Kies are from Melanie Kaye Kantrowitz and Irena Klepfisz, eds., *The Tribe of Dina: A Jewish Women's Anthology* (Montpelier, VT: Sinister Wisdom Books, 1986).

The account of the jarringly hospitable conditions awaiting Marciano when he was brought back to the precinct draws from his interview in Elkaïm, *Panthères Noires d'Israël.*

"the just struggle for the improvement": A copy of the merger agreement is in the appendix of Bernstein's dissertation, "The Black Panthers of Israel, 1971–1972."

"he cried out that he loves his country": From *Maariv,* May 28, 1971.

"The Panthers joined the Moroccan Immigrants Association": From *Maariv,* May 20, 1971.

"They bought us": Quoted in Bernstein's dissertation, "The Black Panthers of Israel, 1971–1972."

"the Panthers will get nowhere by joining other organizations" . . . *"there will be grenades":* From *Maariv*, May 21, 1971.

"will humiliate the whole of the Moroccan community": From *Jerusalem Post*, May 21, 1971.

"I feel like I can be more useful outside jail than inside": From *Jerusalem Post*, May 21, 1971.

"apolitical": From *Jerusalem Post*, May 23, 1971.

"Personally, I am with you. I am sick of all the protests": From the minutes of the meeting, which are in the Black Panthers files at the Jerusalem Municipal Archive.

14. VOTE OF NO CONFIDENCE

The account of the debate over the no-confidence motion is drawn from the May 24, 1971, minutes of the Israeli parliament.

A news article on May 25, 1971, in the newspaper *Lamerhav*, credits Abergel for securing the free medical care. Names of Panthers who were treated at the hospital and what injuries they sustained are from hospital records in the Black Panther files at the Jerusalem Municipal Archive. Additional details of the arrangement and how it came about are from a May 23, 1971, memo written by city hall staffer Shimon Cohen and from the minutes of a meeting at deputy mayor Akiva Azoulay's office dated May 23, 1971, copies of which are also found in the municipal archive.

"Each child will be sent home with a flower": From minutes of a meeting between the Panthers and Azoulay dated May 26, 1971, in the Black Panther files at the Jerusalem Municipal Archive.

"We think Matzpen members threw the cocktails": From *Jerusalem Post*, May 20, 1971.

15. FIRE

The invitations that Abergel printed out . . . *"you who support our struggle"* . . . *"Would you be so kind as to show up":* From a letter from Abergel to Meir dated June 11, 1971, found in the Israel State Archive.

The contents of the *Voice of the Panthers* are from a copy held by Abergel in his personal archive.

Suddenly, a Panther latched on to it. As he began his ascent, someone handed him a banner: From Bernstein's dissertation, "The Black Panthers of Israel, 1971–1972." Additional details from the *Jerusalem Post,* July 6, 1971. A photo of the Panther atop the pole is in the Summer 1971/Winter 1972 double issue of *Flashpoint,* a magazine of the Israel Palestine Socialist Action Group, which is from the archives of the Center for Jewish History in New York City.

"Americans were anxious to get away from their own social problems": From *Jerusalem Post,* July 26, 1971.

"If they go to a development town": Narkis made this comment to Bernstein, who included it in her dissertation, "The Black Panthers of Israel, 1971–1972."

Abergel and a few other Panthers agreed to go along with the proposal and take a tour of the town of Maalot: From newspaper accounts including in *Maariv,* June 25, 1971.

The account of the fire at the Panthers' headquarters and their subsequent march on the television station is drawn from Bernstein's dissertation, "The Black Panthers of Israel, 1971–1972"; newspaper accounts; and official city documents found in the Black Panthers files at the Jerusalem Municipal Archive.

It was reported at 8:17 p.m., and a fire truck arrived about five minutes later: From a letter dated June 25, 1971, signed by a fire-fighting official and addressed to Mayor Kollek, in the Jerusalem Municipal Archive.

This should not have come as a surprise . . . "it was a hot day and thorny brush often catches fire": From *Jerusalem Post,* June 29, 1971.

"They burned our house, we'll burn their house!": From Bernstein's dissertation, "The Black Panthers of Israel, 1971–1972."

Meanwhile, the city engineer's office ruled the house structurally unsafe: From a report by the city engineer in the Jerusalem Municipal Archive.

Details of the clean-up day are from a press release published by the Panthers and found in the Jerusalem Municipal Archive. Additional details are from a police surveillance memo dated June 30, 1971.

A photo from that day captured Abergel and his wife, Rachelle: The photo is in the archive of the newspaper *Yedioth Ahronoth.*

"No ceasefire in the war on poverty": From *Yedioth Ahronoth,* July 6, 1971.

"Are you giving money to Jews in a State of Jews, or to Ashkenazim?": Quoted in Bernstein's dissertation, "The Black Panthers of Israel, 1971–1972."

Seventeen-year-old Tsuberi didn't come from Musrara: Details about Tsuberi are drawn from a letter dated July 11, 1971, signed by the Panthers' lawyer, Shlomo

Segev, and addressed to the secretary of Israel's Labor Party, in the Jerusalem Municipal Archive.

The announcement of a U.S. tour . . . "can foresee being caught in a squeeze" . . . "at present no more than loose ties of sympathy": From a telegram sent by the American consulate in Jerusalem to the State Department. A copy of the telegram and other correspondence by American diplomats regarding the Panthers can be found at the National Archives at College Park, Maryland.

"We copied the fist from the Jewish Defense League": The quote and the fact that this was the first appearance of the symbol of the clenched fist are from the *Jerusalem Post,* July 6, 1971.

16. GOLDA'S SPEECH

The speech is recorded in the minutes of the Israeli parliament, July 28, 1971. A full English translation was published by the *Jerusalem Post* on July 29, 1971.

Reactions to the prime minister's speech are from the *Jerusalem Post,* July 30, 1971; *New York Times,* July 31, 1971; *Baltimore Sun,* July 29, 1971; and *Los Angeles Times,* July 29, 1971.

As would be documented . . . saw their average levels of education and income drop: A summary of the scholarship on this issue is in Chetrit's book, *Intra-Jewish Conflict in Israel,* which credits sociologist Shlomo Swirski as a pioneer of quantitative research on inequality in Israel.

Abergel would point to the absurdity . . . "Who had ever heard of a Jewish criminal in Morocco?": From one of my interviews with Abergel.

"Abergel gave the speech over a bullhorn": The speech was transcribed and translated into English by Bernstein, who featured it in her dissertation, "The Black Panthers of Israel, 1971–1972."

17. EFFIGY

The flyers . . . "Moscow-style show trials" . . . "by any means necessary" . . . "Prepare for a surprise": From the Israeli Left Archives at Amsterdam's International Institute of Social History.

But while the Panthers . . . "Down with the Devaluation Regime!": According to photos from the protest in the archive of *Yedioth Ahronoth.*

promoted a macho environment . . . "disappearing": From Bernstein's dissertation, "The Black Panthers of Israel, 1971–1972."

"Either we'll have our share of the pie—or there will be no pie!": This memorable quote has become so emblematic of the Panthers that its specific context has been forgotten. Bernstein's dissertation, "The Black Panthers of Israel, 1971–1972," says the declaration was made by Marciano on August 23, 1971. I opted for a different translation than Bernstein's.

"Above her figure, the poster proclaimed": From dozens of photos found in numerous archives.

The account of the protest draws from Bernstein's dissertation, "The Black Panthers of Israel, 1971–1972"; contemporaneous news articles; police memos; and other sources.

"Never had I seen, not even on Independence Day, so many people": From an interview with Kochavi Shemesh in Elkaïm, *Panthères Noires d'Israël*, 50.

"We will not move from here until Sapir himself comes": From Bernstein's dissertation, "The Black Panthers of Israel, 1971–1972."

Decades later, a group of Panthers went searching for Amram Cohen, and their quest was documented in *Have you Heard about the Panthers?*, by filmmaker Nissim Mossek (2002). In the end, they find Cohen in the holy city of Safed in northern Israel. He had become religiously devout and appeared placid and jovial, a stark contrast with his former self.

The morning after the protest . . . "urgent" meeting . . . "How do these boys make a living?": From the minutes of the August 24, 1971, meeting of the Israeli parliament's Internal Affairs Committee.

The 23 people arrested during the demonstration: A copy of the indictment detailing their names and charges can be found in the Black Panthers files of the Jerusalem Municipal Archive.

Details about the Panthers who went underground are drawn in part from a police memo dated September 12, 1971, detailing the interrogation of Eli Avichzer.

In an attempt to evoke . . . "going underground": From Bernstein, "The Black Panthers of Israel, 1971–1972."

Marciano responded, "violence and beatings from the police" . . . "The real defendants should be those responsible for poverty": From *Maariv*, August 31, 1971.

And in a pamphlet . . . "If it becomes impossible to eradicate poverty": From a flyer dated August 26, 1971, found in the Israeli Left Archives.

After ten days . . . wearing a black shirt: From *Jerusalem Post,* September 3, 1971.

A survey commissioned by the London newspaper: The survey was published by the *Jewish Chronicle* on September 3, 1971.

His name was Massimo Pieri . . . Abergel was selected as the group's representative: From a police memo dated September 30, 1971.

"We are not going to speak about foreign policy and security problems": From *Jerusalem Post,* October 1, 1971.

Details about the participants and contents at the gathering of revolutionaries are drawn from an account that appeared in the London *Daily Express,* April 17, 1972.

Biton reportedly asked the Americans . . . "discrimination against the blacks": From *Davar,* November 3, 1971.

The Videofreex archive was collected and digitized by the Video Data Bank at the School of the Art Institute of Chicago as part of an 18-year effort completed in 2018.

"I was overwhelmed by the lightness of the portable video camera": From Deirdre Boyle, *Subject to Change: Guerrilla Television Revisited* (New York: Oxford University Press, 1997), 6.

The biographical sketch of Kochavi Shemesh draws from a feature article in *Maariv* on October 29, 1971, and from Shemesh's personal essay published in Matzpen's eponymous magazine on March 10, 1972.

18. KAHANISTS AND COMMUNISTS

A scholarly analysis of the relationship between the Panthers and the Jewish Defense League can be found in Oz Frankel, "What's in a Name? The Black Panthers in Israel," *The Sixties* 1, no. 1 (2008).

One night, a group of Panthers drove out to Rehavia . . . "we have proven ourselves against greater threats": From *This World,* June 21, 1972, and *Jerusalem Post,* June 16, 1972.

"Kahanism is a social disease": From *Jerusalem Post,* September 13, 1985.

"If they only knew the truth, they would have never approached us": An article connecting the Panthers and the Red Army was published June 5, 1972, and Shemesh's response came June 9, 1972, both in *Yedioth Ahronoth*.

In explaining his anti-Zionist bona fides . . . "with obvious delight of a visit paid him by Angela Davis": From *New York Times*, May 5, 1974.

According to an account . . . "black labor" . . . Davis chastised him: From an interview with Shemesh by Oz Frankel, as cited in Frankel, "What's in a Name?"

The story of Yehezkel Cohen draws from articles in *This World* published on December 13, 1972, and in *Maariv* on December 15, 1972.

"Of the four Jewish members, I knew one well": From Shemesh's essay in Matzpen's eponymous magazine published January 10, 1973.

19. A COUNTRY TRANSFORMED

Only about 80 people showed up . . . "Even a few Panthers showed up, of course" . . . "It's sad to see that we are so few": From *Davar*, December 25, 1972.

Among themselves, some of the Panthers were blaming Abergel: From Bernstein's dissertation, "The Black Panthers of Israel, 1971–1972."

"Look," Abergel told the reporter, "demonstrations don't change anything": From the *Canadian Jewish News*, June 29, 1973.

"If an oppressed majority in some development town": From a video recording of a press conference found in the archive of the Israel Broadcasting Authority in Jerusalem.

"Dai's political platform": The platform is described in *Maariv* on January 13, 1973, and in Bernstein's dissertation, "The Black Panthers of Israel, 1971–1972."

"With this significant official gesture": From *Davar*, May 23, 1973.

The group also produced a campaign film formatted as a documentary: A documentary called *Have You Heard about the Panthers?* came out in 2002 after filmmaker Nissim Mossek discovered the original campaign footage, which he thought had been lost. He intertwined clips from the original with newly shot scenes of a group of Black Panthers contemplating the impact of their legacy and searching for old comrades.

"It was the first time a party had chosen the letter zayin as its symbol": That's according to the *Jerusalem Post*, July 11, 1973.

As Cohen explained, "No one dared pick that letter all these years": From *Jerusalem Post*, December 30, 1973.

Sources on Golda Meir include Francine Klagsbrun, *Lioness: Golda Meir and the Nation of Israel* (New York: Schocken Books, 2019); Elinor Burkett, *Golda Meir: The Iron Lady of the Middle East* (London: Gibson Square, 2009); and Meir's memoir, *My Life* (London: Weidenfeld and Nicolson, 1975).

"Plans are taking shape in my head on domestic matters": From a Jewish Telegraphic Agency bulletin, July 3, 1973.

Welfare Minister Michael Hazani . . . with a new $900,000 program: All dollar amounts cited here and below are estimates, converted from the Israeli pound based on a typical conversion rate for the era of 3.5 pounds to the dollar.

As one newspaper headline put it, "The Panthers helped the government find the budget": From *Maariv*, March 7, 1971.

A few days later, Minister of Finance Pinchas Sapir announced $23 million: From *Maariv*, March 11, 1971.

Then, Sapir made last-minute amendments to the proposed government budget: From *Jerusalem Post*, March 15, 1971.

The Ministry of Social Welfare granted the city of Jerusalem $300,000: From *Jerusalem Post*, April 1, 1971.

It would no longer categorically deny enlistment to youths possessing criminal records: From *Haaretz*, May 11, 1971.

Allon's chief adviser said that these educational policies: From *Jerusalem Post*, May 26, 1971.

"There is nothing wrong in the government reacting instantaneously": From *Jerusalem Post*, February 23, 1972.

Some observers . . . "The Budget of the Panthers": From Chetrit, *Intra-Jewish Conflict in Israel.*

It was the first time Israel ever cut defense spending in favor of other priorities: From *Jerusalem Post*, July 26, 1973.

The Ministry of Social Welfare saw its budget increase . . . National funding for local jurisdictions was up 88 percent: From *Jerusalem Post*, February 23, 1971.

As a result, impoverished families received a 20 percent increase . . . 2,575 impoverished families received household appliances: From *Maariv*, January 11, 1972.

By early 1973, the welfare minister said: From *Jerusalem Post*, March 22, 1973.

"In almost every relevant government agency and related institution": From a June 1973 report authored by Benyamin Gedalyahu, director of the youth division at the city of Jerusalem's education department, titled "A Survey of Changes in Attitudes, Policies, and Practices in Services for Distressed Youth in Response to the Black Panthers." A copy of the report can be found at the library of Hebrew University's School of Social Work and Social Welfare.

Later research concluded that the changes were not only correlated with the arrival of the Panthers but caused by it: According to Menahem Hofnung, *Protest and Butter: The Black Panthers Demonstrations and Allocations for Social Needs* [in Hebrew] (Jerusalem: Nevo Publishers, 2006).

In the area of criminal justice and policing, the 1971 Youth Law established a separate court system: From Mimi Ajsenstadt and Mona Khoury-Kassabri, "The Cultural Context of Juvenile Justice Policy in Israel," *Journal of Social Policy* 42, no. 1 (2013).

The police carved out a budget for youth recreation: From Gedalyahu's report, "A Survey of Changes in Attitudes, Policies, and Practices."

"[The Panthers] can be credited with bringing the problem of poverty to the forefront": From *Yedioth Ahronoth*, October 7, 1973.

At the defense ministry . . . A new program was created to teach commanders: From *Haaretz*, May 11, 1971 and Gedalyahu's report, "A Survey of Changes in Attitudes, Policies, and Practices."

A housing ministry program was ramped up . . . The labor ministry began outreach . . . The welfare ministry shifted . . . The National Center for Volunteer Services: From Gedalyahu's report, "A Survey of Changes in Attitudes, Policies, and Practices."

At the National Insurance Institute . . . overhaul the way benefits were calculated: From an Interview with Israel Katz in the *Jerusalem Post*, August 13, 1973 and Gedalyahu's report, "A Survey of Changes in Attitudes, Policies, and Practices."

The report of the Katz commission, officially known as the Prime Minister's Commission on Children and Adolescents in Distress, is available on the website of the Golda Meir Institute for Leadership and Society.

"When I sensed the growing momentum of the unrest and protests": From an interview with Katz that appears in Hofnung, *Protest and Butter.*

All the work of the past couple of years . . . "the natural next step": From the minutes of the parliament's session on July 25, 1973.

Abergel opposed the pursuit of public office . . . "We have yet to convince this population" . . . "I teach not only sports": From *Maariv,* September 7, 1973.

The account of the fight in Musrara is drawn from interviews with various participants, contemporaneous news articles, and court testimony in the trial of Eliezer Abergel. Records of the trial were provided by Eliezer Abergel.

Soon, the Panthers were not only campaigning but also celebrating together: Per a photograph printed in *Yedioth Ahronoth* on September 21, 1973.

"I am dying to see Saadia Marciano serving in parliament": From *Yedioth Ahronoth,* September 22, 1973.

"We have abandoned street demonstrations": From *Jerusalem Post,* December 30, 1973.

From Cairo . . . "What would you like to tell your friends" . . . "Vote for the Black Panthers": From *This World,* November 1, 1973.

The Panthers articulated . . . "Until this war started" . . . "The Panthers to Damascus": From an undated pamphlet in the Israeli Left Archives.

20. THE BALLOT REBELLION

The kidnapping plot was disclosed by the Panthers to a reporter who mentioned it in an article in *Yedioth Ahronoth* on December 12, 1975.

"We believe that the Palestinians are an integral part": From *Maariv,* March 28, 1975.

In the language of the approved resolution . . . "a just peace is possible": From *Yedioth Ahronoth,* December 12, 1975, and *Jerusalem Post,* September 1975.

In the summer of 1975, Menachem Talmi, a correspondent: From *Maariv,* August 1, 1975.

The headline declared that Reuven Abergel: From *Maariv,* January 2, 1976.

They quoted the judge handling Eliezer's arraignment: From *Yedioth Ahronoth,* January 4, 1976.

In his first interview after being released, Olmert agreed in early 2018 to answer questions: I interviewed Olmert at his office in Tel Aviv on January 17, 2018.

The names of those who testified against the Abergels and what allegations were described during the trial come from roughly 200 pages of court transcripts kept by Eliezer Abergel, provided to me during my interview with him.

"Today, I am very bitter": From *Yedioth Ahronoth*, November 28, 1986.

Kellner's article about the mole inside the Panthers was published in *Kol Ha'ir* on June 11, 1999. In my years of research on the Panthers, I did not encounter a single reference to that article; it appears to have been forgotten. On the other hand, Weitz's exposé, which was published by *Haaretz* on December 4, 2007, is an enduring touchstone in the collective memory.

On the day he was sworn in . . . "I am not going to disappear": From an account of Marciano's day published in the *Jerusalem Post* on May 23, 1980.

what some called "the non-respectable poor": From *Jerusalem Post*, July 29, 1977.

Neither Panther managed to pull almost any Mizrahi support, not even in Musrara: From *Maariv*, May 19, 1977.

He didn't want to frighten . . . But he also didn't want to downplay": From an interview with Yavin broadcast on Israel's Channel 12 on May 21, 2022.

The account of the scene at Begin's victory celebration is drawn from an article by Yehuda Avner, published in the *Jerusalem Post* on May 26, 2007. A consummate political insider, Avner served as an adviser to five Israeli prime ministers.

The summary of the debate about the 1977 election and the Mizrahim draws from Avery Weinman's award-winning undergraduate thesis, "Reverberations from 'the Earthquake': Collective Memory and Why Mizrahi Israelis Vote for the Israeli Right" (University of California, Santa Cruz, 2019).

The account of Begin's 1981 speech is also drawn from Weinman, "Reverberations from 'the Earthquake.'"

Mizrahim had begun their migration to Likud: From the *Jerusalem Post,* which published an article on January 9, 1974, with the headline "Oriental Community Shifts Clearly towards the Likud."

"The Panthers could bring the Likud to power": From *Maariv*, June 16, 1971.

Details of Biton and Marciano's activities as young lawmakers in parliament are from profiles of the two published in the *Jerusalem Post* on July 29, 1977, and May 23, 1980, and other news articles in the Israeli press.

The account of Abergel's encounter with Meiri and subsequent recovery from addiction are drawn from my interviews with the two as well as from their personal papers.

"I ask for forgiveness on behalf of the Labor Party": From *Globes,* September 28, 1997.

"Even if we didn't mean to do so": From a copy of the letter found in Abergel's personal papers.

"I am a Black Panther in my heart and soul": From a written speech found in Abergel's personal papers.

Index

Note: Page references in *italics* refer to photos.

and Biton, 265; and Panthers' fractured alliances, 263–64; Sheli and Marciano, 265–66; work of Panthers as parliamentarians, 271–74; Zionist Panthers, 264

Baltimore Sun, on Meir's speech (July 28, 1971), 211

Barak, Ehud, 275

Bardugo, Avi, 77–83, 89, 98, 103, 117, 140–42

Bareli, Daniel, 143, 172

Barkat, Reuven, 194

Basement (municipal clubhouse), 73–74, 76, 81, 83, 87, 94, 216

Begin, Menachem, 267–71

Belisha, Ruben, 153

Bellos, Susan, 59–61, 139

Ben-Amotz, Dahn, 119–20, 122–23

Ben-Dor, Lea, 210–11

Ben-Gurion, David, 9, 24–25, 30, 46, 131

Ben-Haroush, David, 31–32, 43–47, 50

Ben-Harush, Amalia, 24

Ben-Harush, Meir, 24

Ben Simhon, Shaul, 184, 188, 190, 191, 203, 212

Ben Zaken, Rafael, 117

Bernstein, Deborah, 281

Bialik, Hayim Nahman, 88

Bin-Nun, Yigal, 185

Biton, Charlie: and Abergel brothers' trial, 262; arrests and imprisonment of, 117, 182, 221–22, 259; on European trip by Panthers, 259–60; far left associates of, 130; Musrara childhood of, 35–37; and Panthers' inception, 80–82, 88; and Panthers' leadership disputes, 11, 142, 169; photo, 153; political career of, 265, 266, 272, 273, 275; and U.S. tour plan, 208–9, 215

Biton, Eliyahu, 35–36

"Black Is Beautiful" slogan, 151

Black Panthers of Israel. *See* Israel's Black Panthers

Black Panthers of United States. *See* American Black Panther Party

Black September, 233–35

Blue and White Panthers, 217, 254–56, 264

bohemians (walking description), 63

British Mandate of Palestine: Jewish Underground's resistance to, 49; and Partition Plan, 7, 14–15, 105. *See also* Palestinians; State of Israel

Brock, Uri, 117

Brun, Gabi, 94–95

Buhbut, Zion, 124

Central Elections Committee (Israel), 241–42

charity, religious concept of, 91

Chelouche, Aharon, 35

Chetrit, Sami Shalom, 270, 274, 281

Christian missionary activity, 48

class issues. *See* language; Musrara neighborhood (Jerusalem); poverty; racial discrimination against Mizrahim

Cohen, Amram, 220, 262, 263, 301

Cohen, Hillel, 264

Cohen, Levy, 40–42, 48

Cohen, Louise, 186

Cohen, Shalom: and Dai (Black Panthers–Israeli Democrats), 240–42, 248–50, 253–56; and Hofesh (Freedom) Party, 264–65; introduction to Panthers, 132–33; on no confidence vote, 196; transit camps investigation by, 20–21

Cohen, Yehezkel, 235–36

Cohen, Yinon, 295

communism and Rakah Party, 192–93, 195, 196

Cort, David, 227–29

Costello, Seamus, 225

Czechoslovakia, Shimshon Wigoder in, 107

Dai (Black Panthers–Israeli Democrats): campaign of, 240–42, 248–50, 303; election loss of, 253–56, 257

David (king of Israel), 131

Davis, Angela, viii–ix, 82, 234–35

Dayan, Moshe, 14–15, 16, 22, 28

"Dayenu" (song), 149

De Amicis, Edmondo, 85

Deri, Koko, 53–56, 79–81, 103, 111

"diasporic Jews" stereotype, 41–42

Dreyfus, Alfred, 87

drugs: Abergel brothers' trial (1975), 261–64, 274–75; Abergel's arrest and exoneration (1970), 122, 124, 128, 166; drug parties, 103; Meir's impression of Abergel, 156; Musrara neighborhood problem of, 77; and Tourgeman's police work, 127; Zoharim addiction recovery center, 275

Dwek, Moshe, 130

Eban, Abba, xii, 131, 163–64

Edry, Amram, 199

educational system: literacy training at Basement, 73–74, 76, 81, 83, 87, 94; and Musrara teens in reform schools, 27, 72–73; spending and policy change (1971–1973), 244; vocational tracking of Mizrahim, xiii, 20, 25–29, 39; and Wingate Academy scholarship, 238

effigy burning and demonstration (August 23, 1971), 214–22, 218, 219, 222

Egypt: Gaza captured during Six-Day War, 55; Israel's shared border with, 9; Mizrahim from, xi; peace treaty (1979), 265; Suez Canal, 207; War of Attrition, 86–87, 98, 242; Yom Kippur War, 251–53

Elbaz, Yacob: and Ashkenazi activists' split from Panthers, 199–200; biographical information, 144–46, 145; and Blue and White Panthers, 255; characterization of, 144–46, 145, 157; hired by police as "P/51" informant, 134–37; identified as police informant, posthumously, 264; leadership recognition of, by Panthers, 142, 166; at Meir's meeting with Panthers, 155–64; as Molotov cocktail suspect, 185–86, 191; and Night of the Panthers, 171, 174–75; police information provided by, 135–44 (*See also* Israeli police surveillance)

Elbaz, Zion, 185

El-Karif, Akiva, 30–31, 38

Elon, Amos, 223–24

employment: government jobs offered to Panthers, 128, 135, 143, 234, 238, 260; job discrimination, xiii, 20, 25–29, 39, 49–50, 155, 157–58, 161

"Enough!" (Black Panthers), 112–13, 116

Etzioni, Moshe, 37, 46

Etzioni commission, 37–43, 45, 47

Exodus. *See* Passover

Exodus (Uris book and film), 68

permit application for demonstration (1971), 5; and rise of Panthers, 93, 96

Kopel, Pinhas, 2, 5

Kurdistan, Mizrahim from, xi

Labor Party. *See* Mapai (Labor) Party

language: Arabic spoken by Mizrahim, 20, 21, 25; Meir on accents, 161; Panthers' English sign ("Blaks Panther"), 155; Panthers on their "poor Hebrew," 137, 156; Yiddish and Ashkenazim, 149, *150*; Yiddish slur against Mizrahim, 158

law enforcement and criminal justice system: Dai's platform and prison abolition movement, 240–41; and kibbutz program, 28–29, 37; and Musrara teens in reform schools, 27, 72–73; and Musrara teens' thwarted advancement, 159; Panthers' clemency campaign, 275; Youth Law (1971), 245. *See also* Israeli police

Lebanon, Israel's shared border with, 9

Left Camp of Israel (Sheli), 265–66

Leissner, Aryeh, 92

Levit, Dany, 117, 140–41, 199–200, 201

Levy, David, 111, 142, 155–64, 190, 191

Levy, Meir, 111, 117

Likud Party: and The Ballot Rebellion (1977), 266–71; early leadership of, 19; Herut Party as predecessor of, *36*; Knesset representation, during Meir's tenure, 194, 255; modern-day majority of, 268; and Netanyahu, 271, 275–76; and Olmert, 262–63

Little Red Book (Mao Zedong), 151

Lod Airport terrorist attack (1972), 233

Lorincz, Shlomo, 195

Los Angeles Times, on Meir's speech (July 28, 1971), 211

Maariv (newspaper): on Abergel brothers' arrest (1975), 261–63; on Musrara poverty, 260–61; on rise of Panthers, 95–96

MacDwyer, Jane Emmet (Devorah Wigoder), 104

mahapach (upheaval), 267

Maimonides, 204

Malcolm X, 82, 215, 222

Malka, Eddie: and Abergel brothers' trial, 262; Blue and White Panthers of, 215–17, 254–55, 264; at Hebrew University rally, 136, 137; and Night of the Panthers arrest, 190, 191; Second Israel group of, 143–44

Mao Zedong, 151

Mapai (Labor) Party: and Likud's win (1977), 267; majority rule by, 36, 194, 196; and Meir's campaign and re-election (1973), 242, 249–50, 255–56; and Plugot Hapoel, 44; and Wadi Saleb rebellion (1959), 32, 43–47, 50

Marciano, Aliza (mother), 56–57, 120–21, *121*, 186

Marciano, Ayala (sister), 56–57

Marciano, Eliyahu (father), 35–36

Marciano, Rafi (brother): and Ashkenazi activists' split from Panthers, 199–200; and demonstration (March 3, 1971), *119*, 124; and leadership of Panthers, 142; at Meir's meeting with Panthers, 155–64; and Night of the Panthers, 170; at Wingate Academy, 234

Marciano, Saadia: and Abergel brothers' trial, 262; arrests of, 115, 117, 123–24,

Mizrahi Jew, 114; immigration of Moroccan Jews to Jerusalem (late 1940s to mid-1950s), xi, 7–14, 17–18; intermarriage of, 295; Iraqi Jews, oppression and hanging (1971), 71, 162–64; Katz commission report on poverty among, 246–47; Likud's win (1977) and role of, 266–71; Palestinian encounters, following Six-Day War, 55–58; Passover metaphor for migration of, 147–51, 150; segregation and tension with Ashkenazim, xii–xiii, 20–21; Sephardim confused with, xiii, 158. See also racial discrimination against Mizrahim

Molotov cocktail incident (Night of the Panthers), 178, 185–86, 200

Moroccan Immigrants Association, 183–84, 188–91, 199, 212

Moroccan Jewry: immigration of, to Jerusalem (late 1940s to mid-1950s), xi, 7–14, 17–18; Israeli police on "loyalty oaths" of, 34–35; letters intercepted to, by Israel, 43; Meir-Panthers meeting, Moroccan heritage discussion, 157; mellah (Jewish quarters in Morocco), 60. See also Mizrahim

Mossek, Nissim, 241, 303

Mughrabis, 146

Mulford Act (1967, California), 133–34

Municipal Youth Clubs of Social Welfare Department (Jerusalem), 48–50

Musrara neighborhood (Jerusalem): Christian missionary activity in, 48; cleanup program, 199, 202–3, 206–7; early immigration of Mizrahim to, 4, 15, 16–17, 21–26, 23; "French Revolution incident," 88; lifestyle/treatment of

youth in (1967), 58–61, 59; Maariv on (1975), 260–61; "no-man's-land" border with Jordan, 14–15, 22–24, 23; and police violence, 60–61, 127, 139, 163; social hierarchy among men of, 197; street gangs of, 73; "the swamp," 24; Wadi Salib rebellion and effect on, 34–37, 48–50; youth camp for, 84–85

Nachlaot neighborhood, 83

Nagar brothers, 168–69

Nahmias, Yosef, 33

nakba (catastrophe), 14

Narkis, Uzi, 205

National Center for Volunteer Services, 247

National Front for Peace and Equality, 265

National Insurance Institute (Israel), 246–47

National Rifle Association (U.S.), 134

Negba (passenger ship), 9–11

Nehoshtan, Ya'akov, 195

Netanyahu, Benjamin, 19, 271, 275–76

"New Jews," 41

news media: Abergel's house fire, television coverage, 206; Basement and Panthers' early exposure to, 73–74, 76, 81, 83, 87, 94; Egyptian newspaper on Israel's Black Panthers, 129; Egyptian radio on Panthers (1973), 253; and inception of Panthers, 70–72, 90, 92–93, 94–96, 97; in Israel of late 1950s, 34; journalists spied on by police, 138–39; Kies as Panthers' spokesperson for, 187; on Night of the Panthers, 177–78; Panthers' open letter to, 113–14; permit requirements

Hadassah (women's group), 226–29; and Herut Party, 36; "Labor Zionism" vs. "Revisionist Zionism," 269–70; and Machal, 13–14; Meir's commitment to, 99; and "New Jews," 41; Panthers on commitment to Zionism, 204; and Partition Plan, 105; rejection of, by Matzpen, 4–5; United Jewish Appeal, 104; Youth Aliyah, 42, 126; Zionist Congress, 229

Zionist Panthers, 264

Zion (Musrara teen), 102

Zion Square (Jerusalem): Begin's speech in, 270; as Night of the Panthers venue, 171–78 (*See also* Night of the Panthers [May 18, 1971]); terror attack (1975), 260–61

Zoharim addiction recovery center, 275

Zola, Émile, 254